BRICK BY BRICK

BRICK BY BRICK IS A MEMOIR—the tough, inspiring story of a young woman who comes of age in New Bedford, Massachusetts in the 1970s. Lynn Donohue drops out of school at 15 and is heading nowhere, without a plan or a future. Eventually, she takes a masonry course and embarks on a career as a bricklayer. The work is hard and the money is good, but it's the beauty and rhythm of the work that give her a sense of purpose and empowerment.

Lynn breaks into the union, battles prejudice, and helps construct schools, hospitals, and public buildings. But when the time comes, no one will accept a woman as foreman of a building project. Undaunted, Lynn forms her own company, which becomes a multi-million-dollar business and earns her a solid reputation in the construction world.

Behind her tough-as-nails exterior, though, Lynn harbors deep vulnerabilities. As she struggles to make her way to the top of her profession, she begins a much more difficult journey of personal growth. She faces the demons from her troubled past and learns to open her heart to friends, family, romance. With the right amount of tenderness, caring, and forgiveness, she discovers, she can still be in charge and win big.

BRICK BY BRICK

a woman's journey

by

LYNN DONOHUE

with Pamela Hunt

edited by
Marsha L. McCabe

Spinner Publications, Inc.
New Bedford, Massachusetts

Spinner Publications, Inc., New Bedford, MA 02740

© 2000, 2006 (second printing) by Spinner Publications, Inc.
Text © Lynn Donohue. All rights reserved
Printed in the United States of America

Some names have been changed to protect the privacy of individuals.

Cover Photo: Nancy Cole
Design: Joseph D. Thomas, Jay Avila

Cataloging-in-Publication Data

Donohue, Lynn, 1957-
  Brick by brick : a woman's journey / by Lynn Donohue,
  with Pamela Hunt ; edited by Marsha L. McCabe.
  269 p. ; 24 cm.
  ISBN 0-932027-57-1 (cloth)
  ISBN 0-932027-58-X (pbk.)
  1. Businesswomen--Massachusetts--New Bedford--Biography. 2.
  Women-owned business enterprises--Massachusetts--New Bedford--Case
  studies. 3. Argus Construction Corporation--History. I. Title

HD9715.U52 D663 2000   00133444

To Geraldine, my inspiration

ACKNOWLEDGMENTS

Many people have helped me along the way:

The bricklayers (my brothers) who befriended me and were my mentors.

My best friend, Pam Hunt, who taught me the true meaning of friendship. This book would not have been written without her.

Marsha McCabe, my editor, whose dedication to this project and love for this story have inspired me.

Joe Thomas, my publisher, who believed in me and felt this story should be told.

My daughter, Kelsey, and my son, Daniel, whose love and support are my blessing.

And, finally, Geraldine Schultz, who in death became my inspiration.

CONTENTS

THE BELMONT CLUB

Somebody built the pyramids and the Empire State Building—
these things don't just happen. There's hard work behind it. I
would like to see a building, say, the Empire State, I would like
to see on one side of it a foot-wide strip from top to bottom with
the name of every bricklayer, the name of every electrician, with
all the names. So when a guy walked by he could take his son
and say, "See, that's me up there on the forty-fifth floor. I put
the steel beam in."

—Mike Lefevre in *Working*, by Studs Terkel

The first time I read those words about the pyramids and the
Empire State Building, I got goose bumps. I understood the
poor guy perfectly. He just wanted to leave his mark. I can
identify with that. We all want to leave our mark, to be able to point
to something and say: *I wrote that book, I painted that picture, I put the
steel beam in that building.*

As I drive through my hometown of New Bedford, this gritty sea-
port city on the southeast coast of Massachusetts, I realize I have left
my mark in ways I never dreamed. We drive by St. Luke's Hospital in
the West End and I tell my small daughter, "See? That's me up there.
It was the worst winter we'd had in years and I'm shivering my butt
off laying brick for their new building."

Or we go through Weld Square in the North End and I nudge
Kelsey. "Look. That's me and the pigeons, sweating up there on the
staging. We renovated the old trolley barn and turned it into a housing
complex for the elderly, a piece of work, if I do say so myself."

And, hey, put my name on the wastewater treatment plant in Fall
River and the Com Electric building in Wareham and Faneuil Hall
in Boston, too.

I did not set out to become a bricklayer. I didn't set out to become
anything at all. I was adrift, without direction. I wasn't even looking to

get on course. And then one day something happened. It's these random events that change our lives—we go a different route, we bump into somebody, we read something, and this small, unlikely event propels us into a whole new universe.

So it was with me and bricklaying. I saw an item in the newspaper about attempts to recruit women into the trades, and I liked the sound of that seventeen dollars an hour bricklayers made. Simple as that.

But there were other forces at work here, too. I think I had a central core of sanity that asserted itself even in the midst of chaos. Perhaps we all have something like this, a kind of radar, and it allows us to survive. And God knows I had a will.

But this is the thing: laying brick helped me develop a sense of self. Tell that to a psychiatrist. Before I became a bricklayer, there was nobody there. A lost, aimless ghost of a girl with a mouth, yes. But I had no content, no insides.

Through the laying of brick, through the rhythm and precision of the work, and the near-total concentration required of masons, I was also building my self, my life. Outside of work, I began educating myself and gaining self-understanding. Maybe the rhythm of the work helped me to hold back the chaos, like a reprieve, and I got a chance to fill up on the good stuff. However it worked, brick was good for me. Would selling jewelry in a store or doing data entry have done the same? I don't think so. I only know that, in practicing my craft, I was also building my life, brick by brick.

My story begins at the Belmont Club, my father's tavern in the South End of New Bedford, where I was a bartender. The year was 1976. I had imagined popping cans here indefinitely, for lack of a better idea, but things came to an abrupt halt on a languid summer night when I learned that bartending can be a dangerous occupation, and you can die from it if you aren't careful.

I remember that day so clearly, every face at the bar, what Artie said, what Izzy said, my thoughts, oh, especially my thoughts, sunk in despair at the state of my life while maintaining the joviality required of bartenders.

At first it was just another day, just me and the bar regulars, and nothing was happening. I was well into my twelve-hour shift and experiencing my usual mid-afternoon blahs, especially since I'd had my nineteenth birthday the week before and I felt sixty.

School was behind me—I had dropped out of Roosevelt Junior High at fifteen—and nothing much was ahead. Yet things were better than they had been, I have to admit that. At least I had a job and a place to live. The job was pretty secure, it being my father's tavern, and I made $3.10 an hour, which was minimum wage in those days. There was only one real problem with this gig—time dragged, sucking my life away with it.

But on the whole, it had been a good week, money-wise. I had logged fifty hours behind the bar so far. The Belmont had a parade of regulars I'd come to know like a family.

The Belmont Club is dark and smoky, your basic neighborhood dive but with lots of dark wood and brickwork, almost like an English pub. The neighborhood is very English and bowling-on-the-green is a popular activity in the park across the street. A funky buffalo head looked over at me from the opposite wall, his big brown glass eyes glaring at me several times a day. What are YOU doing here? he seemed to say.

Same as YOU, I'd sneer and this is how, in a way, we became good friends. Two lost souls who ended up in a bar. I would have given anything to take him back where he belonged, to Kansas or North Dakota or wherever he was from. It was amazing to think that he once had a life.

"Hey sweetheart, gimme a f__kin' beer!" yelled Dave, his voice competing with the jukebox as Jim Morrison sang *Light My Fire* for the tenth time that day. I popped the cap from a cold bottle of Miller and set it in front of him, then filled some time doing chores: checking inventory, washing glasses, plunking empty cases of Budweiser bottles down next to the padlocked rear door.

Time for a break, I told myself, as I slipped out from behind the bar and perched on a stool, casually thumbing through a newspaper someone had left on the bar. A story immediately caught my eye. Not too many stories grab me. I wasn't into politics or world news or anything like that, but I did like those human interest stories. This one was about the need to get women into nontraditional jobs and my heart jumped when I saw the union pay scales for carpenters, electricians,

14

and especially bricklayers. Seventeen dollars an hour! Jeez, I'd have to work nearly six hours at the bar to make that. It was like fantasy land. Wow, I thought, and I had one of those moments where I was laying brick and pulling in money like that. Just a flash.

"Hey! What the hell you doin'? Get up and get me a f__kin' beer!"

I didn't have to look up to know who was giving the orders. Zack was already drunk at two-thirty in the afternoon and his usual nasty self. This once-handsome athlete and ladies' man couldn't handle life after high school and it was all downhill from there. A commercial fisherman, he went to sea for ten days at a stretch, then came into port and blew all his money at the bar.

"Yeah, yeah, keep your cool," I mumbled out of earshot and placed the folded newspaper behind the bar for safekeeping so I could check it out later. After tending to Zack, the phone rang and I recognized the voice right away. It was the wife of one of the regulars and she wanted her guy home.

"Sorry, he's not here," I said sweetly, a standard reply in most bars. My father, an ex-cop, had owned the Belmont since I was a child, and my mother had been given the reply more times than she could count before their divorce. My father's tavern lifestyle had ruined our home life, and my mom and we kids—there were five of us—had suffered the consequences. We hadn't spoken to him in years.

Then one day last spring, my father saw me trudging through heavy rain in downtown New Bedford, a sorry sight if there ever was one, and offered me a ride. Even after all the heartache he had caused our family, I was still glad to see him. When he learned I was job hunting, traipsing from restaurant to restaurant looking for a waitress job, he offered me work at the Belmont and I jumped at it. Yeah, I needed the money but I knew I'd also win points with the hippie crowd I hung around with. They thought bartenders had it made— free drinks, party- hearty, all that. But the day-to-day reality behind a bar is not what it seems. You see too much of the dark side of life, people going down the tubes and you're helping them along.

Strangely, I couldn't stop thinking about that newspaper article. As soon as I found a minute, I grabbed the paper and reread the article.

At that moment, Artie barged in the front door and announced, "Hey guys, I'm here," as if we couldn't see him. He was the local bookie and he must have finished his rounds because he always rewarded himself with a few drinks. A short, stocky man with a gravelly voice and a stump for a left arm, he was always sharply dressed in polyester leisure suits. Polyester was big in the seventies and he wore it well.

Artie was not alone today. "Hi, guys," said Diane, who hung on his good arm. The two made quite a picture. Her once-beautiful face was buried under layers of makeup, not quite concealing the puffiness from years of alcohol and drug abuse, and she was only twenty-eight. The guys joked—if you slept with Diane, her facial features would be permanently imbedded on your pillowcase. She had a sad history. When she got pregnant at seventeen, Children's Protective Services gave custody of the boy to her mother-in-law. After that Diane was a train wreck, as they say. Artie felt sorry for her and bought her a drink or two occasionally.

"Dewar's and water for me and whatever Diane wants, honey," said Artie, who regularly sat on the barstool closest to the front door. We all knew he took that seat in case there was trouble so he could make a quick exit. Diane dumped Artie as soon as she saw another opportunity—a fisherman who came in with Zack. She hoped to get drinks or grams of coke in exchange for her favors.

I counted out Artie's change and sought his undivided attention before he got too wasted. "Hey Artie, you go to the Embassy Lounge once in a while, right?"

He looked at me curiously. "Yeah, yeah, I do. Those hard-hats love playin' the football cards, so I'm down there on Fridays and Mondays usually. Why?"

"Did you ever see any female hard-hats hanging around there?"

"Heh, heh. Only the hookers who put the hats on as a teaser." Artie started to sip his drink, then looked at me oddly and said, "You're kiddin', ain't ya?" "Yeah, just kiddin'," I replied.

"Good afternoon, dear, I'll have the usual, please," said John, who arrived right on schedule, greeting everyone in a charming English accent as he removed his jacket and took his usual place. A small kindly man of seventy-five whose wife had recently died, he was a fixture at the Belmont. He nursed a small Bud and told me in great detail about his breakfast and morning walk, then returned after lunch and filled me in on the news of his grown children. I listened attentively to his domestic sagas because the man exuded charm, and charm was in short supply around here.

Occasionally, he splurged on a few shots of blackberry brandy and stayed longer than usual, reluctant to return to his lonely apartment. Diane watched him like a hawk. If she noticed him drinking brandy, she'd come around and act interested in his stories, expecting a few drinks as a payoff. Eventually John would catch on and dejectedly make his way home.

"You ready for another, Harold?" The quiet man on John's right looked up from his beer and nodded. Harold was a mystery man, hiding behind his long unruly hair, scruffy beard and thick wire-rimmed glasses, never speaking unless he absolutely had to. There must be a lot of soul there, I thought, for he was a talented painter who created wall-sized murals in oils and watercolors. But he didn't pursue a career in art; he just did menial jobs and frequented the bar regularly.

The previous spring he presented my father with a twenty-foot-long mural in vibrant oils, depicting a lively crowd of people enjoying the park and beach across the street from the bar. "Wow!" I said when I first saw it, and that was my response every time I saw it. It was so detailed you saw something new every time you looked at it, and he even painted the faces of several Belmont barflies into the scene. But he didn't want any payment or thanks. He didn't even want to be pointed out as the artist if anyone inquired.

I served up the drinks, then opened the newspaper to show Artie the article, but he was in the middle of a heated discussion with Brian, a guy whose handsome, chiseled looks could have made him a model if he hadn't started smoking pot and hanging with the druggies in ninth grade. Now, at twenty, he was a full-fledged heroin addict. The regulars avoided him because he was a nuisance, always begging for money.

"Do I look like a bank to you?" Artie said, annoyed.

"Come on, Artie, I'm good for it."

"Ask me again and I just might kill ya before the smack does."

Brian, agitated and desperate, took up his usual post at the entrance to the Belmont, begging money from all who entered, but no luck. Everyone knew they'd never see their money again. His chance of getting a fix would improve at nightfall when the hard-drug crowd gathered across the street in the park.

The front door banged open and this time stayed open, the daytime light blinding us. We were always in the dark, and I squinted like a mole emerging from a tunnel into the harsh sunlight. Oh, it was just my father showing Brian the door.

"Out," he said firmly with a sweep of the hand.

He was a handsome, charming man, my father. The patrons held him in high regard, not only because he owned the place but because he was kind to them and treated them with respect. And he often bought a round for everyone.

"Hi, dear," he called over to me, then exchanged greetings with some of the regulars.

"Hi, Dad," I yelled over the din, "can you watch the bar for me while I go get a sub?"

"Sure. Any problems?"

"Nope, but I could use another case of vodka if you get a chance." The beer cases were stacked in a storage closet in the back, but the hard liquor was kept in my father's office under lock and key. He nodded as I grabbed my purse and newspaper and walked a few doors down to the pizza shop. It was late summer and people were out in the streets. A slight mist drifted up from the sea and I could feel my hair turn to frizz, but the fresh air smelled good after leaving the smoky bar.

I ordered a ham and cheese sub and turned back to the newspaper again. My eyes kept drifting to the wage information in the inset box. It's not that I was money crazy, it's just that I couldn't imagine making seventeen dollars an hour, and the article was practically begging me to do it. Come on, it cried out, this is your chance to earn some real money. Well, I have to say, it was incredibly appealing.

True, bartending was the only job I knew, not counting the month I spent in a factory on an assembly line wrapping wire around television tubes all day. When I hit my stride as a bartender and told my dad I felt comfortable at it, he said, "Stick with it and the club may belong to you someday." This was the only time I ever felt a twinge of job-related motivation.

That's what was wrong with me—I just wasn't motivated. Heck, I didn't know what success was. I can't explain what was happening to me, except to say that seventeen dollars an hour made a huge impression on me. I headed back to the bar, singing, "Seventeen dollars an hour" to the tune of *Come on baby, light my fire*. Something weird was going on deep inside of me and I knew I would take the next step. I was going to call the newspaper and see what this was about.

I was so preoccupied, I failed to notice the screaming-red Harley-Davidson parked outside the bar until I nearly fell over it. "Oh, great, Izzy's here," which meant the end of a "no problem" day. A Janis Joplin look-alike, Izzy could drink most men under the table. The red Harley belonged to her and she would kick the family jewels of any man who came too close without her permission.

Izzy would drink her way through a pint of Southern Comfort, then pull up her blouse and show her breasts. "Bet you puppies would love to get your hands on these, eh?" she'd say to the men who looked her way. But the rolls of fat around her midriff and her obnoxious personality left her with few takers. Her night was never complete unless she started at least one fight and she didn't care who she punched out, as long as it was somebody. She'd been barred from the club so often I lost count, but Dad always relented and let her back in. One night she threw her shot glass at some guy and broke the full-length mirror behind the bar, apologized tearfully the next morning and actually paid for a new one. Dad forgave her and she was soon back.

After just two drinks, Izzy got up to leave. "See ya later, sweetie. This place is a graveyard."

I tried not to show my mood brightening at her departure. It was almost seven o'clock, nearing the end of my twelve-hour shift. Dad had collected the day's receipts and returned to his apartment for supper—he would be back later. Artie and Harold were still hanging on, but most of the daytime crowd had drifted out and now the night crawlers began huddling around the jukebox and pinball machine.

During a lull, I whipped out the paper to show Artie the article and ask him what he thought about women in the trades. His little red mustache went up and down as he regarded the question.

"Well, Izzy could handle construction, no sweat," he joked, "but the work's too hard for most broads, and they'd be sittin' ducks with all those horny guys around. But damn, the money ain't bad, is it?"

Our conversation came to an abrupt halt when Gail and another woman blew in and asked for some quick drinks. She was breathless, her hair flying. "Whew," she sighed. "That was a close call, wasn't it?"

"Yeah," said her friend.

"We've been cruising the Avenue, up the North End," she explained to anyone who would listen, "just looking for something to do."

Oh, sure, tell us about it. That's what everyone was saying under their breath. She was married to Pidge, a fisherman, and people joked that her drinks were not the only thing on the rocks. When Pidge was out to sea, everyone knew what Gail was up to.

"We planned to have a few drinks at the Martinique, but it turned out to be a bad idea. Five bikers from the Sidewinders gang showed up and started coming on to us."

"Yeah, they were pigs," said her friend.

"We gave them the finger and got out of there. We took off so fast, we were really flying, but then I noticed in the rearview mirror they were following us. We lost them on Brock Avenue. Those guys are so grubby they turned my stomach."

"Yeah."

Biker gangs grew like weeds in the North End of New Bedford—the Sidewinders, One Percenters, Devil's Disciples, Gypsy Jokers—and they all loved to fight. Each gang wore their "colors," denim jackets with ripped-off sleeves and the club insignia on the back, and they protected their own turf with their mouths or fists. They never hassled the peace-loving crowd I hung out with in the West End, but sometimes I saw them at the Portuguese Feast in the summer, getting hauled away in handcuffs by the police.

I looked at the clock, then locked eyes again with my friend, the buffalo head. I'm outta here, I bragged. Dennis, my father's right-hand man, would be here in fifteen minutes to cover the night shift. These twelve-hour shifts wore me down. I was ready to go home and sleep.

BAM! The front door burst open and five Sidewinders strode in, pumped for battle. What a sight! Some had teeth missing or rotted, one had a black eye, and two looked like they did their hair with Crisco. None of them looked like they'd ever washed. Tension crackled in the air as the loudest, tallest guy barked "Millers!" at me. I quickly uncapped five bottles and lined them up on the bar. A fat biker with a bald head marched up to Gail and grabbed her arm. "Hey, bitch. You wanna flip me off again NOW?"

"Ow!" she cried as he yanked her up from the barstool by her hair.

One of the bikers blocked the front door while the tall, loud one, who looked insane, confronted quiet Harold. "What the f__k are *you* lookin' at?" Harold lowered his head and stared at his drink. The biker knocked him to the ground, smashed a beer bottle on the bar, and with its jagged edge sliced a four-inch gash into the right side of his face.

It was a nightmare and I was in it. As I watched a pool of blood form on the ground under Harold's head, the fifth biker came behind the bar toward me. My mind clicked into gear and I ran wildly, hiding behind a stack of empty beer cases in the rear hallway. He opened the cash register and filled his pockets with bills. As I cowered behind the boxes, I prayed, "Oh God, please don't let me die."

Everything happened so fast. The regulars stood frozen in disbelief, then began running for cover as two of the Sidewinders picked up chairs and began smashing everything in sight. Another was swearing and kicking over tables, while a fourth held a switchblade and hollered, "Awright, you motherf__kers, who ELSE wants to play?"

I saw the biker guarding the front door turn around and take a step back as Dennis, the night bartender, arrived with three young regulars behind him. Dennis quickly assessed the situation and grabbed a steel trash can next to what was left of the cigarette machine. He used it as both a shield and a weapon as he attacked one biker after another, yelling, "GET OUT!" at the top of his lungs.

Two of the newly arrived regulars grabbed whatever they could get their hands on and followed Dennis's lead. The third backed out of the bar and I prayed he was going for help. Dennis tossed the trash can aside, grabbed the baseball bat we kept behind the bar for protection and shouted "GO!" as he swung the bat at them.

The bikers flew out, revved up their motorcycles and sped away, the brawl ending as quickly as it began.

Artie bunched up his jacket and pressed it hard against Harold's face. "Somebody get an ambulance," he called, but Harold shook his head no. "Who's got a car then?"

Barry, who had come in with Dennis, gave Harold a clean towel for his cheek and drove him to the hospital.

"Jesus Christ," Dennis exclaimed as he surveyed the damage, "what a f__kin' mess! Anybody else hurt? Is everybody all right? Lynn, call your dad." He ran around checking everyone's condition.

"I'm so sorry," said Gail in tears, "I'm so sorry, so sorry."

Most of the customers had made a hasty exit. I stood up shakily and picked my way through the rubble, then called my father from the pay phone.

"Call the South End precinct," Dad instructed. "I'll be right there."

Every Christmas Dad donated a case of top shelf liquor to the South End police station, his home before he retired, and their response time was fairly quick. I tried my best to tell my story to Dad and the police, but I was shaking and my voice quivered. When I got in my car and headed home, I said to myself, "That's it. Tomorrow I'll get that bricklayer information. It's gotta be easier than this."

THE SOUTH END

I grew up in a white Cape-style house on a dead-end street in the South End of New Bedford, just blocks from the sea. The house wasn't imposing or fancy but understated, with a kind of working-class simplicity, and it was roomy enough for the six of us. The street was quiet and orderly with its neat rows of small Colonials and cottages, and you'd think nothing was happening here at all. A typical middle-class neighborhood. But there was lots of heartbreak going on behind those doors. Deeply buried in the mythology that all was well here, we were living the American Dream, or at least doing better than our immigrant grandparents who worked in the textile mills.

In the yard was a rock garden with tall grasses and wildflowers, and a giant red cedar that bore the imprint of my hands and sneakers, for this was my own personal climbing tree and I nearly wore it out. Late afternoon on a summer's day, I'd play around the yard and when I ran out of things to do, I'd begin my ascent up the old cedar—up, up I'd go, high enough to see the whole world. And what a world it was! Squinty-eyed and patient as a snail, I'd try to guess the types of boats that emerged at the edge of the horizon. Was that a catboat, a barge?

For sure, New Bedford had seen better days. The old whaling port was once the richest city per capita in the world but had fallen into decline, suffering one loss after another, losing its whales, its textiles, and now in danger of losing its fishing industry. But nothing could take away the city's harsh beauty, a city that smelled of the sea and was populated by characters right out of *Moby-Dick* who roamed the downtown and waterfront. The maritime trades still lived down there on Water Street, in the old buildings currently used by the fishing and stevedoring industries. New Bedford was the real thing, the real nitty-gritty thing. You could go down to the docks and see fishermen bring in their catch, smell the lacquered salt air of the Atlantic, and witness grizzled men who looked like they had just emerged from the deep.

The South End was a mixed bag, at least where I lived. Many residents were descendants of the English from Lancashire, an Old-

World center of finely woven cotton, who arrived here as highly skilled craftsmen and took leadership positions in the mills. That's how come there was still bowling-on-the-green across from the Belmont in Hazelwood Park with its large clubhouse and velvet lawns.

Cotton mills were built all along New Bedford's beautiful shoreline, including the South End—a three-mile-long peninsula that juts into Buzzards Bay. Across the bay in South Dartmouth, the grand homes of the mill owners stood watch, their own wooded coastline still pristine for easy living, undisturbed by these hulking beasts that surrounded us. Over the years, the great brick buildings became home to garment shops and other industry. A smattering of Irish, French-Canadians and Portuguese lived in the three-decker tenements near the mills, but we lived "towards the point" in a more suburban setting. We kids thought of ourselves as American as apple pie.

The view from my perch in the cedar tree was not spectacular but it was pretty and picturesque and gave me a sense of calm that washed over my life. I'd climb up high enough to spot the white beach two blocks away, then crawl gingerly along the huskiest limb until Butler Flats lighthouse came into view. There I could see the boats steaming through the channel and hear them sound their horns—draggers, freighters, tugs, toylike sailboats, and sometimes majestic yachts. Dawn, my younger sister, played on the swing-set below, listlessly swinging back and forth as she watched me climb.

Through the open kitchen window I heard the can opener and knew what was for supper tonight—creamed tuna over toast. Mom didn't have much interest in cooking and she worked full time at the library, so we usually had three choices—shepherd's pie, American chop suey, or creamed tuna on toast. Dave, my older brother, didn't seem to mind the same stuff all the time and ate heartily. Dawn and I ate whatever was put in front of us, but Steve was a picky eater. He liked his spaghetti with butter, not sauce, and he stirred coffee syrup into his milk, then drank only the foam at the top. Mom sat at the table while we ate, but she rarely ate with us. She was usually absorbed in a paperback and oblivious to the activity around her. When we were done, we put our plates in the sink and scattered.

If there was tension in the air, we each carried it in our own way, and not until I was well into adulthood did I understand how heavy that burden really was. Mom was resourceful, she could escape from our domestic trauma through sewing or books, but we kids had fewer inner resources. We walked on eggshells, our antennae always up, listening, looking about, ready to scurry at a moment's notice. The great fear nobody talked about was my father.

We ate quickly just in case he came home for dinner. When he was around, we made ourselves scarce, but at mealtime we were sitting ducks with no escape in sight. He was a massive presence the minute he walked in. He'd sit down next to picky Steve and shovel forkfuls of food into his mouth, yelling, "Open! Chew! Swallow!" The rest of us would keep our heads down and eat as fast as we could so as not to be the next victim of his wrath. We never knew what made him so mad all the time, but in my heart I thought I knew. We existed. We had the misfortune of being born in his house.

Breakfast was predictable too. Mom hurriedly made toast or dished out Carnation Instant Breakfast as she tried to get us ready for school and herself ready for work. The invention of Pop Tarts made a big impact at our house and gave us a third breakfast option. Peanut butter and Fluff sandwiches were for lunch, always. On school days I tried to trade my sandwich and milk money for my friends' lunches, my mouth watering at the thought of bologna, ham, tuna salad, or roast beef. Sometimes I think I chose my closest friends based on the contents of their lunch boxes. Our mom's mom, Grandma Mary, baby-sat for us after school and we relished the cookies and snacks she brought from home, often filling up to make us less hungry at dinner time.

I was a sad-looking kid no matter how you looked at it. Mom made my clothes and she was a very good seamstress, but I always felt like plain-Jane next to my classmates who bought the latest styles in the department stores. Worst of all was my hair. Dad cut our hair himself, the way he wanted it, and we had no say about style or length. He cut my bangs very close to my scalp and I hated it, but I didn't dare say anything. In class, I scrunched up my forehead to make my bangs look longer but my schoolmates weren't fooled. Mrs. Correia, my third-grade teacher, must have interpreted my forehead scrunching as wide-eyed enthusiasm and she often called on me, to no avail. I wasn't a great student because I had trouble concentrating. I was always off somewhere else in my mind.

Dad, as a city cop, was popular among his fellow officers because he also owned a tavern. He fit the cop stereotype—a tough, hard-drinking man's man. In truth, we didn't see much of him at home, but he seemed to rule the house whether he was there or not. When he did show up, we felt the tension. None of us wanted to make a mistake, say the wrong thing, look the wrong way, have a wrong expression on our faces, or the place would explode. We had already seen enough explosions in our young lives to last forever.

My mother tried her best to raise four kids alone and hold a responsible job, despite constant criticism and ridicule from Dad. She found great comfort in pouring her talent and energy into decorating our little white house, which she loved dearly. Altogether, she must have felt a terrible strain. I admired her tremendously though I would never tell her. To me, she was really beautiful, with gorgeous red hair and sparkling green eyes and just the right size. And she knew a lot, she was always reading. She knew the answers to all the questions on *Jeopardy*, she knew things about geography that nobody else knew, she knew about politics and history. She was tolerant of people who were different and she accepted all my friends. And she was funny. I just couldn't understand why Dad didn't see her as we did.

My parents probably had a good marriage for about two years. He had fallen in love with a smart, pretty redhead in her twenties, and she had fallen in love with an older cop who exuded charm. He probably drank too much with the boys but she didn't see it as a problem; he would settle down into family life as time went by. He was a charmer and a gentleman, but it didn't last. His demons were unleashed soon after Dave, their first child, was born. As time went on, the drinking got worse and she tried to fight it, but she was powerless; the Bottle always won. How could Dad be so kind to his drinking buddies but not to his own family? Did he use up all his good qualities before he came home? He was a street angel and a house devil, we used to say.

He put Mom down, criticizing the way she looked, the way she kept house, the way she took care of us, and things drifted into chaos. Her only means of fighting back was by bickering, and, later, forcefully arguing, but she was no match for him.

In those days, a family stayed together because of the children, no matter how bad things got. Marriages didn't end because Mom or

Dad was abusive or alcoholic. They endured, no matter how difficult the circumstances. The family needed a man's paycheck to survive. Even when a woman worked, she earned a pittance of what her husband earned. Going on welfare was unthinkable and humiliating. In a woman's mind, her family would end up in the streets if she did not stick out the marriage. This philosophy of endurance was buttressed by the Catholic church and ingrained in every family I knew.

No one ever asked the children—the family had already died in their psyches. Anyway, the important thing was that we didn't feel any different from any other family in our neighborhood and, in many ways, we weren't. Lots of families had alcoholics living in the house and they endured too. In those days, if you had problems in the family you didn't say so. Everything was kept secret. Mom did the best she could, trying to keep the peace, trying to keep us out of the way of danger but not really protecting us, juggling fiercely to make everything turn out right, pretending we were doing all right. But we weren't.

Since my father's days at the police academy, he and Fred Bishop had been best friends and drinking buddies. The two men had gone through training together and were stationed at the same precinct. They were married about the same time and their wives, both librarians, became best friends too. They bought homes one street apart in the South End and the four Bishop children were born in the same succession and time frame as the kids in our family, so we each had a friend close in age and upbringing. Our families even had the same breed of dog, black Labrador retrievers.

There was a major difference, however. My mother welcomed my father's absence from the home. When she came home from work, she made supper, then retreated to the den to sew or read, leaving us kids to fend for ourselves. Sue Bishop took a more assertive approach, calling her husband repeatedly at the Belmont Club, urging him to stop drinking and get himself home where he belonged. When that failed, she hauled the kids to the tavern, shoved them inside and left, hoping to shame Mr. Bishop into playing a more fatherly role. My mother thought that was a terrible thing to do, but Mr. Bishop went home more often than my father, so perhaps it had its merits—or maybe not, depending on how you look at it.

After his shift on the police force was over, Dad went straight to the Belmont to begin his second job. Running a bar is a lot of work but Dad was a workhorse and the bar was his favorite place in the whole world. It gave him something to do, plenty to drink, and constant companions who asked nothing of him. He rarely came home, unless Mom called him home for a particular reason. Whenever we heard his car pull up, we scattered like bugs, looking for the nearest place to be out of sight and out of range of his wrath.

I don't know where his demons came from, or if it was just the alcohol, but his rage seemed to threaten our very survival. He was pleasant enough in the neighborhood, fixing people's plumbing or doing light carpentry, and he was jovial at the bar, but at home he was a holy terror. Dawn and I were seldom his targets, but we didn't want to be in his range either, so we ran to our room and played quietly. Dad usually went after Steve or Dave.

One rainy Saturday we were all in the living room playing the board game *Sorry*. Preoccupied, we didn't realize Dad was home until we heard the back door open. We scattered, leaving the game in disarray. Dad started yelling, "Get out here and clean up this mess NOW!"

Dave, Dawn, and I crept out of our hiding places and began putting the game away, but Steve lagged behind. Dad marched upstairs and gave him a backhand that sent him tumbling down the stairs. Head over heels he went, crashing against the wall at the landing. I had left my prized possession on the landing, a ceramic beer-barrel bank my father had given me for my birthday. After Dad left, I peered out of my room to see if the coast was clear and saw my precious bank in pieces, the coins scattered. Steve had hit the wall with such force he broke it. I ran down the stairs and picked up the broken pieces, tears running down my cheeks, then I flew out the door and threw the pieces in the street, shouting, "I hate you! I hate you!" as my father drove out of sight. I don't know if Steve felt rage too, or if he was just too numb and broken up inside to feel anything at all.

I loved Grandma Mary and Grandpa Charlie, my maternal grandparents, and always felt safe in their care. Grandpa had an adventurous spirit and a keen intelligence, and, best of all, he was a rebel. Everyone in New Bedford knew Charlie was coming when they heard the roar of his Indian motorcycle. An inventor of sorts, he could usually be found in his basement workshop, building electronically controlled model airplanes, boats, and other machines long before such things were commonplace in toy stores. Their house was our sanctuary. Dave and Steve spent long hours in the basement with Grandpa, taking apart broken alarm clocks and transistor radios, recycling the parts for use in one of Grandpa's new projects. Here they felt safe and happy too. Dawn and I played outside in the yard, climbing trees and waiting for the boys to come out so we could play hide-and-seek or tag.

We saw Dad's parents only once or twice a year. His biological father died when Dad was two years old, and his mother was not a person you'd want to see very often. She was a tough, demanding woman who worked in the mills and she and Dad didn't have much of a relationship. I think he was afraid of her. But there was one good thing in this picture. After Dad's father died, she remarried a surprisingly nice man. Dad liked his stepfather, but he was estranged from his only sibling, Joseph, who grew up to be a drinker and a gambler like his deceased father. So Dad's family life left something to be desired.

I was afraid of Nana, but Granddad (my step-grandfather) was always kind to us. He drove a bread truck and lavished day-old doughnuts on us when we visited. Maybe Dad's demons came from the ghost-father he never knew and from a mother who was so mean she made her own grandchildren shake in their boots. Throw in the alcohol and the picture becomes more clear: We were a family paying for the sins of the fathers.

We kids kept the family secrets and acted like the *Leave It to Beaver* Cleavers whenever we went anywhere, which was usually only on holidays. On Easter and Christmas, Mom made matching outfits for herself, Dawn, and me. The boys wore white shirts with clip-on ties, plaid jackets, and navy-blue slacks. Hats, coats, shoes, and underwear were store-bought, but Mom made most everything else. Steve wore Dave's hand-me-downs and Dawn inherited mine. We always ate at Grandma's on holidays and I felt like a princess when I saw Gram's fancy table with so many beautiful things on it—plates, sparkling glasses, cloth napkins, serving dishes, a colorful tablecloth, scented candles, matching utensils, and a centerpiece—it was soooo beautiful. Dad wasn't there so we ate without fear. My mother smiled a lot and paid attention to us when we spoke. Uncle Jerry, Mom's twin brother, and his family came from their home in Connecticut to our holiday dinner too so it was just about perfect.

Christmas was not Dad's best day. Though we always got presents for him, he'd ignore us and the presents and head for the Belmont. Mom would put his gifts on his bureau where they sat unopened until she quietly got rid of them, usually on the day she took down the Christmas tree. We could never figure out why he would not open any gifts from us. It hurt but we got used to it, with little hope that next year would be different. In spite of this bad beginning each Christmas day, the new outfits, the toys, and the trip to Grandma's made everything good.

Although my parents were not churchgoers, Mom took us on Christmas, Easter, and other special occasions. She dropped us off at catechism classes, then met us later when Mass began. Catechism was okay because it gave me an opportunity to fool around with my friends. Our church life ended abruptly after Dawn made her Confirmation. My father was absent during our brief churchgoing days—the first and last time he went to church was on his wedding day.

St. James Church sits on County Street, a bustling thoroughfare that runs from the South End to the North End, twisting and turning along the way. Mom-and-pop stores and Portuguese bakeries nestle snugly between three-decker tenements, interspersed with a funeral parlor, bank, and used-car lot. I always felt the majestic church building was out of place in the humble neighborhood. It was like the castle Tinker Bell flew out of at seven o'clock Sunday night on *The Wonderful World of Disney*. The interior was intimidating to me with its statues of solemn-faced saints on platforms looking down intently on the congregation below.

On the whole, church was not a bad experience for us, and during Mass I felt comforted by the atmosphere of reverence and order. The sermons about a loving God and a peaceful heaven made me feel calm for a moment, masking my inner turbulence. Luckily, the nuns' lectures about hell did not put fear in me—I knew a thing or two about fear, and hell seemed easy. Best of all, when my turn came to receive the sacraments, I was thrilled with the special attention from Mom and the beautiful outfits she made for me.

The first two aisles in church were filled by Mrs. Malloy and her fourteen children. Her husband had recently died of cancer and one of the parish priests, Father Porter, became a surrogate father to the clan and was often a guest in their home, a huge gray house at the bottom of my grandmother's street. Mrs. Malloy attended Mass every morning and her sons served as altar boys. Her devotion to the church was total and unwavering. She cleaned the rectory, cooked meals for the nuns and priests, made crafts for the bazaars. Wherever there was a need, Mrs. Malloy could be counted on to fill it.

The Malloy children were a lively bunch, friendly and full of fun. We loved playing with them, especially because we had enough kids between our two families to make up two sports teams. But after their father died, things changed and they were no longer the carefree children we had known. They spent evenings and weekends at home or at church, often under the watchful eye of Father Porter, while their mother immersed herself in volunteer work. Thirty years later, Father Porter made international headlines when he was sentenced to prison for sexually molesting hundreds of children during his tenure as a priest. Among his victims were several of the Malloy children.

If no First Communions or Confirmations were on the agenda, we spent Sunday mornings with Dad at the Belmont. Since the so-called Massachusetts blue laws forbade liquor sales before noon, the club was closed to patrons. Dad's idea of quality time with his children was to bring us to the bar and put us to work cleaning the place. Dave and Steve scrubbed the bathrooms while Dawn and I swept the floors and washed down the tables and chairs. Later, the boys hauled cases of beer and restocked the coolers. Being in his favorite place put Dad in a civil mood and he was nice to us. If we did a good job, he gave us a few quarters.

While Dave and Steve played pinball, Dawn and I headed for the jukebox. We climbed up on the barstools and spun around as we listened to the Beatles sing *She Loves You and I Wanna Hold Your Hand*. When the quarters ran out, the boys hunted for loose cigarettes and coins dropped in odd places by tipsy customers, stuffing them into their dungaree pockets before Dad caught them. At noontime, Dad locked up the bar, dropped us off at home and headed back to greet the afternoon crowd.

The sound of shouting woke me early one Tuesday morning and I heard Mom say, "And who's going to clean up after her? I have my hands full already!"

Dad hollered back, "What's it to you? The house is a pigsty anyway!" as he slammed the door and left.

Curious, I tiptoed down the stairs and peered over the railing. There was Mom standing over a cardboard box with her hands on her hips, shaking her head. I made my way over and squealed with delight as I saw a small black puppy sitting inside. Mom slowly smiled and said, "Well, she is cute..."

Dawn and the boys stumbled down the stairs, still groggy with sleep but curious about the clamor. "We have a puppy!" I told them, and they were instantly wide awake, all talking at once and reaching down to pet her. Lady was a black Labrador retriever, friendly and playful. We raced home from school each day to see her, anxious to be showered with the unconditional love that only a dog can give. She was chained to her doghouse in the back yard when we were off at school and work, and she barked in frustration each time she spotted a squirrel, bird, or other back yard intruder.

When Lady was eight months old, we arrived home from school one day and she was gone. She had wriggled free from her collar and disappeared. We ran frantically throughout the neighborhood shouting, "Lady! Lady! Come here, girl!" to no avail. When Mom came home, she called Dad at the police station and he checked the day's reports. A dog fitting Lady's description had been killed by a hit-and-run driver. Dad went to the Animal Rescue League and called to tell us it was indeed Lady.

We were devastated by her loss and uncertain about where she had gone in death. From our short-lived catechism classes, we knew people like Mr. Malloy went to heaven or hell when they died, sometimes with a short layover in purgatory, and we knew limbo was for babies who hadn't made it to church in time to be baptized. But dogs had never been mentioned, and we hoped Lady had gone to heaven, a section set aside for canines, heaped with bones and chew toys.

A few days later, Dad came home with another cardboard box containing another black Lab puppy. We again named the puppy Lady and quickly fell in love with her. She was quieter and not as playful as the original Lady and when she was six months old, we learned she had distemper, contracted before she came to live with us. When she died one night in her sleep, we were crushed all over again. Our second chance at a regular dose of love and affection was gone. As we watched Dad take her away, the prospect of a doggie heaven didn't seem as likely now that we had seen the finality of death with our own eyes.

When Dad showed up with a third black Labrador puppy we, of course, named her Lady. The third try was the lucky one and Lady grew to be strong and healthy. We taught her to avoid cars and to stay beside us as we ran and played in the neighborhood. She was housebroken but content to spend most of her time outside in the back yard. Unlike Lady One and Two, she didn't mind being tethered to her doghouse and serenely surveyed the yard as she lay inside on an old wool blanket. The boys tossed a ball for her and she retrieved it over and over, dropping it at their feet with a solemn let's-do-it-again look. I confided all my troubles to her while she listened patiently, laying her head on my lap. Dawn dressed her in hats and scarves and played house. She obliged, looking humiliated but never shaking off the odd costumes. In later years, Lady stayed inside at night, curled up on a wool blanket in front of the fireplace. She died peacefully in her sleep at the age of fifteen. I will always remember Lady as a stabilizing force and a faithful provider of love and devotion to me during my tumultuous childhood.

Finally, June arrived and school was over. Although we had fun playing in the neighborhood and taking lunch to the beach on the long, hot, lazy days of July, we all looked forward to the highlight of the summer—the annual camping trip. Myles Standish State Forest in Carver was only thirty miles from home, but it was like another country with woods and ponds as far as the eye could see. Oh sure, there were campers, tents, trailers, and hundreds of people vacationing at the reserve, but to us it was a frontier with endless possibilities for exploration and discovery.

This was heaven—no sirens, no car horns, no traffic lights. We loved breathing fresh air, listening to the birds, and smelling the sweet smoke of campfires. We were explorers of a new world—following dirt paths, discovering fresh water ponds and wild animal tracks. And we loved seeing old camper friends again and meeting new ones. Most of the families were from Massachusetts, but we were fascinated by out-of-staters and questioned them as if they were from foreign countries. Amazingly, they were just as interested in us. They even seemed to like us.

Some days we spent more time in water than on land. The ponds were plentiful, each with its own personality. College Pond was choked with water lilies and boaters got their oars tangled in leaves. Barrett's Pond was the warmest, clear and clean and heated by the sun all day long. Curlew Pond, our favorite, was the largest and drew throngs of children toting inflatable swim toys. Teenage lifeguards watched over the youngsters, leaving parents free to enjoy some peace and quiet.

Nighttime was even more magical in the forest. We hunted frogs, shining our flashlights along the edges of the pond, tiptoeing quietly and whispering to each other. The lucky finder let out a whoop and we ran to inspect his quarry amidst high-pitched squeals from the girls, raucous laughter from the boys. A few minutes shushing each other and we were off in pursuit of the next unwary victim. Empty mayonnaise jars, holes poked in the lids, became home to the hapless frogs.

The kids without flashlights used mayonnaise jars to trap fireflies, a hunt that required more patience and observation. The bugs glowed for a lightning instant and, if you lost sight of them, they'd be off and away before flashing again. When they flew over a bush or a pond, no one could get them and the forest roared with the moans and groans from frustrated trackers.

Back at the campsite, things were a lot like home. Mom and Dad bickered constantly, but there were no doors for Dad to slam. For starters, Dad always brought two cases of beer, and replenishing the stock wasn't difficult since he traveled back and forth to the Belmont Club each day. Mom somehow kept him from drinking at home in the city, but she had little control here.

Although she was used to seeing him drunk, she rarely watched him drink because he did his serious drinking at the Club. Here at the campsite, she had to watch him down bottles of beer, one after another. Clearly, she hated the sight of him guzzling and didn't want us kids watching either. When she chastised him, he replied, "But I never get drunk," and he proceeded to do just that.

His drinking lessened when my grandparents came to visit, but as soon as they left, he became himself again. In spite of these problems, Mom enjoyed the country life and kept herself occupied with a book or hand stitching. At sunset she retired to the pop-up camper and read until she fell asleep. Dad drank by the campfire as we roasted hot dogs on whittled sticks, then toasted marshmallows. Dawn and I liked ours barely browned, but Steve plunged his into the flame until it was coal-black, then ate it off the stick, yelping as it burned his mouth.

We kids slept in a tent, safe and happy, breathing in the smells of mildewed canvas, wood smoke, and the cool night air. Dawn fell asleep instantly. Dave and Steve briefly played around, pillow fighting or poking each other, but sleep came quickly to them too. I drifted off to sleep like an angel, wishing I could live this way forever.

Our fun doubled the summer the Bishop family joined us. Camping with our best friends at Myles Standish! We each tried to be the first to show off our favorite places or recount our past exploits. Mom loved having Susan Bishop there and Dad was just as glad to be with Fred. The constant bickering ended and they enjoyed the company of their best friends. Fred and Susan Bishop had a small camper. The kids brought their own tent and we pleaded with our parents to let the girls have one tent and the boys the other. They relented and we eagerly rearranged our sleeping bags for the night ahead.

At dusk, our parents sat around the campfire talking and laughing. Mom was the only one not drinking. As the evening progressed and the other three got tipsier, she drowsily bid them good-night and went into the camper. We kids were exhausted but unwilling to end the day's fun, so we kept up the pranks between the girls' tent and boys' tent until one by one, we nodded off. The anticipation of tomorrow made me smile as my eyelids closed and I fell into a deep sleep.

At some point, I awakened to the sound of loud, angry voices. At first I thought I was having a nightmare and I sat up in my sleeping bag, startled out of my wits. I tried to focus. Jeez. They were the voices of my parents and the Bishops. What was going on?

"For God's sake, Bill, she's your best friend's wife!" my mother cried. My father, his speech slurred, said, "I was just walking her to the bathroom and one thing led to another, it's no big deal."

"I'm so sorry," mumbled Mrs. Bishop to Mom.

"Shut up and get in the car," Mr. Bishop said disgustedly. Slam! Slam! The Bishops drove off, leaving the children behind, still asleep. A stony silence ensued, broken only by the shutting of the camper door as my mother went to bed and the pop of a bottle cap as my father opened another beer.

The next morning, Mom acted as if nothing had happened. Dad left early for the Club, and Mom told the Bishop children their parents had gone home. No one questioned why they went and I was grateful for that. We played through the rest of the week and took the Bishop kids home with us at the end of our vacation. Although Dad and Mr. Bishop remained co-workers and drinking buddies, it was the end of the friendship between my mother and Susan Bishop. It was also the end of our camping trips.

Shortly after my ninth birthday, I noticed Mom was putting on weight. I didn't think much about it until Steve told me she was going to have another baby. As her belly grew bigger, the more she and Dad fought at night in their bedroom, often waking us with their yelling.

"This is all I need right now, another mouth to feed!" I heard him shout one night.

"I didn't do it alone!" Mom yelled back as Dad slammed the bedroom door, marched out of the house and drove away.

When Mom went into labor, she called Dad at the tavern and he sent one of the bar's regulars to drive her to the hospital. Grandma came and stayed with us until Grandpa brought Mom home. We were thrilled to meet our new baby brother, Mark. Mom doted on the new baby and sewed custom-fitted bedding for his bassinet. Dad never did go to the hospital. He came and went from our house, but didn't talk to Mom for three months, angry because she had taken offense at his sending a customer to drive her to the hospital. From then on, my parents were physically and emotionally separated, even though Dad continued to live at home for several more years. As for Mark, Dad ignored him right from the start and continued to do so throughout most of his childhood. We kids thought Mark had it made, the luckiest of us all.

TURBULENCE

Young girls never see danger up ahead because the world is good, and nice people don't hurt, at least those outside the family. When I was nine, I learned otherwise, and I also learned to keep quiet and protect the perpetrator. It probably wouldn't happen like this today because children are encouraged to be honest and open about what happens to them. Then again, there's probably a lot of silence today too.

When my brother Dave was in high school, he got a summer job working at Circle K Ranch in Carver and he fell in love with horses. Dawn and I began taking part in the trail rides offered for children on weekends and school vacations. For five dollars each, we could ride on three different trails and hang around the ranch for most of the day.

The ranch's owners, the Farrells, became our surrogate family and we spent lots of time there. When Mom became concerned about the cost, the Farrells agreed to let us pitch hay, shovel manure, and groom the horses in exchange for riding time. The gentleness of the horses, the beautiful countryside, and Mrs. Farrell's kindness and delicious cooking made me blissfully happy.

The Farrells had a perfect partnership. Mr. Farrell was the cowboy, a weathered Clint Eastwood type who could be abrupt and impersonal, but he had the knowledge to help us become real rugged Western riders. He trained the horses and led the trail rides while Mrs. Farrell, plump and perky, kept on top of the business. She did the books, scheduled rides and ran the household. Three paid employees helped keep the place going and there were always kids around who fed and mucked and groomed to pay their way. A few times each year, the ranch bustled with excitement as the Farrells prepared to participate in local horse shows and parades.

One of the biggest was the Fourth of July horse show in Marion. Only a few chosen young people were allowed to ride and they trained with selected horses months before the event. My brother Dave was chosen, and before long he fell head over heels for Beth, one of the prettiest riders on the team. They were inseparable and I loved watching them hold hands and smile shyly at each other. One day as I entered the barn, I overheard them talking in tense, pleading voices.

"Please don't say anything to him, Dave—you'll ruin everything," Beth begged. "I'll just stay away from him—I want to ride in the show more than anything."

Dave spotted me and cut the conversation short. "We'll talk about this later," he told Beth as he turned and walked past me, eyes filled with anger. Dave was a gentle soul and I had never seen him so mad.

"What's the matter?" I asked, running after him.

"Nothing, just forget it." He left no doubt that this subject was not open for discussion. Ten minutes later I really had forgotten it, lost in my own thoughts as I brushed my favorite horse, Amigo.

Beth and Dave won blue ribbons and Dave added his to the collection pinned up along one wall of his bedroom. He and Beth went their own separate ways a few months later, but stayed friends. I was brokenhearted to see true love die. Was this the way it worked? You're crazy in love one day and the next day you're not? I think I was more depressed by the breakup than Beth and Dave were.

Time passed and life went on the same as before. The year after Dave and Beth broke up, I decided I wanted to ride in the Fourth of July show too, even though I was much younger than the other competitors. Dave's blue ribbon collection was a challenge to me.

Mrs. Farrell was rolling out pie dough at the kitchen table when I approached her and asked the million-dollar question. She looked up and smiled. "Well, dear, you're a little young, but you do ride real well. You'll need to speak to Mr. Farrell about it. Why don't you go talk to him and see what he thinks?" She returned to her pie-making, humming along with Tammy Wynette on the radio as I skipped off to the barn, elated at the possibility of actually riding in a show.

"Mr. Farrell?" I yelled.

"Over here in the feed room," he responded. The feed room was a small enclosure in the rear of the barn and held fifty-gallon drums of oats, barley, and pellets. Mr. Farrell sat on a threadbare couch, filling feedbags with a mixture of the three grains. I stood in the doorway for a minute, watching him. He looked up and said, "What's on your mind, girlie?"

I was giddy with anticipation as I strode up to him. "Mr. Farrell, I want to ride in the Fourth of July show. Can I?"

He looked me over and sized me up. "You're mighty young for that, ain't ya?"

"I know I am, but I can ride better than some of the high-school kids."

He stopped filling the feedbags. "Well, come on over here and sit down while I think about it."

I sat next to him on the couch and for a moment thought he might be estimating my size for a riding outfit as he put his hands around my waist. A moment later, he had slipped one hand under the waistband of my jeans and slid it down further. I was shocked and frightened and confused and paralyzed. Finally, I managed to say, "I gotta go, my sister is waiting for me."

Afterwards, I pretended nothing had happened and I didn't tell anyone about it. I rode in the Fourth of July horse show but didn't win any ribbons that year. I erased the incident with Mr. Farrell from my conscious memory and continued to go to the ranch and ride with Dawn for several more years, but I made sure I was never alone with him again.

The year I turned twelve, Mr. Farrell, was accused of child molestation by a high-school girl who boarded her horse at the ranch. Mrs. Farrell, certain the charge was false and worried sick about the ranch's reputation and financial situation, asked several young riders to testify in court about Mr. Farrell's wonderful character. It was upsetting for me to see my surrogate mom in such distress.

"Please, Lynn, will you come and testify on his behalf?" she pleaded, her eyes brimming with tears. I agreed. Court was an intimidating place and my voice shook just a little when I stated under oath that Mr. Farrell had never approached me in an inappropriate way.

"You did a great job," said Mrs. Farrell, who rushed over to me during the recess. Two young girls from the ranch trailed behind her, all smiles. I have to say it was not my finest hour. In spite of my testimony, Mr. Farrell was convicted and served a six-month jail sentence. Convinced of his innocence, Mrs. Farrell ran the ranch herself until he got out of prison. He died of cancer a few years later—I had the feeling his life was over anyway.

Meanwhile, in the neighborhood, we found a new group to chum around with—the Hastings kids. Like the Bishops, the Hastings children closely matched us in age, and my perfect match was Lisa. Mr. Hastings worked in a bank and he was an alcoholic, but not the sort we were used to. He was very kind to us, speaking softly and politely whenever he came home. This amazed me, since chances were good that a dozen or so neighborhood children were playing in his house at any given time. Mr. Hastings had his own bedroom on the second floor. To get to it, he had to pass through a large, open room where most of his children slept. Whenever we slept over, which was often, he'd say, "Good night, children, pleasant dreams," as he passed through the room. I found this nightly ritual comforting.

"Ma" Hastings was a short, stocky woman who reminded me of a bulldog. Her jet-black hair was cropped like a man's and she wore jeans and men's T-shirts, her cigarette pack rolled up in the cuff. She was nearly toothless and she smoked like a chimney. I was fascinated by the way she could smoke a cigarette right down to the filter without the ashes falling.

Her sister Lucy, who was a younger version of Ma Hastings, came by to visit sometimes, and she was amazing in another way. She had taken in Ma's fourth child, a boy born with a spinal disorder who was not expected to live more than a few months. Tommy was now twelve years old and Lucy carried him everywhere in her arms.

When we went to their house on a Saturday or Sunday morning, Mr. Hastings' brother Roland was often there. Ma would still be in bed, nursing her hangover from the night before, and Roland would go into her bedroom and shut the door. They would both emerge hours later for coffee and cigarettes. Lisa told me that the three youngest Hastings children were fathered by Roland. I was a little shocked, but Lisa explained it so matter-of-factly, I took it as a fact of life, just the way things were.

Before Ma woke up, we kids trekked back and forth from the corner variety store with jumbo loaves of white bread and tubs of margarine. We made toast, glopped margarine on it and dunked it in cups of weak tea, sweetened with sugar and milk. Before long, we'd hear a roar.

"This place looks like a f__kin' tornado hit it. You kids get to work and clean it up or I'll beat the shit out of ya." These were Ma's first words of the day. We scrambled for brooms, mops and dust rags and went to work. Everything had to sparkle, and I learned how to clean a house from top to bottom during these cleaning frenzies. Lisa forgot to empty the dustpan once and Ma whacked her in the face so hard she flew across the room, the back of her head smashing against the wall.

The Hastings kids didn't eat well. Ma knew nothing about nutrition and Mr. Hastings didn't pay much attention. Poor Lisa was plagued with ear infections and toothaches and often couldn't sleep at night because of the pain. She always had a tube of Orajel with her. No school nurse or social worker ever intervened. The kids wore clean but worn hand-me-downs, so Lisa wasn't a dirty child, just a neglected one. Ma had a routine she stuck to like glue. She slept most of the day and woke up around four in the afternoon, immediately heading out to the First Base Cafe to drink. When I visited the Hastings, we ate cold cereal for dinner and sometimes macaroni and cheese from a box. Mr. Hastings bought the groceries but didn't have a clue what to buy. Soon Ma would call on the phone and tell Lisa to bring her some money. This was our signal to hop on her brother Bobby's Stingray bicycle and head down to the bar to retrieve her. There we'd find Ma, propped up against the doorway, drunk as could be, yelling for Lisa to hurry up.

We'd tug at her arm. "C'mon home. It's time to come home. We have NO money," we'd tell her.

"You little brats, what'd ya do with my money?" she'd yell. She'd continue yelling like this and when she was all yelled out, Lisa and I would struggle to position her on the bike seat and peddle her home.

Despite everything, I felt safe and comfortable at the Hastings house. The craziness was predictable and familiar and I always felt accepted there, but I dreaded returning to my own home each day. My brother Mark, now three years old, was still shunned by my father, who barely acknowledged his existence. Mom and Dad's fighting was constant. Dawn was learning all the wrong things from me, and she began to hang out with troubled kids, just as I did.

When it came time for my two older brothers to leave home, they had no specific plans; they just knew they wanted to get away. Dave left as soon as he graduated from high school and moved into his own apartment. He and his friend Gary thought they might launch their careers by holding a rock concert in an old movie theater in the North End. At the least, they'd make some big bucks and get promotional experience. Gary's father fronted them the money and they booked Canned Heat and a local band called Pleasant Street. As it happened, Canned Heat wasn't all that hot at the time and Pleasant Street played free at many local places so ticket sales were slow. Gary's father ended up paying most of the expenses and Dave was indebted to him for years.

But this unhappy experience was not a total loss. Dave was bitten by the concert bug and landed a job with Virgo Lighting, the company that worked the Canned Heat concert. Dave was soon on the road, traveling from state to state with Virgo, providing the elaborate lighting and special effects demanded by popular bands. I envisioned Dave as the star behind the scenes, the one who lit up the stage in psychedelic colors, casting the bands in shocking pinks and moody blues, the one who released the helium balloons at outdoor concerts, which flew all the way to Brazil or Zanzibar, making rainbows wherever they went. Months went by without us seeing or hearing from him, and I missed him.

Steve found salvation by toughening up. Picked on in the neighborhood and the object of Dad's wrath at home, his life had been difficult. Struggling to rescue himself, he began lifting weights in a friend's basement and pouring down weight-gain drinks. Soon he was healthier and hefty enough to try out for the high-school football team. He made the team, and the following years held the peak moments of his life. After his senior year, he moved to Martha's Vineyard, rented a small room, and sold jewelry on the Wood's Hole ferry. I think he felt safe and happy on that small island, away from the city.

Dawn and I were restless, aimless teenagers, biding our time until we were old enough to move out too. My grandparents sensed trouble and tried their best to help, but our family life was beyond repair. However, life did change in one important way; Dad left home for good, and I had something to do with it.

As Dawn and I were being driven home from our friend Anita's house by her older brother John, we saw our dad pass by, driving in the opposite direction from the Belmont and from our home. Dawn and I exchanged curious glances.

"That's our dad's car! We can ride the rest of the way home with him." John shrugged and turned around, following Dad as he drove down Brock Avenue. Dad parked, got out of the car and rang the doorbell of a house we didn't know. A strange woman opened the door, kissed him on the cheek, led him in, and closed the door behind him.

Dawn and I looked at each other in shock and dismay. "Oh, I guess it's not him after all," I said, embarrassed nearly to death. When John dropped us at home, we hurried inside, said hello to Grandpa, ran up to our room, and shut the door.

"Oh my God. How could he do this to Mom?" I couldn't believe what I had just seen.

"What should we do?" Dawn asked, devastated.

Our reaction seems naive, of course, these many years later. Mom and Dad lived in the house but they didn't have a real marriage, so it figures he'd sow his oats elsewhere, but at the time we were shocked. Even with all the bad stuff that happened at home, cheating with another woman was still crossing a line. Or maybe it seemed extra bad because it made our situation public.

"Let's look in the phone book and find out who lives there—I saw the number on the door when she opened it—51 Brock Avenue." Dawn got the phone book from the kitchen and we spent an hour going page by page, looking for a name to match the address. By the time we got to the letter *B* we realized how futile this method was. Just as we were about to give up, Dawn spotted the name *Baker* at 53 Brock Avenue.

"Let's call them and ask them who their next-door neighbor is."

We scanned the living room to make sure Grandpa was engrossed in his TV show and crept down the cellar stairs to use the phone on Dad's workbench.

I had a plan and dialed slowly. "Hello, is this Mrs. Baker?"

"Yes, it is, dear. How can I help you?"

"Our dog Lady got loose and we think we saw her in your neighbor's yard. We wanted to call your neighbor but we didn't know her name."

"Oh, you mean Sylvia? Sylvia Poyant? She has a poodle. Maybe your dog went over to make friends. Would you like me to look out the window and see if your dog is still there, dear?"

"No thank you, we'll call her ourselves." I quickly hung up and passed the news along to Dawn.

"What do we do now?" Dawn groaned.

"I think we should tell Mom. Then she'll have a good excuse to get rid of him." I never hated my father as much as I did at that moment. When Mom came home from work, we told her what happened. She defended him like she always did, saying, "Your father has his faults, but he's a hard worker. He gets a little carried away sometimes but he would never cheat on me."

"Ask him yourself then," I challenged her.

She did exactly that. She called Dad at the bar and asked him to come home right away.

When he arrived, she said, "You girls go out and play for a while. I have to talk to your father alone."

Dad did his best to deny the facts, claiming he had been doing some plumbing work for Sylvia, whose husband had been a Belmont regular before he died the year before. When Mom threatened to confront Sylvia, Dad finally admitted his affair. After a lot of yelling, my father packed a bag and left, telling my mother he'd be living with Sylvia for the time being.

Mom was in shock but she acted fast; by the end of the week, she had filed for divorce. She also discovered she was the last to know about Dad's infidelity and she had the sympathy vote in the neighborhood. I was brimming with rage at my father. For years he'd made our lives miserable and this final betrayal just added fuel to the fire.

I was so angry, I decided to pay Dad a visit at the Belmont and tell him exactly how I felt. All the swear words I knew weren't bad enough to describe him. We weren't allowed in the bar during business hours, but this time I didn't care. I marched in. He was sitting at the bar, drink in hand, laughing with a customer. I strode up to him, tapped him on the shoulder, and, as he turned around, saw the smile leave his face.

"Are you happy, Dad? It wasn't enough to make Mom's life miserable at home, but you had to humiliate her in public too?" My voice broke and tears welled up in my eyes.

"You don't belong in here," he said, trying not to make a scene. Conversation quieted down as customers began looking our way. "Go home now, Lynn—go on!"

"Your days of ordering me around are over!" I was so hurt and angry I hardly realized what I was saying. But these were the words

I'd wanted to say my entire life, and I wasn't about to stop now. "So, hey, why don't you just go have another highball?" I spat out.

At that point, Dad got up from his barstool and chased me out the door.

Meanwhile, life didn't get better. I was thirteen and going through puberty. I felt ugly and awkward and hated my nose, my teeth, my ears, my freckles, and my shape. Mom was so pretty and stylish, always wearing the latest fashions. I was sure I'd look awful for the rest of my life and could never hold a candle to her beauty. My destructive attitude put me at odds with the world and Mom blamed me for setting a bad example for my kid sister. She was right.

After that awful summer of my parents' divorce, I entered seventh grade at Roosevelt Junior High School and things began to look up. I met Barbara Arruda in homeroom, a petite girl with green eyes, a dark complexion, and the most beautiful hair I had ever seen. It flowed past her waist in a cascade of black, shiny ringlets.

Barbara invited me to her house after the third day of school and I became a frequent visitor to her third-floor tenement on Nelson Street. Her parents were from Portugal and didn't speak much English but they thought I was wonderful. A pot of kale soup simmered on the stove every day and her mom loved to see me dig into a steaming bowl. Barbara, as weary of kale soup as I was of peanut butter and Fluff sandwiches, laughed as I slurped the delicious soup loaded with fresh kale, kidney beans, linguiça, and onions. Mrs. Arruda buttered thick slices of Portuguese bread for me and I dunked them into the broth as I wolfed it down.

Because they didn't know the language or culture, her parents trusted Barbara to make her own choices in friends and activities and, unfortunately, I was not the best influence. We began spending a lot of time with the downstairs neighbor, Jody, a bleached blonde of eighteen whose mother was seldom home. Jody wore a purple-fringed suede jacket and was already involved in sex and drugs. We looked at her as mature and worldly.

When my mother came looking for me at Barbara's one day and found me at Jody's, she hit the roof. "You are not going to hang around with a tramp like that," she scolded as we drove home. That did it.

Everything else in my life had been ruined and now Mom wanted to take away my best friends. I had told my father I wasn't taking orders from him anymore and, right then and there, I decided I wasn't going to take them from my mother either. I began skipping school and hanging out at Jody's during the day. Soon my grades dropped and the truant officer was having a talk with Mom.

Mom tried to make me go to school, but I had already given up on myself; I felt like a complete loser. I was sent to a juvenile detention center in Chelsea for two weeks because of my truancy, and that experience took away the last threads of hope I had for a normal, happy life. I didn't try to run away from the program as some girls did, mainly because the food was great. I still remember the baked chicken dinners with hot gravy and creamy mashed potatoes.

The program didn't reform me. When I returned home, I headed straight for Jody's. She and most of her friends had quit school so I had plenty of company during the day. Mom finally gave up trying to make me go to school and hired a tutor to work with me at home. When I didn't show up to meet the tutor, she realized I was unwilling to cooperate and she resignedly signed the papers that allowed me to quit school at fifteen. It must have been a heartbreaking moment for her, but I was only seeing my own side of things.

Headstrong and adventurous, I just wanted to have fun, but it was a desperate kind of fun. At my young age, I had no self-understanding and didn't know why I caused Mom such grief. I was full of confusion and longed for a warm family life. With Dad out of the house, I might have had it. All I had to do was work hard in school and stop giving Mom so much trouble at home. But she always tried to control me and I was out of control. I just wanted to run away from everything. So I told myself Mom would be better off without me in the house and I left. Dawn followed my lead and left school after she finished the ninth grade. Mom kept working and focused her attention on taking care of Mark. Her heart must have been in pieces as she watched her family fall apart.

I didn't go home much after that and for awhile I slept at Barbara's or Jody's. Oh, I was always welcome at home, if I followed the rules, but I chose to leave. Now that I was on my own, eating regularly became a problem so I had to remedy that. Lying about my age, I got hired as an assembly line worker at a sweatshop in the South End. Eight hours a day I stood on my feet and wrapped thin wires around television tubes, then put the tubes on a conveyor belt for the next worker in line. I hated the job—the awful monotony of the work, the smell of burning plastic filling the factory, the downtrodden older people I worked with, the way time dragged and minutes seemed like hours inside the dark, dingy plant. As soon as I got my paycheck at the end of the fourth week, I quit.

One night when Barbara and Jody weren't home, I had nowhere to go and I walked up and down Brock Avenue trying to ward off my hunger and the chilly night air. At two o'clock in the morning the avenue was deserted, so I walked down a side street and saw the framework of a house under construction. I approached cautiously, then loosened one flap of the plastic sheathing around the framing and crawled inside. In the blackness I couldn't see a thing so I curled up in a corner and waited for daylight, terrified, like a small animal cornered by a bigger one, afraid to move. It was the longest night of my life, but it was still better than going home.

The people I met through Jody were older and many were heroin addicts. Everyone accepted me as a tag-along but a good-hearted kid. I spent my time walking around the South End with Jody, whose good looks attracted a lot of attention. We often stopped to talk to people she knew along the way, like Rico, the Cuban, who was one of the biggest heroin suppliers in the city. Lots of cars pulled up to conduct business on the avenue and many customers shot up drugs right there in their cars.

My mother worked at the library across from the Ritz Cafe, where most of the illegal drug transactions in the South End took place. One day when Jody and I were talking to a friend outside the bar, I looked over and saw her staring out the library window at me, a pile of books in her arms and a heartbroken expression on her face. I turned away and felt a deep stab of guilt, rapidly replaced by feelings of loyalty to my friends, who never hassled me the way I got hassled at home.

TRUCKIN'

Though New Bedford was far removed in geography and temperament from San Francisco, the Age of Aquarius had arrived here too, and teens and young adults wore long hair, patched bell-bottom jeans, and love beads. At the Electric Grape, one of several downtown "head shops," you could get psychedelic posters, black lights, India import clothes, and drug-related items. High-school kids, once bound for college, were choosing to be free spirits and become one with the universe.

Barbara was still going to school, but on weekends she'd tell her parents she was sleeping at a friend's house. On Friday nights we'd hitchhike to Newport and on Saturdays to Provincetown. The drinking age was eighteen and lots of younger teens frequented the nightclubs that didn't check I.D.'s. One Friday night, two long-haired boys from the North End picked us up and as we drove toward Newport, the driver playfully flirted with me. His name was Phil and he was nineteen. I thought he was very cute. He was also the first boy who had ever really shown a romantic interest in me. He had his own car and asked if we could get together again sometime.

"Sure. How about tomorrow?"

I soon learned that sex was one way to get affection and attention, two things I desperately needed. My choice of friends and boyfriends began to follow the same pattern as that of a loyal pup. If anyone showed me kindness or attention, I was their faithful companion forever.

As time went by and the thrill of first love began to wane, Phil and I became less a couple and more a part of the gang. We'd pile into his car and ride around, looking for adventure. Each section of the city had its own public park and special hangout spot where young people gathered: Hazelwood Park in the South End, Brooklawn Park in the North End, and Buttonwood Park in the West End. I became bored with the Hazelwood Park crowd and Phil was bored with the Brooklawn Park gang, so we started hanging around Buttonwood Park in the West End. This choice proved to be life-changing, as I would meet two very important people at the park: my future best friend, Pam, and my future husband, Tim.

There was a zoo in the park and one day I decided to stroll over and take a look at the new seal pool. As I walked through the playground, I struck up a conversation with an attractive young woman named Pam, whose long, blond hair sparkled in the sun. She was friendly and vivacious, and she seemed so right with the world as she pushed her little boy, Jason Blue, on a swing. He was an adorable child with blond hair cut in a bowl shape. Clearly, he was the light of her life and he won my heart too with his shy, sweet smile. Pam invited me to join them as they snacked on fruit and cookies and I felt suddenly connected. Something good had come into my life.

Pam was four years older than I and had already been married and divorced. She worked at odd jobs, trying to provide for her son without any financial help from her ex-husband. When I asked her what she did for work, she replied with a laugh, "Well, let's see. I baby-sit, sell embroidery, do phone soliciting for vacuum cleaner sales, shelve groceries at a food co-op, substitute at a day-care center—I guess that's it." We talked a bit longer and then I headed over to the basketball court where the hippies hung around, sitting on park benches or lying on the grass, soaking up the sun.

Phil and I got to know the West End crowd and learned that many of them lived together in a big house called "Rounds Street." When two guys needed a ride there one day, Phil and I dropped them off and they invited us in to meet everybody. The minute I walked in I knew I had found a home.

About a dozen long-haired men and women were busy with various activities. Some were playing guitars and singing peace songs, a few women were baking organic wheat bread, and one really cute guy, dressed only in cutoff denim shorts and a puka shell necklace, was drinking Boone's Farm apple wine and reading *Be Here Now* by Baba Ram Dass, the ultimate hippie guru of the time.

The walls were draped with psychedelic posters and macramé dream catchers. Sweet-smelling candles and incense filled the room and the couches were covered in Mexican blankets. Everyone greeted me warmly and as I wandered into the kitchen, a woman offered me some freshly baked bread with homemade apple butter on top.

"Hi, my name's Crystal," said the woman as she went on working in the kitchen.

"Jeez, this is great. Who lives here, anyway?"

Crystal stopped what she was doing and offered me some herbal tea. "Now, that's a story. The house is owned by Warren, left to him by his grandmother. Warren, his two brothers, and three cousins originally moved in, and then their girlfriends joined them. Next came several friends and acquaintances with nowhere to go after leaving home. I live here with my sister and our boyfriends. There's also a revolving group of about twenty people, coming and going. C'mon, I'll show you the upstairs."

We trooped upstairs and I could hardly believe my eyes. "Wow, this is far out." The bathroom walls were painted day-glo purple with black trim, and mattresses ran wall-to-wall in the four bedrooms. We continued the tour in the back yard where Ben, a gentle German shepherd, was stretched out on the grass napping. As she lit up a joint and offered it to me, Crystal showed me the organic garden she and her sister had planted and said they were vegetarians and tried to eat only their own homegrown produce.

I knew, without a doubt, I wanted to live here and I thought I'd better make my case right now.

"Um...Crystal," I stammered. "I'm, well, kind of on the move and I never know where I'm going to be sleeping from one night to the next. Do you think I could maybe stay here for a while?"

Crystal's blue eyes were like the sky on a summer day and her long India-import skirt gave her a mystical look. I was enchanted.

"I don't see why not. Let's go talk to Warren."

We wandered through the rooms and found Warren, a tall man with a gentle manner. His long, curly brown hair and horn-rimmed glasses made him look like a '60s pseudo-intellectual.

Crystal smiled benignly. "This is Lynn and she wants to know if she can stay for a while."

He looked me over. "She can stay."

I was so excited I started to babble about all the cleaning and cooking I would do to earn my keep.

"It's not the Army," Warren chuckled, and everyone laughed. People began introducing themselves, making me feel at home. Phil, happy about my decision, already had his eye on a pretty brunette who was embroidering a peace sign onto a faded denim jacket.

Since I didn't have any belongings other than the clothes I kept at Barbara's, I moved in on the spot. Late that night I stayed up listening to a guy named Tommy play guitar, especially impressed that he knew my favorite Crosby, Stills and Nash songs. After a while I went upstairs and found an empty mattress in a small room next to Crystal's. I'm so glad to be here, I thought as I curled up on the bed and fell asleep.

As the months went by, I became a full-fledged member of the commune and had never been happier in my life. Here was the acceptance I had always longed for. They didn't care where I came from or how smart I was—they liked me for who I was, no questions asked. Because I was the youngest member of the group, everyone watched out for me and I felt safe. Everything was shared at Rounds Street—food, clothes, drugs, and sex. A constant stream of people came in and out of the house, all part of the party that never ended. Most of them lived by the "peace, love and do your own thing" philosophy and didn't want to hassle or be hassled.

Once in a while, someone would overindulge in wine or drugs and disturb the peace. On a few occasions, guys who visited the house got more interested in me than I in them and one of my roommates would intervene. Warren's cousin Danny, one of the oldest residents of the house at twenty-two, was like a father to me. We spent a lot of time together, talking about the books we were reading—J.R.R. Tolkien, Carlos Castanada—and life in general. Even when I went to Buttonwood Park to hang out all day, I brought a book along. As with many of the guests at Rounds Street, my opinions and values came from books, rather than parents and friends.

Unlike most of the others, who were strictly party people, Danny had a thirst for knowledge and a desire to make a difference in people's lives. There was something in me that wanted more from life too, and maybe that's why I was drawn to him. He became a close friend and stabilizing force in my chaotic life.

We all lived hand-to-mouth, eating mayonnaise sandwiches one day and baked fish the next. Warren was the only person with a job. He drove an oil truck and paid most of the house expenses such as the electric bill. There was no phone, of course—we were too poor for that luxury. He occasionally donated to the collections we took for food, wine, or drugs, but since we all lived at his house rent-free, we felt he already contributed more than his share. The rest of us worked only when necessary. If there was a shape-up at the state pier for longshoremen, most of the men in the house went. One good-sized freighter could mean three days of steady work—unloading cargo for seven dollars an hour and taking home a box of frozen fish or Granny Smith apples when they could slip it past the gang foreman. The women made money as part-time waitresses or barmaids and brought food home from work at the end of the day. If we were really desperate, one of us would visit our parents and return with some groceries or a few dollars.

At Rounds Street, I fell in love for the first time and also suffered my first broken heart. His name was Richie and he was quiet and shy, with long black hair and hazel eyes. He worked full-time in a factory, which seemed mature to me, and he lived with two friends in an apartment, which seemed really mature. I met him at one of our nightly parties and was instantly infatuated, inspired in part by my deep need for an anchor and security. To make him like me, I offered him food and drink and tried to become a good listener.

He took notice of my desperate, awkward advances, and before long we connected. Most of my experiences with boys had been shockingly brief, but this one was going to last, I was sure of it. No matter how hard I tried, the relationship always seemed fragile. Clearly, my feelings for him were deeper than his for me. He refused to commit exclusively to me and, because I was dumb about these things, I persisted.

Though I officially lived at Rounds Street, I now spent as much time as possible at Richie's apartment, even when he wasn't at home. I cooked for him and his roommates, cleaned the apartment, washed the dishes, and did the laundry—anything to make myself indispensable. When I was at Richie's one day, the local narcotics detectives raided the Rounds Street house, but no drugs were found. That's what you call a miracle! The drugs were getting harder and more plentiful at the house. After that, I spent even less time there as I didn't want problems with the law. I had enough problems as it was.

But Rounds Street was great for meeting people and I had begun hanging out with an exotic-looking girl, Kara, who was sixteen, and we became fast friends. She was wild and always looking for adventure. The two of us hatched a plan to hitchhike to Florida to visit a friend of hers, Steve Bonner, who lived in a trailer in Sugarloaf, in the Florida Keys. I told Richie about our plan and said I'd be back in a week or so.

"If you don't want me to go, I won't," I promised. I wanted him to say—Please don't go. I can't live without you.

"Sure, go ahead. Just stay out of trouble."

Good advice, but we didn't follow it.

A Boston radio station had a *Keep on Truckin'* spot that announced drivers looking for riders on long-distance trips, and vice versa. We hooked up with a lanky hippie named Dana who had stringy blond hair trailing past his waist. He was looking for riders to go to Miami with him in his Volkswagen bus. "We're it," we laughed and we jumped in and off we went. Dana was a little weird but, hey, the trip cost us twenty dollars for gas and he got us there safely. In Miami we took a bus to Sugarloaf and the driver dropped us off at midnight. The whole town was asleep.

Right away we knew this wasn't the party we were looking for. Walking down street after street, we finally came upon Steve's trailer, looking abandoned in the middle of a dirt lot with no lights on inside. Garbage and debris were heaped in front of the door and filled the entire area so we couldn't get within twenty feet of the place.

"What a mess," I groaned.

Kara was just plain speechless. Sitting on the ground, we put down our knapsacks and wondered what to do next. Huddled together, we swatted bugs, listened to strange animal calls and prayed no snakes or alligators were nearby. Come daylight, we could figure out what was going on.

Sunrise was probably pretty in Sugarloaf—we wouldn't know. All we could see was the trailer, vacant but filled with the same trash and debris that was strewn outside. We asked a neighbor about Steve's whereabouts and were informed he had been evicted a month earlier. With nowhere to go and no money left, we made our way to the beach and spent the day lying around, discussing our options. We knew the sunset in Key West was a big event and the waterfront would be crowded with people at dusk.

"We could panhandle," said Kara.

"Yeah, good idea."

We waited for the evening crowds and after an hour of begging, we made $2.75 between us, but it looked like gold. Kara bought a loaf of bread, two bananas, and a bottle of soda and we sat on the beach and feasted. That night we covered ourselves with our clothes and slept in the sand. In the morning, we finished off the rest of the bread and soda and talked to beachcombers, trying to find a ride back home.

Things didn't get better. After a third night on a different beach, we were even more desperate and very hungry.

"We could steal," said Kara.

"Yeah, I suppose." I assumed she would do the deed. After all, she was the wild one.

"You do it, Lynn. You're more innocent looking than I am. There's nothing to it, go ahead."

"Oh, jeez."

Nervously, I walked over to the nearby store and looked up and down the aisle in my most nonchalant manner, then quickly shoved a jar of peanut butter into my knapsack and headed for the door. A clerk with a stern look on her face stopped me and marched me straight to the manager's office. Oh, shoot, I thought, I'm busted! Luckily, I had no identification and lied about my age so they wouldn't call my parents. The next thing I knew, a deputy was taking me to the sheriff's office, and I spent the next fourteen days in a Key West jail.

Kara visited regularly and said she'd hang around until I got out, and she'd try to get us some money to get us home. Meanwhile, I was getting a firsthand look at jail and the other unlucky souls I shared my cell with. One girl was arrested for making love with her boyfriend in the sand dunes. Another was caught with drugs and waiting for her father to post bail. Another was in for disturbing the peace. Nobody had committed murder or anything. I consoled myself with the thought that I had a safe place to sleep and three meals a day. Yeah, there were certain advantages to being in jail. Out there on the beach, Kara had nothing to eat at all.

When I was released, Kara and I started hitchhiking home, occasionally spending the night on a beach and eating fruit from trees along the roadside. Sometimes our drivers would feed us. One nice family picked us up and took us to a roadside diner with them. I ordered a giant cheeseburger, fries, and a chocolate milk shake and it seemed like the most delicious meal I had ever eaten in my entire life.

When we finally got back to Rounds Street, all hell broke loose inside me. Richie already had a new girlfriend, someone he'd worked with at the factory. I cried for days and had no shame, trying to convince him to break up with her, but he gently told me no. The anguish seemed unbearable. Not long afterwards, Richie married the girl and they had a baby boy. After the initial hurt subsided, I just became angry and tried to drown my sorrow with wine, but nothing worked to stop the hurt. All the hurts of my life came rushing back to haunt me.

I returned as a full-time resident to Rounds Street, the only security I knew, and when I was feeling especially down one night, Warren sat beside me and tried to cheer me up.

"I don't know what I'm doing," I told him, with great angst. "I can't go home. My boyfriend went and married somebody else. I feel so bad I could die." He listened compassionately as I talked and put his arm around me. The next thing I knew, he was trying to kiss me.

"Warren, what are you doing? I just like you as a friend." I pushed him away, but I could feel the sizzle of hurt pride. He got up and left the room.

"Uh oh, you better be careful," Crystal warned. "He can really hold a grudge."

"What? Well, I'll tell him tomorrow I'm sorry if I gave him the wrong impression," I responded, thinking it was no big deal.

"Very good idea," Crystal replied as she headed upstairs to bed. A lot of people were still there, playing guitar and singing, so I stayed up a while longer. The next morning when I went downstairs to the living room, Warren looked at me coldly.

"Where's my guitar?"

"Your guitar? How should I know? The last time I saw it was last night."

"Well, it's gone, and you were the last one up last night."

I felt a twinge of fear but tried to keep my composure. "Warren, the house was full of people partying. Did you check out on the porch?"

"Yes, I checked the porch. I checked the bedrooms and bathroom, too, and the guitar is gone. Whoever you gave it to, you'd better go out and get it back NOW," he ordered.

My mouth flew open. "How could you think I'd do something like that?" By now I was holding back tears.

"Look, I'm not stupid, so stop lying to me. You have until tonight to get it back or else you can find another place to stay," he ordered with ice in his voice.

I tried desperately to think of all the partygoers that came and went last night, but I didn't even know some of their names. Some of the Rounds Street crew had been getting involved with the harder drugs lately—Quaaludes, speed, and other stuff—so just about anyone could have taken the guitar. Convinced I was the culprit, Warren made good on his threat that same night and told me to move out now. Crystal was sympathetic and tried to change Warren's mind, but to no avail. I tearfully packed my clothes and left.

Things couldn't get any worse and I felt betrayed that no one but Crystal had come to my defense. For the next few weeks, I stayed with friends who had their own apartments. I slept on couches and cleaned their bathrooms, then left after a few days so I wouldn't wear out my welcome. Obviously, I needed a more permanent solution. A car!

I sold some albums for fifty dollars and bought an old Buick station wagon from a farmer in Westport and it became my home. I didn't have a license and the car wasn't registered, but no problem. It had a license plate on it, so I asked the farmer to show me how to drive it, which he did. I drove it sparingly since I had no money for gas and no license. At night, I'd park the car on a quiet residential street and sleep. I moved it every few days so I wouldn't arouse suspicion.

Lonely and frightened in the car at night alone, I decided I needed a companion, but I wasn't having much luck with people. A junkie I knew had a dog that was neglected and rarely had a good meal. Well, I got the dog, a German shepherd, and we took to each other like long-lost friends. From then on, Jake lived with me in the car and I spent many nights curled up in the back of the station wagon under a quilt with Jake asleep at my feet.

Things began looking up when a young woman named Christine, who sometimes visited Rounds Street, offered to let me stay at her house. Her parents had divorced and moved out of her childhood home but the house was not empty. Christine, her boyfriend, Greg, and their young son lived there, as well as her sister Debbie. I stayed there for a few months and my dear dog Jake was adopted by a friend who had the money to feed him and a big yard for him to play in.

At Buttonwood Park, I continued to see Pam and her little boy and we began developing a close friendship. She must have seen something good in me, some vague potential, that made her take me under her wing. Not that she had a lot of time to rescue anybody. She was now attending Southeastern Massachusetts University, the local college in nearby Dartmouth. I looked way, way up to her and watched how she managed her life. She actually had goals! Even her job status rose as she worked part-time at the college. Pam and Christine often baby-sat for each other and I grew fond of their sons, Jason and Matthew. I thought I'd like to have a baby of my own someday, but I had a lot of trucking to do first.

Most afternoons I hung around Buttonwood Park with my Rounds Street friends—they were all I had. Warren worked days so I didn't worry about running into him and feeling further humiliation. Through the grapevine, I heard that Larry Mello, a junkie, had stolen Warren's guitar and fenced it for dope money. When Crystal told Warren the story, Warren replied that I had probably given the guitar to Larry for a few bucks. Warren was definitely not interested in pursuing the matter further and I was furious when Crystal told me this. Was he punishing me for spurning his advances or did he really think I was a thief? Either way, I was very upset that he didn't welcome me back into the family. I was in exile.

Life in Buttonwood Park had its perks. A group of guys from the West End, many of them former basketball players from Holy Family High School, played ball there. If enough Rounds Street guys were hanging around, they formed teams and played each other. One guy caught my eye, tall and muscular with black hair and pale blue eyes.

I asked Christine, a Holy Family grad, who he was. "That's Tim Donohue, but forget it—he's way out of your league."

Tim had been a varsity basketball player on a championship team since his freshman year in high school and she had dated his older brother, John, also a basketball player. Although my wounds from Richie were still fresh, I felt the familiar stirrings of a giant crush developing, and I made up my mind to do everything I could to make Tim Donohue notice me.

"Introduce me," I begged Christine.

She did, and I made a great effort to be friendly with him and his friends every time I ran into them in the park. If I had money, I made sandwiches for the teams, and this was a big hit. In early May, Christine was planning a party and I invited Tim and his friends. That night, Tim and I did a lot of talking and soon after, we started dating. I had never been out on a real date before and I was so uptight, I thought I was going to have a nervous breakdown. But once I relaxed, we clicked. We became boyfriend and girlfriend. How had I managed to pull this off?

Tim was different from other guys I'd known—he had goals and a job working in a silver factory. I felt so grateful he had chosen me to be his girlfriend. As I got to know him, I discovered his family situation was as painful as mine. Tim had quit school and given up a potential basketball career. When he was younger, his father left the family, and his mom worked as a nurse to support her five children. She was severely depressed. I met his older brother, John, and John's twin, Maureen, his younger sister, Sharon, and the youngest, Meg, who suffered from cerebral palsy and was confined to a wheelchair. I took to the Donohues like a duck to water.

Now that I was spending most of my time with Tim and his friends, I didn't see my Rounds Street friends as often. My new friends all had jobs and though they drank and some used drugs, they kept in shape by bicycling and playing basketball.

Tim's best friend, Sean Sullivan, became a close friend of mine too. He worked at Acushnet Company, manufacturer of Titleist golf balls, and I'm not sure why he didn't go to college because in high school he was always on the honor roll and was voted "Best All Around." He had a sharp wit, loved to goof on people, and was very artistic in drawing and illustrating. He never gossiped or said anything malicious about anyone. Sean had a beautiful girlfriend, Alison, whom he'd met in high school. I liked the way he looked at her—his face lit up the room, even though they had been sweethearts for almost five years. Alison looked like a movie star and seemed out of place in New Bedford but I guess Sean was worth staying around for.

Meanwhile, it was time for me to relocate. I couldn't stay at Christine's much longer; she had been a great friend, but my time was up. Since the lease was also up on Sean's winter rental cottage on the beach in Mattapoisett, I suggested we get a place together and share the rent. Of course, there were certain problems.

"I don't have a job but, you know, I could get one."

"Okay," said Sean, who liked the idea.

We found a small beach front cottage on West Island in Fairhaven and moved in.

When I was hanging around Buttonwood Park one day, I told my friend Steve I was looking for a job. He nodded and filled me in on the program he was in, studying passive solar energy at BCC, Bristol Community College, in Fall River. My antenna went up when he said he was going to school with grant money that didn't have to be paid back! Hey, I could do that too. I began reading everything I could find on the subject, and Steve and I shared a brief dream of getting a grant from the Carter administration to build solar energy homes. But then my interest waned as quickly as it had driven me a few weeks earlier.

This was a crazy time for me, as I set about trying to pay the rent and do something with my life. I had no idea how to go about it. There were lots of programs around for people like me and I applied for anything that offered money in exchange for training. I even found myself in a six-week, grant-funded cooking class, training to be a chef. The important thing was the money, not the cooking.

Eventually I got a continuing-education grant to study library science at BCC, subconsciously trying to emulate my mother in her field of work. What was I thinking? Anyway, I found it quite a jump from eighth grade to college. The kids I went to elementary school with were now seniors in high school—class of '74! I also earned a little money through the work-study program, which helped pay the bills. But my lifestyle interfered with the demands of schooling. I stayed out late, I drank too much, I was late for classes, I found it hard to focus, but, amazingly, I muddled through from September to April. Then, bam, I quit! Just up and quit. I was convinced that I was too messed up inside to ever accomplish anything, and that was that.

I returned home now and then to pick up my things or to hit my mother up for money, but my comfort level in the house was zero.

"Lynn, what are you doing to yourself?" Mom would say in exasperation. "You're ruining your life."

"Don't worry about me, I'm fine," I'd reply.

I couldn't help but notice how well she was getting her own life together. She was doing fine, just her and my brother Mark. I admired her a lot but I'd never say so. She had a new self-respect, making great efforts to better herself and advance her career.

She had become a student, a true student, maybe inspired by economics at first, but it turned into a real love of learning. In the library she had to train younger workers, and the ones with college degrees immediately began making more money than she. This hurt—after all, she had been there for years and was so smart. So she began taking courses at night in library science at BCC in Fall River when she was still with my father. Though it was part-time, he hated her going to school and threatened to move out if she continued.

Now that Dad was no longer around, she decided to become a full-time student and work for an associate's degree in library science. Well, Mom was always a student at heart and now she had found a place where she could come alive. She loved going to school. I had to hand it to her. She graduated as class valedictorian, then entered SMU, Southeastern Massachusetts University, to work for a bachelor's degree.

With growing confidence and self-respect, she began applying for better jobs and ended up reaching higher than even she had imagined. The position of city clerk of New Bedford was open and posted. She decided to go for it, presenting herself as confident and capable, but never dreaming she would actually get it. She not only got the job but received a substantial increase in pay. Soon after, she got her license to become a justice of the peace and began performing weekend ceremonies. She had accomplished wonders for herself—my father had not killed her spirit.

At the same time, Pam was working toward a degree in social work at SMU and paying the bills by bartending and doing odd jobs. She enrolled Jason in day care three days a week and took him to school with her the other two. While she took notes in class, he played happily with his Matchbox cars. I stopped at her apartment whenever I was in town, but I missed her and wished we could spend more time together. So did she, which I found amazing.

What a great day it was when Mom and Pam both graduated from SMU with high honors.

Soon after, Sean and I moved into our rental cottage. Tim moved in too. Alison visited often and that made things just about perfect. I relished domesticity and fixed up the cottage, cooked and planted a garden. The landlord had minimal standards regarding the upkeep of his property, but we were young and hardy and oblivious.

The cesspool in the front yard constantly overflowed, so the place didn't exactly smell like roses. And the cottage wasn't insulated, so we kept the wood stove burning all winter. If we slept through the night without someone stoking the fire, we woke up to find frozen water in the toilet bowl and could see our breath in the bathroom mirror.

Despite all the inconveniences, we laughed and joked and had the best time of our lives. I grew close to Sean and loved him like a brother, while my love for Tim deepened. We made it through the long cold winter and when sprightly daffodils broke through the ground in April, we were as excited as school kids.

"Spring," Sean sighed.

"Beach weather is right around the corner," Tim put in.

"I'm high on life," I said, and I meant it, sort of. I was half-happy. Yes, I had found love but what about the rest?

One afternoon, I decided to apply for a waitressing job at a diner in downtown New Bedford. Though it looked like fair weather, I got caught in one of those sudden, relentless rainstorms and ended up soaked and bedraggled from top to bottom. As I walked quickly down Pleasant Street toward the city's makeshift bus station, a car passed, then slowed down and I recognized it as my father's. He backed up, rolled down the window and shouted, "You wanna ride?"

I eagerly hopped in, more concerned about the drenching rain than about any lingering grudges from the past.

"Where are you headed?"

I told him about leaving school and needing to find a job.

"I can always use another bartender at the Belmont Club if you're interested."

He looked straight ahead at the road. This was the closest he had ever come to showing me kindness. He dropped me off and said he'd meet me at the bar at eight o'clock in the morning.

I hadn't seen my dad for over three years and I had mixed feelings when I told Tim about our meeting. Although I felt abandoned by my father, I still loved him and wanted his approval. Tim listened but warned me not to set myself up for more heartache and disappointment.

"Leopards don't change their spots," he said, as if recalling his own litany of hurts. "Don't expect a big, happy family reunion because it isn't going to happen."

I expected nothing but a paycheck, which was what I needed most at this moment.

Change kept happening. When Alison received an offer to pursue a modeling career in Florida, at first we were thrilled, then concerned. What about Sean? After much thought and agonizing discussion, she told Sean she was going. He put up a good front, smiling and joking as always, but inwardly he was devastated. Meanwhile, our lease was up at the end of May and we began to discuss where we would go from there.

Tim and I felt the need for more privacy than we had in our communal living arrangement, so we found a third-floor apartment in the West End of New Bedford. We explained things to Sean and he understood perfectly. He was able to move into an apartment in the South-Central area with his younger brother, Leo.

Bartending at the Belmont was working out fine so far, and I was thrilled to be back in my dad's good graces. Tim worked as a groundskeeper at the Oak Grove Cemetery, not far from our apartment, and we carefully budgeted our money so we could pay our $120 monthly rent.

I was also depositing money in a savings account each week from my tips, and before long I had two thousand dollars saved up. One of the regulars at the Belmont had a new Datsun 240Z and I thought I'd use my savings as a down payment on one of my own.

"Not a good idea," said Tim. "It's not a good long-term investment. Let's look into buying a house instead."

Wow. Buying a house seemed too far out to even consider. Then again, maybe it wasn't such a bad idea. For the moment, the seed was planted, and all we had to do was save three thousand more for a down payment.

We still saw a lot of Sean, but things were not good. There was a sadness in him since Alison left and he couldn't seem to emerge from the darkness. He wouldn't even look at another girl. Then he was laid off from his factory job just before Christmas. Despite his troubles, he still laughed and joked and was the same old Smilin' Sean we knew and loved. We were not savvy enough to see the danger signs.

In early January, Tim was on his way out to his mother's house when the phone rang. I answered it and heard Leo dazedly say, "Lynn—it's Sean—I came home and—he's dead."

Shock and confusion overwhelmed me as I tried to absorb the horrible news. "What do you mean? What hap...oh my God...we'll be right there."

I stammered the news to Tim and we jumped in the car and raced to the apartment. When we arrived, Leo stood on the sidewalk looking bereft and in agony while police cars and an ambulance sat ominously out front.

Leo looked at us with a distant, glazed stare and tried to get the words out—"I came home from work and saw his car outside, but when I went up, he wasn't here. I called out but he didn't answer, so I kept looking around and I noticed his closet door was open a little. I opened it and that's when I saw his legs, and I looked up, and he was...hanging there." Leo began sobbing inconsolably. I grabbed my stomach and doubled over, feeling like I had been kicked. Tim just stared at Leo—"No, oh God, no." Tears streamed down his face.

The next few days were a blur. I thought I would die of grief and couldn't get past my own anguish to know how to comfort Tim or Sean's family. Tim and I felt such guilt; it was our fault for not knowing the depth of Sean's depression and we never should have moved out on our own, leaving him to fend for himself. We felt responsible, knowing he was too kind to burden us with his problems, and devastated to think he had been in so much pain. The worst part was that it was so final. There was nothing we could do to bring him back and tell him everything was going to be all right.

Sean, Tim's best friend since childhood, was buried in New Hampshire next to his grandparents. Ten of us, his closest friends, drove up for the funeral. Nothing I had been through was as difficult for me to cope with as Sean's death. As I said a final goodbye at the cemetery, I vowed that, for as long as I lived, I would try to be as kind and giving to others as Sean had been during his brief stay on earth.

I found myself going to my childhood church, St. James, on weekdays. Sean and Leo's apartment was right across the street, and I wept silently when I looked over there. The church was usually empty around noon and I sat in a pew near the back and prayed for Sean. Even though I did not have much faith or religion, sitting in the church comforted me.

Tim felt a lot of anger over Sean's death and began to talk about getting out of this miserable city. It was not really the city's fault, of course, but we both felt this need to blame something "out there" and flee. Nothing in our lives seemed to matter in comparison to the loss. We both needed a change. Tim had always loved Lakeville, a farming town about fifteen miles from New Bedford. Every Sunday his family drove there to drop off his sister Meg for therapy at a children's rehabilitation hospital.

We began driving around Lakeville looking at houses and one afternoon we came across a tiny home on an acre of land with a For Sale sign out front. We called the number and learned the price was nineteen thousand dollars. After a lot of calculating, we figured out we could afford the mortgage if we didn't eat much and kept the heat low, two things we were already used to doing.

With the five thousand dollars my savings account now held, we made the down payment on the bungalow and moved in that summer. Luckily, the mother of my brother Dave's ex-girlfriend Beth, from Circle K Ranch, was a loan officer at the New Bedford Institution for Savings, so when I went to apply for the mortgage, I made sure to see her. It was unusual for a woman to be a loan officer in those days, but then, it was unusual for a single woman to apply for a mortgage. I was prepared for questions like "How will you pay off the loan if you get pregnant?" but thankfully, they never came. My savings were more than adequate to use as a down payment and the mortgage payments were manageable.

Our new home was solace for the soul, and slowly but surely we began to rebuild our lives. The resilience of youth was on our side and we gradually began to feel hope for the future. The house was a "fixer-upper" so whenever we weren't working, we spent our time sanding, wallpapering, painting, and repairing. Our bedroom was so tiny we bought a bed with drawers underneath because we couldn't fit a bureau in it. The physical labor was therapeutic, especially for Tim, who needed time to work things through. It also took us further and further away from the dead-end lifestyle we had been living in New Bedford.

I loved living in the country and immediately set to work planting a garden of tomatoes, butternut squash, cucumbers, and carrots. My excitement at seeing things grow was quickly dampened when rabbits invaded my garden and ate all the new seedlings. A neighbor suggested I plant marigolds around the garden perimeter to keep out the rabbits, but they apparently liked the flowers, and after they dined on my vegetables, they had the marigolds for dessert.

I drove out to a nearby farm one day to get some replacement seedlings and was charmed by the newborn goats for sale. When I rode away in my station wagon, I had my seedlings and a cute baby goat, too. We built a little pen for it in the back yard and set out food and water. Waddles seemed to like his new home, but that night, we were awakened by a constant and plaintive "baaa, baaa" coming from the yard. Unable to stop the incessant crying, I called the farmer for advice.

"He's lonely," said the farmer. "Why don't you come back and buy him a companion?"

Tim and I decided we weren't quite ready to become dairy farmers and reluctantly gave Waddles to my dad's friend Carl, a farmer.

Money was tight since we both earned minimum wage and, although our combined paychecks covered the mortgage, in our youthful naivete we hadn't planned on property insurance, furnace repairs, tools, lawn equipment, and all the trappings of home ownership. When we found ourselves siphoning gas from our lawn mower to put into our car, we knew we needed more money.

The only way we could survive was to work weekends, so I added two more days of bartending and Tim painted houses on Saturdays and cut cords of wood on Sundays. After a few months of tedious, constant work, we managed to put a few hundred dollars into a savings account and felt comfortable returning to a five-day work week. The sudden shift in our lives from our carefree leisurely days to the responsibilities of adulthood was a difficult transition, and we missed our friends and the parties that were so much a part of our lives.

The Fourth of July was coming up and I had an idea. Why not give a party ourselves? We were proud of our renovations, so we could invite our friends to a housewarming. The Fourth of July was also Tim's birthday so the date seemed more than perfect. I passed the word along to the old gang and told everyone to bring drinks and side dishes and we would supply meats for the grill.

Friday I took off work to get ready for the big day. I borrowed a large barbecue grill from my dad, an old fifty-five-gallon oil drum cut in half lengthwise, propped on metal legs, and covered with an old wire grate from a storm door. The only thing missing was the charcoal. Then I borrowed a canoe from a neighbor and filled it with ice from the Belmont Club, a perfect cooler for drinks. Dad let me take a few boxes of hot dogs and hamburgers from the Club and I bought day-old buns from the local bakery thrift store. The owner of a nearby strawberry farm offered all the riper berries crated in back of his barn. I made strawberry sauce from the good parts of the berries and used it as a topping on my homemade cheesecakes, following a recipe on the back of a graham cracker box.

I put up signs that said Rest Rooms, pointing to the woods behind our house, then picked wildflowers and arranged them in empty wine bottles for the food table centerpiece. Tim's mother presented us with a hodgepodge of paper plates, cups, napkins, and plastic utensils left over from years of parties with slogans like "Have a Happy Howdy Doody Birthday," "Merry Christmas," and "It's A Boy!" The last thing I did before collapsing into bed that night was check the weather report on the eleven o'clock news—sunshine and blue skies predicted for the weekend.

Saturday arrived at last. Pam and Jason came early to help, but I'd already done most of the work, so we traipsed out back to the oak tree and pushed Jason on the rope swing. We figured thirty people would show, a calculation based on how many people had cars, who had gas money, and who could follow the directions to our house. The first carload arrived around noon, our old friends from Rounds Street, including Crystal, who carried a large bowl of potato salad. Ten minutes later a Volkswagen van pulled up, filled with Tim's buddies from school, and they brought a volleyball net that Tim helped them set up in the yard.

Our families came next and I was relieved and happy to see my mother. She sat and talked with Tim's mother and Meg, who was parked beside the picnic table in her wheelchair. As I set up the food table, I noticed my brother Mark playing a game of horseshoes with Tim's brother John.

By two o'clock, fifty guests had arrived and more cars were pulling up every few minutes. My friends from the old neighborhood, the South End, helped Tim lug the record player and eight-track tape deck from our house and set it up on a table near the garage, running extension cords from the house. Several people brought albums and tapes, and the Allman Brothers and Grateful Dead blared from the speakers. Everywhere I looked, people were engaged in activity—playing volleyball, eating, drinking beer, dancing, and talking. A few friends brought their toddlers and everyone felt the magic as they blew soap bubbles and chased them around the yard.

By five o'clock over a hundred people filled our yard. Someone set up three tents near the woods so those who overindulged could sleep it off in private. Whenever the food ran out, a new carload of people arrived with still more food. Every so often the hat was passed for someone to zip over to the package store across the street. It was a great party and we relished being in the company of our friends.

As the sun set, we lit some citronella candles and shared a can of bug repellent; some people stayed outside, some slept in the tents, and others went inside to keep on partying. How amazing that our tiny house could hold so many people! At ten o'clock the police showed up and told us to turn the music down, which we did, but not until they made a second trip to refresh our memories.

By one o'clock in the morning about forty people remained. Some retired to the tents and others curled up on the floor in sleeping bags or blankets brought in from their cars. One van had a mattress in the back that became a bed for two people. Tim and I were happily exhausted and went to our bedroom—only to find four people asleep on our waterbed. We thought it was hilarious and went outside to see if there was room in one of the tents, which there was. We quickly fell asleep, lost in the night sounds of the woods and the beauty of the stars.

Sunday we awakened to the sounds of Van Morrison singing *Tupelo Honey* on the tape deck. Several people were up and about, cleaning up the yard. We put on a pot of coffee and sat on a blanket in the morning sun, laughing and talking about the festive day before. An odd assortment of leftovers sat forlornly on the food table—potato chips, hamburger buns, onion dip, and chocolate cake. Perfect! We added it to the food in our refrigerator and came up with a weird but tasty breakfast buffet.

Several people who had gone home on Saturday night returned and we lazed about in the sun, ate leftovers, and listened languidly to music. "Let's make this a yearly party," someone said, and the group agreed unanimously. Later we plunged into the lake at the end of our street. At ten o'clock at night, the last guest said good bye and Tim and I collapsed on the bed, exhausted.

I had been too busy planning the party to get Tim's birthday present before the event, but I knew exactly what I wanted to get him. I had seen a sign on Route 105 in Lakeville advertising puppies for sale. After work on Monday, I stopped in at the farmhouse and was told there was only one puppy left, a male golden retriever with a gentle disposition. I explained that I didn't have much money and the kindly farmer's wife agreed to let me have the dog for fifty dollars. I took him home, hoping the new puppy would help fill a void in Tim, who was still suffering from the loss of his best friend. Tim was delighted with the puppy, named him Mugsy, and the two became inseparable. He took the dog everywhere and Mugsy brought joy and laughter into our lives. In time, with the help of family and friends, our new dog, and the rhythms and routines of ordinary life, our grief over Sean lessened so we could once again remember the good times without the acute pain.

THE FIRST BRICK

The night the Sidewinders barged in and tore up the Belmont Club was the first time I knew I was done with bartending—there was just no future in it. For a few more months, I dragged myself reluctantly between the bar and home, not quite sure where the future was. It didn't help that business at the Belmont had slowed to a crawl and the merry Christmas season with all its painful memories was upon us.

Old-timers like John stayed home during the harsh New England winters, afraid of slipping and falling on icy sidewalks. Younger regulars who just got by on meager salaries took seasonal Christmas jobs to supplement their income, working in warehouses or sorting and delivering parcels. Construction workers who had plenty of work in spring and summer did snowplowing to get them through winter. And the bikers were grounded until the roads were once again safe for their motorcycles. Even Izzy and Diane were scarce.

I spent my time watching dreary soap operas in the near-empty tavern, and suicide seemed to be a recurring theme this year. Three bartenders were on staff, and we knew one of us would be laid off until business picked up in spring. The other two assumed my job was safe since my father owned the place, but Randy and Dennis had families to support and I was ready for a change anyway. We talked it over and I volunteered to be the one to go.

Randy was in a sweat, as if he'd just avoided a collision.

"Thanks, Lynn. Jeez, the price of toys today, I'll be workin' here the rest of my life just to pay for all the Christmas toys I bought for my kids." He shook his head in exasperation.

Dennis, my father's right-hand man, gave me a slow smile. "Yeah, Lynn, thanks. But are you sure you can stand to give up this glamorous job? The customers ain't gonna be too keen on lookin' at my ugly face instead of your pretty one, and my figure is no competition for yours either." We all laughed as he gave a mock sway of his hips and, I knew they were overwhelmingly grateful I was the one leaving and not them.

Before I was out the door, I gave them one final reason for going. "I'll miss you guys but I won't miss the job. The thing is, I'm still freaked out by the Sidewinders trashing the bar, and it could happen again come spring and summer. I don't want to be around for a replay." Clearly, I was making this decision in my own self-interest as well as theirs and I wanted them to know that. But most of all, I didn't want to reveal the truth about myself: I wasn't able to stick with anything very long. Once I mastered a thing, I had to move on.

"Yeah, I hear ya, and look on the bright side," quipped Randy, who was still on a high about his new job security. "Ya can still come in and have a few beers, but ya won't have to be behind the bar takin' any crap."

My father agreed to lay me off and said I could collect unemployment until spring, then decide if I wanted to return to the bar. The time off would give me the perfect opportunity to look for something that paid better and left me fuller in the heart. Yeah, that was it—I needed a fuller heart.

The unemployment office sat in a dismal concrete building near the old downtown train station. The interior walls were painted green-blah, a nondescript shade often used in factories and government offices, which appeared to sedate the employees as well as the clients. Here I began a dreary routine, bumping into old friends and several Belmont regulars in the unemployment line each week, where I became accustomed to the familiar banter, "Hey, how's it goin'?" "What's up, man?" "Hey, can I bum a ride?" "Wanna get a few beers after we cash our checks?" "Yo, buddy, can I have one of them butts? I'm a little short this week…"

As I listened week after week, I began to realize how far I'd moved from where they were, but I still wanted out of the rut I was in. As I stood in line one day, a new poster on the wall leaped out at me from among the yellowed ones with curled edges. It fairly shouted: "Women in Construction, look here." I moved closer to read the details—women interested in learning a trade could enroll in a twelve-week regional training program. Though the course paid minimum wage, I recalled the newspaper article I'd read at the Belmont and remembered those high union wages for people in the construction trades. Maybe, just maybe, this could be the beginning of something better.

Without hesitation, I waltzed up to the counter and boldly said, "I'd like to sign up for the women-in-construction training." A puzzled look crossed the clerk's bored face, bringing him back to life.

"What are you talkin' about?"

I pointed to the poster. He shrugged his shoulders and mumbled, "I don't know anything about it—hold on a minute." After talking to his supervisor, he shuffled back to the counter and pulled out a fat folder of paperwork from an overflowing file cabinet. Clearly, he was less than enthusiastic about filling out forms to enroll me in the class.

"You want carpentry, painting, or masonry?"

I paused to think it over, while he tapped his pen on the scratched-up counter, as if I were keeping him from something far more important. But I was doing some heavy calculation here. Since money was my chief motivation, I decided to choose the masonry course, remembering the seventeen-dollar hourly rate for bricklayers. I eagerly signed the forms, grateful I would not have to stand in the unemployment line again for at least three months. "You should get a letter by next week telling you where to report," he informed me grimly.

Five days later a letter of confirmation arrived, noting the course would begin the following week in nearby Carver—cranberry country and home to the woods of Myles Standish State Forest, where we camped as children. I did some more calculating and tried to estimate my gas money for the first week of classes so I could put it aside from my unemployment check. If my old Buick station wagon ran out of gas on the deserted back roads in Carver, I couldn't count on being rescued. What should I bring to class? Not a clue. A pencil and note pad would do for starters, and I'd have to figure out the rest as I went along.

I was filled with trepidation that first day of class as I drove to Carver, located the building, and parked near the entrance. A few other women arrived at the same time and we exchanged greetings as we walked in. "This place is really out in the middle of nowhere. I hope I can find my way back to the highway after dark," said a petite redhead in high heels, a casual suit under her long dressy coat.

"Where are you from?"

"My friend and I drove down together from Brockton. It's supposed to snow tonight and I don't want to be marooned out here in the woods."

Her friend, also dressed to the hilt, said, "We figured today would just be orientation, so we didn't want to dress like slobs."

"Uh-huh," I mumbled as they glanced at my blue jeans and flannel shirt. We walked down a long corridor and hung our coats on a freestanding coatrack in the corner of a large open room. About thirty women were already sitting on bleacher seats chatting. Most wore jeans or corduroys and long-sleeve shirts, so I felt okay about my outfit.

From my seat, I listened to the hum of conversation around me, anxious to know who these women were. Several from the Taunton area said they'd been laid off from their factory jobs. A few said they were waitresses, and two sisters were laid off from their teaching jobs.

A young woman named Robin, about six feet tall with long blond hair, introduced herself to me and I thought she must be some kind of model or something. She was pleasant enough, but my attention was drawn to a slight, unconventional woman sitting apart from the crowd who looked like a teenage tomboy with her short dark brown hair and no makeup. Her rough-looking hands were wrapped around a paperback. I went over.

"What are you reading?"

She looked up and gave me a once-over to see if I was worth talking to, then replied, "This book is incredible. You wouldn't believe the poisons they're pouring into our rivers. The factories are dumping sludge that's going straight from our water into our soil and into the atmosphere. And they're getting away with it!"

"Wow." I was genuinely impressed by her interest and passion.

Just then a tall, middle-aged man marched into the room with a clipboard. "Okay, can I have your attention? I need you to break into groups. Painting on the left, carpentry in the middle, and masonry over here on my right." The chatter slowly dissipated as everyone found her way to her designated area. Painting and carpentry were the most popular—only six brave souls stood with me in the masonry area. After taking attendance, the man led us down a long corridor and directed each group into their classrooms.

The woman with the paperback signed up for the masonry course too, and I learned her name was Nancy. "I just finished potting some onion plants at home before I came," she told me as we walked along. "I grow all my own food organically."

"Everything?"

"Just about. I'm a vegetarian and what I don't grow, I buy at the natural food store," she explained as our teacher entered the room.

Gary, a pleasant man of about thirty, was our instructor. He had been a bricklayer for ten years but had been injured on the job and now taught training classes for the state as well as the union. Some of the women exchanged anxious glances when he mentioned his injury. "Any job is dangerous if safety rules aren't obeyed, and bricklaying is no exception. We'll learn more about that as we get further into the course."

Although we'd have a fair amount of book work, we'd be spending a lot of time actually laying brick, he explained, and he handed out a course outline and textbooks.

"Read all of chapters one through four and we'll discuss them on Wednesday. By Friday, we'll be working with some basic tools and building a practice brick panel."

"So what do you think?" Nancy asked excitedly as we headed out to our cars.

"It seems okay so far."

"I'm anxious to start the hands-on brickwork. I'd like to build myself a greenhouse before summer if I can learn the ropes." We stood shivering for a moment in the cold night air and then said goodbye. I looked forward to the next class with my new friend.

As promised, Gary announced on Friday that it was time to put our newly acquired knowledge into action. We lined up next to a practice wall, and he laid a course of brick, showing us how to scrape the right amount of mortar onto the trowel, how to spread it like butter onto the intended surface, and how to place the brick properly on top of it. He then took another brick and repeated the process, demonstrating how to line it up with the first brick and finish it off by scraping away the excess mortar. He continued down the length of the practice wall, explaining every move and giving tips for accuracy as he went along.

"Any questions?" The women all shook their heads.

"Any volunteers?" Again, it was no, except for Nancy and me. Gary asked me to step forward.

The bricks felt awkward and unwieldy in my hands, and I had a difficult time trying to hold the trowel in one hand and pick up a brick with the other. I kept at it and after I successfully butted a few bricks up against each other, I began to get the hang of it. The trick was to find a comfortable rhythm to your movements.

In fact, the process reminded me of another rhythm I knew well—popping the cap from a bottle of beer with one hand, grabbing a glass with the other, and putting them both in front of the customer in one easy sweep. When I reached the end of one course, my fellow classmates clapped and I felt proud. Nancy tried it next and, one by one, the women began taking turns.

As the weeks went by, I got into the routine of getting up at six o'clock in the morning in order to get to class on time. I found I really liked the early morning hours and the drive to Carver, watching the sun melt the dew that lay like a blanket over the cranberry bogs. The class was going well and Gary was a terrific teacher, both supportive and patient. He praised my work often, which was a new experience for me. Because of his encouragement, I embraced the challenge of learning this new art. We laid brick the first week and worked with concrete blocks the second week. I struggled a bit with the weight of the materials and this was tough for the others, too. By the third week, three women had dropped out, commenting that the work was too tough.

The large cement blocks did not seem any heavier to me than the cases of beer I once lugged around at the Belmont Club, but I wondered if my petite build and light weight would be a hindrance on the actual work site. Gary assured me that many men of small stature were successful bricklayers. If they could do it, I figured, then so could I. Nancy liked the work as much as I did. The other two women complained a lot about their hands and clothes getting messed up from the mortar and rough bricks. I had the feeling they wouldn't last very long.

On graduation day the few women who completed their courses sat in the first row of the assembly hall. Behind them sat a handful of loyal family members and two trade union representatives, a sparse audience. Nancy arrived with her brother, and they sat beside Tim and me. The audience cheered for Nancy and me when we went up to get our certificates. As I walked back to my seat with the certificate in hand, I felt a surge of pride and accomplishment. Here was proof that I had followed through and completed something significant.

After the ceremony, Tim, Nancy, her brother Jimmy, and I all went out for pizza. Tim and Jimmy smiled as they listened to my plans to pursue a career as a bricklayer. Nancy decided to use her new-found skill to build a greenhouse, then take an electrician's course.

"That way, I can work indoors all year round if I want to. If not, at least I'll be able to fix the crummy wiring in my own house—that's a yearlong project in itself," she quipped.

"That's for sure," said Jimmy. "Have you guys seen her house? It looks like it was lived in by the Addams Family."

"It's not that bad," Nancy countered. "It is a fixer-upper, but I'm going to knock out a few walls and put sliding glass doors in so I can grow more plants inside. Jimmy said he'd help me, but I have to pin him down first," she teased as she punched her brother playfully in the arm. As we left the restaurant, we agreed to stay in touch and I promised to call her the following week. Tim thought she was a bit eccentric, but I liked her determination and self-confidence.

As I lay in bed that night, I thought about the ways I'd changed over the last three months. Something entirely new was happening to me. It was like love at first sight, which sounds ridiculous, but that's sort of the way it felt. I had fallen in love with bricks, and I wanted more than anything to become a bricklayer. I liked the rhythm of the work and knew I had a knack. With a lot of practice, I could become really good at it. I even started to dream about building skyscrapers and brick walls that went on for miles.

I had never had a sense of direction, much less a dream—life just happened to me and I adapted myself to whatever came my way. But now I had a goal and a dream—to become a bricklayer. And, yeah, to make a lot of money. And to be proud of myself.

How did I get so hooked? Was it the timing? The good teacher? The thought of making seventeen dollars an hour? Whatever it was, I was obsessed with learning more about the trade. When I looked into the future, I saw myself as successful, a somebody, able to support myself. In reality I was living hand-to-mouth and could barely afford the gas to get to class, but it didn't matter. In my mind, I was somewhere else. I had left my dead-end lifestyle and embarked on an exciting new journey, full of promise.

THE BROTHERHOOD

The thought of walking into the Bricklayer's Union Hall to inquire about work was frightening, but I promised myself I'd do it the following Monday. That morning, I heard Tim's voice at seven-thirty.

"Lynn, wake up." He stood over me, coffee cup in hand and I looked up at him and groggily replied, "Okay, just give me another minute or two." I had slept fitfully and didn't have my usual morning energy. For a moment, I thought about pulling the covers over my head andgoing back to sleep. I'd listened to the weather report the night before—scattered showers and cool temperatures, great conditions for shutting out the world and drifting away.

It didn't work. I could hear Gary's voice in my mind and itsurgency got me up—start looking for work NOW, he said. Spring is right around the corner, the busiest time of year for masons. My excitement at beginning something new and important was at war with my nervousness and fear of the unknown. What would I wear? What would I say? Would I be turned away or, worse, laughed at? I took a deep breath and headed for the shower.

The confidence and excitement I'd felt at graduation two weeks before had waned since I was no longer in the safety zone under Gary's supervision and I hadn't heard from two of the other women who had completed the course. Nancy and I kept in touch, but she had no plans to pursue masonry as a profession, and I needed to know how theothers were doing. I was like a kid on the first day of school, not knowing what to expect, nervous as hell.

After trying on several outfits, I chose a flannel shirt and khakis, in case they wanted to put me on a job that day. I brushed my long hair and tied it in a ponytail. No makeup or perfume. My course certificate was stuffed in my pocketbook, in case they wanted to see my credentials.

"Are you sure you don't want me to go with you?" Tim offered. I told him no. I would drive alone to the union hall and practice my speech along the way.

"Do you have any bricklaying work available?" No, that's no good, I thought.

"Hi, I'm Lynn Davidian and I want to be a bricklayer." Even worse, I decided.

"What do I need to do to join the union?" Too amateur.

"I just graduated from a women-in-construction masonry course…" No, it's obvious I'm a woman. I don't need to start out by bringing that to their attention. Oh, hell, I would just have to figure it out when I got there.

The union hall, located in the West End of New Bedford, was tucked away behind Newport Creamery, an ice cream parlor where I'd spent many hours hanging out with my friends. As I approached the parking lot, I abruptly turned the wheel and drove past, unable to muster the courage to park and actually get out of the car. After another drive around the block, I entered and parked near the door, in case I needed to make a quick getaway. I was keenly aware of my body and not quite sure what to do with it. Thank God for the flannel shirt! I tried to carry myself like a soldier, toting a pocketbook instead of a gun. A pocketbook! Oh, well, I took a deep breath and headed for the entrance.

I don't know what I expected but I didn't expect "normal." Yet here was a scene out of Main Street. A pleasant middle-aged woman sat at a desk talking on the phone. Addie Grenon, union secretary, said the name plate on her desk. She smiled and motioned for me to sit down. I was too nervous to sit so I scanned the clippings on the bulletin board, mostly news about insurance and pensions. She hung up the phone and turned my way.

"Hello, dear, how can I help you?" She probably thought I was a bricklayer's daughter on an errand for her dad, but I managed to get the important words out.

"Yes, please," I said, probably a little too eagerly. "I'd like to join the union and find a job laying brick. I just finished a training course." I pulled my certificate from my bag and she politely looked at it, holding her astonishment in check.

"You'll need to speak to Mr. Ripley." She directed me down the hall to the office of the business agent.

I tapped lightly on the door marked George Ripley, Business Agent and stepped in. Behind the desk sat a gray-haired, slightly balding man of medium build, signing papers from a tall stack on his desk. He looked up questioningly. "Yes, miss?"

"Hi, I'm Lynn Davidian and I'd like to join the union," I stammered. He stared at me for a moment, then put down his pen and offered me a seat in front of his desk. I began to tell him about the women-in-construction course, leading up to my desire to begin practicing the trade. He took my certificate, glanced at it quickly and said, "Hmmm, very nice," as he handed it back to me.

Mr. Ripley was a kind man, and as he removed his glasses and rubbed his eyes, I suspected he was formulating a reply to let me down easily. "I'm sorry, dear, but the books are closed right now," he politely informed me.

"What does that mean?" I asked in a very small voice.

"It means there are no apprenticeships available right now. To join the union, you have to start out as an apprentice and work your way up to journeyman."

"Well, when will the books be open again?"

"It depends on the economy. If there's more work available than union masons to do it, we accept new men as apprentices on an as-needed basis."

We spoke for a few minutes more, and I asked him about other alternatives. Apparently there were none. Trying my best to hide my disappointment, I thanked him and left the office. Addie, who was on the phone, looked up and smiled sympathetically as I passed her desk on my way out. Dejected, I drove back home thinking about my visit and the expression on Mr. Ripley's face when I told him I wanted to be a mason, like that of a grownup listening to a child's wish to be a ballerina or an astronaut. I would become quite familiar with that expression in the months ahead.

After relating the details of my failed mission to Tim, I swallowed my disappointment and formed my next plan of attack. Scanning the yellow pages, I made a list of all the local companies I could find under Mason Contractors. If I visited each one, I would find an opening and get some experience under my belt, then return to the union office and get that apprenticeship.

The next day I got up at six o'clock with steel in my veins, dressed in my flannel shirt and khakis again and set off for the first company on my list, this time without the pocketbook. It was located on Acushnet Avenue in the North End, a long busy street packed with family-run stores, ethnic bakeries, and three-decker tenements. I drove up to the front of the building, where a sign directed customers to the rear. I parked and walked around back to a small, fenced-in lot. An elderly man supervised two younger men as they loaded supplies into a pickup truck, yelling at them in rapid-fire Portuguese, waving his arms, and pointing at different pieces of equipment.

"Excuse me," I interrupted, and they all looked up startled. They gave me the once-over, starting at my feet and moving up, lingering on key areas before their eyes reached my face.

I quickly told them I had completed the masonry course and was looking for work. One of the younger men translated for his father and they all hooted with laughter. The elder man said something in Portuguese to one of his sons, who laughed uproariously and then told me in broken English, "My father say he don't need no help." Something certainly got lost in the translation, I thought. I thanked him and left, certain of two things—my rear end was being ogled by all three men and my visit would be joked about for the rest of the day.

The next stop on my list was nearby and looked to be a similar setup. No one answered the door, and the gates to the lot were locked up. I continued on and found only two businesses that had regular offices and large inventories of equipment and vehicles, but I was turned away at every stop. By the end of the week, I had hit every company on my list. This was going to be harder than I imagined and money was becoming an issue. I had to earn money doing something else while I looked for masonry work, and it had to be flexible hours. After some thought, I talked to my father and two other tavern owners and got them to agree to let me sell sandwiches to their customers. It wasn't easy. After numerous trips to the grocery store, I woke at the crack of dawn each day, laid out bulkie rolls over the kitchen counters and filled them, assembly-line style, with roast beef or turkey, cheese, lettuce, tomato, and mayonnaise. Then I wrapped them in cellophane and piled them in cardboard beer cartons, storing them in the garage fridge.

As soon as the bars opened in the morning, I dropped off the boxes and the next day collected the money from the previous day's sales. At a dollar a sandwich, I wasn't going to become rich but it helped pay the bills and left me some free time to continue my serious job hunting. As time went on, I became more courageous, more determined that I was going to break into the masonry trade come hell or high water. I became a frequent visitor to the union hall and to some of the larger masonry companies in the area, still hoping for a chance. As the weeks and months went by, I was no longer greeted with kind amusement but with a hint of irritation.

I was catching on to how the game was played—the union was like the Mafia. You were either born into it or recommended for membership, but only if you fit the mold. Undesirables like me were kept in a state of limbo. The union would let me join if I had a job, but I couldn't get a job unless I was in the union. I felt excluded, as if the women-in-construction program were a sham and the newspaper article encouraging females to enter the construction trades were a lie. But I wasn't giving up. I was absolutely not giving up. I was just going to try a different approach.

Even though I'd treated my mother with little regard and even less kindness throughout my teenage years, she was still the one whose opinion I respected most. And she was the one I turned to now. Thanks to Tim's mother, who had given me an earful about the pains and perils of raising five children alone, I began to see for the first time what I'd put my mother through. Mom had done the best she could, and when she could no longer do anything with me, she gave up trying and only hoped I would one day come to my senses.

As New Bedford's city clerk, she was admired by everyone and, over the years, I had begun to feel her strength. I desperately needed her advice and I arranged to have lunch with her—her treat, of course. We met at City Hall and crossed Pleasant Street to Maxie's Delicatessen, home of the best sandwiches in town. While I had my favorite, hot pastrami and cheese on rye, and Mom a chef's salad, I filled her in on my experience at the union hall and my unsuccessful visits to local contracting companies. She listened, then said matter-of-factly, "You know, Lynn, there are laws to make sure that people are given equal opportunity for jobs—that's part of what civil rights and the women's movement are all about. Didn't they talk about that in the masonry course?"

"Well, they told us there were laws, but they didn't really go into much detail about it."

We ate heartily as we talked about my dilemma. Although she never came right out and said it, I knew Mom was proud to see me back on track and pursuing an occupation, no matter how unorthodox. Now that I was more mature, our relationship was more adult and I was amazed at the personality change in her. She was no longer the submissive woman she had been under my father's rule. She had a wonderful assertiveness and self-respect. In leaving our house, my father had set her free and she was flying.

"Let's go back to my office and make a few phone calls," Mom suggested as we left. Back in her office, she called the city's equal opportunity officer, Ed Ames, and crisply inquired, "Ed, is the city currently meeting their quota of women and minorities on labor contracts? Sure, I'll hold." She began to tap her fingernails on the desk impatiently. "Well, all right, but I need to know as soon as possible," and she hung up and turned to me. "He's got to pull some statistics together and promised to call me back tomorrow. Why don't I call you when I hear from him and we'll take it from there?"

I thanked her and headed home, hopeful this new approach would get me somewhere.

She called the next day with great news. The statistics showed that although some minority quotas on labor contracts were currently being met, the number of women was virtually zero. There were no women bricklayers in New Bedford now or ever! When Mom informed Mr. Ames of my failed attempts with the union and local companies, he was surprised to hear a woman wanted to be a bricklayer, much less the city clerk's daughter. Mom insisted she did not want any special treatment but she expected the letter of the law to be met.

Mr. Ames performed a miracle and broke down a wall. Shortly after their conversation, he called my mother and described in detail the hoops he had to jump through to get MF Construction to take me on as an apprentice. For its part, MF had been fairly accommodating, but the union balked at allowing me in. An agreement was reached after much negotiation among the three parties. In truth, I wasn't as interested in the mechanics of it all as I was in the possibility of actually getting my foot in the door. Mr. Ames informed my mother that MF would be in touch with me. Whoopee! I was grateful to Mom for all her help and let her know.

"I didn't do anything, Lynn, it's the law—the men just need to be reminded of that. I won't lie to you. It won't be easy, but stick with it—and remember, when someone tells you no, that doesn't mean they're right."

The next few days dragged on as I waited for the phone to ring. Whenever I was out of sight of the phone, I began to feel anxiety. I woke up at dawn and waited all day for the call. I fit in my sandwich route, of course, then rushed home and waited some more. I thought twice about going out in the yard and I didn't dare turn on the vacuum cleaner. I couldn't even take Mugsy for a walk. When Friday arrived and I hadn't heard anything, I was discouraged but not about to give up.

"Here you go, Mugsy." I filled the food dish in his kennel and patted him on the head. Shutting the gate behind me, I began loading sandwich cartons into my car, a signal to our golden retriever to begin his usual morning howling, long enough to let his feelings be known but not enough to annoy the neighbors. Just as I was about to turn the key in the ignition, I heard the phone ring and ran back inside.

Breathless, I picked up the receiver and an unfamiliar voice asked for Lynn. "Who's calling?" I asked cautiously, hoping it wasn't a bill collector. The man said his name was Larry Ferreira, the owner of MF Construction, and Mr. Ames from equal opportunity had arranged for him to hire me. His firm was now replacing all the sidewalks in the downtown waterfront area of New Bedford.

I could hardly believe my ears—a masonry job, finally! I listened eagerly to the details. The union still maintained that their books were closed to apprentices, Larry informed me, and so they asked him to pay me bona fide bricklayer's wages, but my lack of experience made that unrealistic. After more negotiation, the union agreed to let Larry pay me the apprentice rate, which was fifty per cent of the bricklayer's rate, and also reluctantly agreed to accept me as an apprentice.

"That all right with you?" Larry asked.

I stifled a whoop of excitement and answered, "Yeah, sure it is."

"Okay, report for work next Thursday morning at seven o'clock at the downtown job site."

I thanked him politely and hung up, then jumped up and down, shouting, "Oh my God! I got a job! A real masonry job!" Then, good grief, the sandwiches! For a moment there, I forgot I was still a sand-wich delivery girl! I ran out to the car, still talking a blue streak. "I can't believe it. Mugsy, do ya believe it? I'm gonna be a bricklayer!" Mugsy resumed his howling as I drove off, upset at being abandoned twice.

"Keepa Go—Make Money for Larry!"

The nervousness I felt on my first visit to the union hall paled before the sheer panic I felt now. Taking on an actual bricklaying job, I thought, would be like laying a pipeline in Siberia. I did not know the language, how to dress, what tools I needed, or what the work expectations were. Overwhelmed by the whole, I decided to break it down into manageable pieces. First, what to wear? Calling Larry for fashion advice didn't seem like a good idea. My bartending outfits—India import tops over Danskin leotards, patched bell-bottom blue jeans and Earth shoes wouldn't do. It was July, so flannel shirts were out too.

Off I went to Mars Bargainland, a discount department store in the North End, sandwiched between textile factories and fish-cutting plants. It was a no-nonsense store, just the basics, no art deco or designer evening gowns. After fruitlessly searching the women's department, I moved over to the men's department and spotted a rack of Dickie work clothes.

Nope, too heavy, too stiff and confining, just not practical in the summer sun. A little farther down, I found a few pairs of painter's coveralls. Nope, the white, lightweight material wouldn't work either.

I finally settled on a thick pair of dungarees on sale in the boys' department. Tan, pockets in the right places, looked like they might hold up. Since all the work shirts had long sleeves, I settled on men's T-shirts in small sizes and dark colors. Now for some heavy-duty work boots and gloves. Again the only possibilities were in the men's department, and even the smallest sizes were way too big for me. I spent the day wandering through every store in the city and suburbs without success. I even called a few stores in the Boston area that specialized in construction clothing, but no luck there either. I finally believed what the salespeople were telling me—there was no such thing as heavy-duty work boots and gloves for female construction workers.

Back I went to the boys' department at Mars Bargainland, where the closest thing I could find were Tyroleans, mustard-colored vinyl shoes with a rippled tread. Lightweight compared to real work boots, they had no steel reinforcement to protect my toes, but it was this or nothing. Next I tried on the smallest men's work gloves and found I could put both my hands into one glove. This was a more serious problem than the boots. If I was going to be laying brick every day, I absolutely had to have a decent pair of gloves.

I expanded my search to Fall River, roaming from store to store, asking hopefully, "Do you sell women's work gloves?" Most clerks wrinkled their brows and shook their heads no. I thought I hit pay dirt when a clerk at the Fall River five-and-ten-cent store smiled and said, "Oh, yes, we have quite a selection." She escorted me to a display of flowered gardening gloves in lovely pastel shades.

Finding the right tools was a piece of cake compared to finding clothes. A few basic masonry tools like a trowel for spreading mortar, a measuring tape, a small level to check the walls, and a tool belt to hold them would get me started. I hoped MF Construction would provide the rest. At Grossman's Building Supply, where my dad bought nuts and bolts, the salesman asked if I was buying tools for my husband. I said yes, and he jumped to help.

I was a bundle of nerves anticipating that first day. Jeez, I hoped they didn't expect me to be as quick at laying brick as the experienced guys. Please, please give me clear directions and put me next to someone I can learn from, I prayed. You bet I'll work hard and get up to speed as quickly as possible. It was Wednesday night and I went to bed early, so I'd be bright-eyed and bushy-tailed in the morning.

At six in the morning I was ready to go, but when I checked myself out in the mirror, I saw a woman dressed up in a Halloween costume as a bricklayer. I was too young to remember Rosie the Riveter and had never seen any woman dressed this way. I wanted to feel self-confident, not like I was about to go trick-or-treating. Just then, Tim came into the room with his cup of coffee and looked me over.

"Hey, you look just like one of the guys. Did you have breakfast?"

"No, I'm too nervous to eat."

"Don't worry, you'll do just fine."

"If not, you'll see me in an hour."

I climbed into my old gray station wagon and turned the key. On the third try, the engine caught and I drove off. I felt like I was going to a funeral, possibly my own, and I was filled with apprehension. Settle down, I kept telling myself, relax.

Approaching the corner of William Street and Acushnet Avenue, I noticed a group of workers standing around a fenced-off area that I thought must be the construction site. I drove by without stopping. What possessed me to think I could ever pull this off? Okay, try again. I drove distractedly down a nearby street, took a few deep breaths to calm myself, and saw a car pulling out of a metered parking space. Since I had only a few dollars, I continued on down the street to a free parking area. The last thing I needed today was a ticket. Besides, parking this far away would give me an easy escape if I decided to turn tail and make a run for it.

"Well, it's now or never." I grabbed my tool belt and headed for the work area four blocks away.

Sawhorses and yellow caution tape encompassed two city blocks where the old sidewalks had been jackhammered out, leaving long troughs with a dirt and crushed stone base. A black pickup truck with MF Construction stenciled on the driver's door was parked nearby, its bed filled with buckets and tools.

I held my head high, squared my shoulders and walked toward the group on the corner where eight or nine men were gathered around an orange and white striped barrel, using it as a makeshift table for their coffee and doughnuts. They wore T-shirts and jeans or short-sleeve cotton shirts and work pants, and their sturdy work boots made my Tyroleans look like baby shoes in need of bronzing.

Most of the men looked to be in their thirties, but a few seemed younger. The dark curly hair and olive complexions told me they were mostly Portuguese, and I heard the familiar dialect as I approached. The Portuguese are known for being hard workers, locally famous for their work ethic in construction, fishing, and farming. Many Portuguese families, including women who worked in the textile factories, pooled their money and stuck it in the bank, saving to buy three-deckers in the city and, later, one-family houses in the suburbs. I couldn't imagine how I could keep up with these men! But there was no running now. I eyed various hand tools and makeshift toolboxes made of five-gallon buckets next to the barrel and thought maybe I'd got this part right. I seemed to have the right tools.

Since I was the first and only woman to work for MF, I was sure my hiring would be the hot topic of conversation among the workmen. I felt like Daniel heading for the lion's den and figured they had already formed their opinions about me, but as I drew closer, I wasn't so sure. A few glances of mild interest were thrown my way. One man with arms crossed leaned back from the circle and I walked up to him and said, "Hi, is Larry around?"

He replied with a thick accent, "No, he don't come here today. I'ma da foreman, Domingos—whadda you need?"

I felt my face flush as all eyes turned on me. "Well, I'm supposed to start work here today," I said nervously.

The words hit the group like a bolt of lightning and they all took notice. Some men laughed out loud, others raised their eyebrows in disbelief. One young man stared at me, slack-jawed, and a younger man with a handlebar mustache and kinky Afro broke into a wide grin and said, "Awwwright!"

Domingos, bewildered, said, "Yeah? You talka to Larry?" as the man beside him shook his head incredulously.

"He told me I could start today." I wished the earth would open and swallow me.

"Stay here, I come back," Domingos muttered as he walked to a nearby pay phone, glancing back at me skeptically.

I hadn't bargained on this reaction and couldn't believe they hadn't been told I was coming. I was mortified, but I tried to look nonchalant in order to get through the painfully long minutes it took for Domingos to return. I could see him in the phone booth, holding the phone with his right hand and gesturing wildly with his left arm as he spoke.

He finally walked back with as much composure as he could muster and declared, "Larry say is okay. The truck is comin'. You worka da chute." Turning to the men who were watching in stunned silence, Domingos said, "Geta ready. The truck gonna be here any minute."

Luckily, the cement truck turned the corner seconds later and got their attention. The men grabbed their tools and headed for their work areas.

"You know how to do?" Domingos asked as he headed over to speak to the truck's driver. I walked along with him and said, "No, this is my first job."

"Aye, Zazoosh," he said in Portuguese, shaking his head and rolling his eyes skyward.

"Okay, come, I show you." We walked over to the truck and Domingos yelled up to the driver, "Hey, you puta over here, okay? She gonna hold da chute."

The young driver, God bless him, smiled at me reassuringly and said, "I'm Mike. How ya doin'? You just signal me to dump or hold up, okay?"

"Okay, I will, thanks." The cement was mixed in the huge spinning top mounted at an angle on the truck, which kept turning so it wouldn't harden. The truck rumbled noisily and Domingos yelled over it, showing me how to operate the chute, a stainless steel open slide that jutted from the back end of the truck. It weighed about forty pounds and looked awkward to maneuver, especially with freshly mixed cement rapidly pouring from it. Several extender chutes stored on the sides of the truck were used to create a narrower channel for the cement as needed. Domingos attached two of these to the truck's main chute, and I watched closely so I wouldn't have to ask too many questions later on.

I tried to concentrate one hundred percent on Domingos, but I noticed the rest of the men standing a short distance away studying me. Now that the initial shock had worn off, they were talking amongst themselves, trying to figure out what the hell I was doing here. Why don't they get to work on their own jobs? Yikes! It finally dawned on me that they couldn't do their jobs until I did mine, since they had to follow behind me and spread the cement in the sidewalk openings. Great. That's all I need, an audience looking at me like I'm an animal in the zoo. Well, they'll have plenty to laugh about if I screw this up so I'd better pay attention to what I'm doing.

I put both arms under the chute as Domingos demonstrated and directed it towards the first open space in the sidewalk. Using one hand, I signaled Mike to begin pouring the wet cement. It looked fairly easy when Domingos did it, but I quickly realized the cement flow caused the chute to wriggle and bounce unpredictably and I needed to keep a tighter grip on it.

Domingos stood beside me, shouting, "Eeeh careesh! Holda tighta!" and "Aye, yigh yigh! You spilla so much! Is no good!" Distracted by Domingos and by the laughter of the men who were watching me, I waited too long to give Mike the hand signal to slow down the flow. Luckily, he had been keeping a close eye on things in the truck's side mirror and slowed the cement flow at just the right time—about one minute before I signaled him to hold up.

After a few more trials, I got the hang of it and Domingos left me on my own. The truck slowly crept along the length of the sidewalk and I did my best to keep the flow of cement evenly distributed. It was almost like pouring cake batter into an oblong pan, trying to get it even and smooth before you pop it into the oven.

As I filled in the last section of sidewalk, one of the men took a tool that looked like a giant windshield scraper and began leveling off the cement at the opposite end. This toothless rake was called a "come-along" and it was used like a rubber spatula smoothing out cake batter. Several other men began to do the same task with the come-alongs at various points along the sidewalk's surface. Domingos yelled, "Keepa go, make money for Larry," every so often, but it didn't seem to speed anyone up or take their focus off watching me.

I filled in the last section and was watching the smoothing process when I noticed Domingos motioning me and yelling, "Clean 'em up, fold 'em up now," as he walked toward me.

Unsure what he meant, I waited for further instruction as Mike shut the engine off and climbed down from the driver's seat. "Time to clean the shit from the chute. Come on, I'll show ya, there's nothin' to it. I got it, Domingos."

After a moment, Domingos nodded his head and walked back in the other direction, barking to the men as he passed, "Keepa go—make money for Larry!"

"Did I do all right?" I asked Mike as he pulled a hose over to the truck.

"Ya did great. This your first job?"

"Yup, my first and maybe my last." He laughed and turned on the water supply and began hosing down the chute, letting the water run down into the nearby gutter.

"Don't let them get to ya. They'll get tired of gawking at ya in a day or two. Now grab this hose and clean the other chutes just like ya saw me do this one."

While I washed down the remaining extension chutes, Mike began detaching and folding them up. I shut off the water, replaced the hose, and followed his instructions on folding the sections and clamping them back into position on the side of the truck.

"Thanks a lot, Mike. You really helped me out."

"No sweat. Another truck should be along any time now so you're gonna get a lot of practice today. By tomorrow, you'll be an expert." He climbed back into the truck and, with a wave, drove off just as Domingos yelled, "Break!"

I looked twice at my watch. It was already nine-thirty and the temperature was eighty-five degrees, the beginning of a real scorcher. Even so, I loved being out in the fresh air and sunshine instead of in a dark, smoke-filled tavern. The men paraded across the street to a canteen truck and I went in the opposite direction in order to be alone and gather my thoughts. Woolworth's was one block away. I had a quick cup of coffee at the lunch counter and tried to quiet my jangled nerves. My hands and eyes were still working, I was filled with adrenaline—I could barely sit still after the fast-paced cement work.

As I approached the work site after the break, the men stomped out their cigarettes and dumped their coffee cups, glancing at me warily, not quite sure what to make of me yet. They probably expected me to be crying over a broken fingernail and heading home by now. Another cement truck was approaching as Domingos came over to me and said, "Same t'ing now, okay? Keepa go."

Nodding, I went over to the empty frame on the next city block and signaled to the new driver as he backed the truck up to it.

Across the street, Domingos barked, "Manny, Paul, you work da bull floats!" Two of the older men hopped to it, carrying two long strips of heavy metal over to the leveled cement. They dropped the bars onto the inside edge and dragged them across the sidewalk. A thin layer of water remained atop the surface of the drying concrete and shimmered like glass. Manny and Paul made their way down the stretch of sidewalk, repeating the same moves until they reached the last section.

Meanwhile, I repeated the process I'd learned that morning, attaching the chute extensions and guiding the flow of cement as the truck inched along. The task went much smoother this time, but the heat was wearing me down. I looked like a contestant in a wet T-shirt contest, perspiration running down my face as I held the chute with both hands. I was getting a good sunburn too, and I made a mental note to wear a loose dark cotton shirt with pockets the next day.

Finally, the last segment of sidewalk was filled with concrete. I turned on the hose and splashed some of the cool water onto my arms and face before I began cleaning the chutes. Hurting from being hunched over for so long, I stood up straight, stretched my back, and noticed a few of the men leering. They reminded me of the customers at the Belmont.

I also saw several elderly people with shopping bags standing nearby, pointing at me and commenting in voices loud enough to be heard by their hard-of-hearing companions:

"I'm telling you, Gertrude, it's a girl!"

"Well, as I live and breathe!"

"That work is much too heavy for a girl. She shouldn't be doing that."

"Don't forget, Oscar, I worked in the steel plant when you went to fight in the war."

I smiled and waved in their direction. They waved back as they continued discussing me. Just as I finished clamping the cleaned extensions back onto the side of the truck, I heard Domingos call out, "Okay, lunch!"

On my way back to Woolworth's, I saw a few of the men sitting in the shade of a nearby tree with their metal lunch boxes. The rest were heading for the Embassy Lounge farther down Acushnet Avenue. I kept thinking about the Cheeseburger Special for $1.25 I'd seen advertised on the chalkboard and thought about getting a large, icy vanilla Coke, too. It was cool at Woolworth's and it felt great to take a break from the scorching heat and staring men.

The cheeseburger and Coke were just what the doctor ordered. As I lingered at the counter, soaking up the air conditioning, I thought about how time flew on this job. Not like at the Belmont, where minutes turned into hours—no wonder they called it a "lounge"! There was no lounging on this job—hours seemed like minutes. The physical labor was constant, you were always in motion. When a break was announced, it was like, wow—I deserve it.

The thirty-minute lunch break raced by and I was back slaving in the midday sun. The mild ocean breeze that blew in from the State Pier didn't help, just increased the humidity as it blew up the hill to our construction site. The third cement delivery of the day arrived, and I was happy to see that Mike was driving the truck. "You're still here, huh?" he joked as he watched me in his mirror and maneuvered the truck into position.

When I gave Mike the signal to slow down the cement flow at just the right time, he said with a slow grin, "See, what'd I tell ya? You're an old pro already!"

I beamed, grateful for the encouragement.

The cement that Manny and Paul had leveled before lunch was just the right consistency for brooming. Phil and Alan, two young Cape Verdean masons, hoisted thick brooms and began sweeping them with practiced strokes across the shiny surface, leaving a uniform texture of straight parallel lines to create traction on the sidewalks. Carlos and Victor followed them, using finishing trowels to smooth out the edges. Antone acted as the "caboose"—he used a groover, a tool shaped like the capital letter "T," to cut dividing lines every five feet along the sidewalk. It was like cutting brownies while they are still warm in the pan.

Domingos walked over to inspect my work now and then, but usually said no more than "Okay, keepa go." He was still looking at me like I was an alien creature, one who could actually pour cement. When he announced it was time for the afternoon break, Mike had just driven away in the cement truck. I rolled up the hose and was too hot and weary to walk back to Woolworth's so I decided to buy a soda from the canteen truck and take my chances with the crew.

Manny and Paul passed me, carrying their thermos jugs to a cool spot in the shade. I smiled, but they gave me the cold shoulder. Victor looked my way with a guarded expression as he spoke to Domingos. In spite of my nervous stomach, I kept on walking to the canteen truck. Antone, a wiry Portuguese man who looked about twenty-five, stood under the awning, downing a can of root beer.

"How ya doin'?" he said between gulps.

"Okay. I'm Lynn."

"I'm Antone and that's my brother Carlos," he went on, nodding in his direction. A thick gold necklace with a Playboy bunny pendant nestled on his hairy chest, framed by his partially unbuttoned, sweat-soaked shirt. It didn't do much for me, but I could tell he thought of himself as quite the ladies' man.

Carlos looked at me curiously. "What are ya doing here? The union send ya?"

I stood at the window and ordered a Coke, slowly counting out fifty cents and stalling for time.

"You a reporter?" Alan asked as I turned around.

"Far from it," I laughed.

Carlos tried again, "So are you union or not?"

I took a sip of my soda as the men looked at each other in puzzlement, then Phil spoke up, "Your old man's in the union, right?" He looked proud at having solved the mystery.

"Nope." I felt like a guest on *What's My Line*. "I'm here to work, just like you."

"No shit," mused Phil, still confused.

I took a swallow of Coke just as Domingos hollered, "Break's over," then guzzled down the rest, wiped my brow and walked back to my spot, grateful the ice had broken.

The last hour was spent mostly on cleanup. It must have been too hot for the elderly spectators—they were gone. At three-thirty, Domingos yelled out, "That's it," and the men gathered their belongings and headed for their cars and trucks. There were no good-byes, they just packed up and left.

I stood alone, looking at the finished sidewalks with great satisfaction. Having something, well, concrete to show for my hard work was new to me and I loved this sense of accomplishment. I drove straight home.

Tim was waiting for me, eager for a report, and we sat out on the back porch as I filled him in on the details of my day. He listened attentively, amused by the men's reactions but proud of me for holding my ground.

"You sure you want to go back?"

"Yeah, I'm sure. I hoped I'd be laying brick right away, but at least I got my foot in the door. I just hope the guys get used to me—I hate feeling like I'm under a microscope."

"Well, just remember, you can quit any time you want."

"Quit? Did you say quit? The only thing I want to quit right now is talking. I'm ready for a hot shower and a good night's sleep." I felt braver than when I had awakened that morning and looked forward to going back to work the next day.

PAYING DUES

On Tuesday, Domingos handed me my first paycheck. I didn't expect to be paid so soon, as I had only worked for three days. I took a quick look at the dollar amount—and wow—$136! My pay from the Belmont for a forty-hour week was $124 and this check was for only sixteen hours! If I needed encouragement to stay with the job, this was it. If I could make this kind of money in two days as an apprentice, imagine what I could make as a certified bricklayer working full time! I folded the check reverently and stuffed it in my shirt pocket.

By the end of the second week on the MF job, I hit my stride. My previously unused muscles, the ones I didn't know I had, stopped aching relentlessly, thanks to the BenGay I applied each night. As I poured cement, my movements were smooth and fluid and, as my proficiency grew, so did my confidence. The waitress at Woolworth's knew my routine by now and had an ice-cold drink waiting for me at break time. I even received a few lukewarm greetings each day from a small group of men I overheard commenting about how hard I worked—for a girl.

The worst was over, I sensed, and I continued to pour all my energy into the work. Even though I was still pouring cement and hadn't learned any new skills, I observed what the men near me did so if I got a chance to do that, too, I'd be prepared.

One morning, my co-workers were telling dirty jokes, much to the amusement of all, and I joined in and told an off-color joke I'd heard at the Belmont. Two of the men misconstrued my intent and began making personal sexual comments to me. A few others looked insulted and repulsed. This was one area where I would not tread again! My full attention would stay on my work.

I occasionally stopped by the union hall to check the bulletin board and ask questions. Addie had the patience of a saint in the face of my constant interruptions. One day she surprised me by asking if I'd be interested in attending the union meetings held twice a month at the main building downtown.

"What? Apprentices can go?" I figured that these meetings were restricted to bricklayers and union officials.

"Certainly, dear, anyone in the union can attend, but just a word of caution—there's no ladies' room there, so it's best to be aware of that beforehand."

"Thanks for the tip, Addie. I'll stay away from the coffee pot."

A week later, I marched up the steps of the stately old building in downtown New Bedford on a sultry summer evening. The union rented this labor hall for meetings because its own building was too small to accommodate the entire group. Meetings were held the second and fourth Tuesday of every month and, from now on, I planned on going to each and every one. My excitement over finally glimpsing the inner workings of the brotherhood was tempered by my fear of sticking out like a sore thumb.

I arrived early, hoping to get a parking spot out front so I could see the guys arrive. Bad idea. One look at the row of gleaming pickup trucks with running lights ablaze convinced me to park my yellow Volkswagen Bug a few blocks away and slink back on foot, blending in as best I could. My beloved station wagon was in the junkyard, and although I was excited when I got my used VW, I now longed for a truck of my own.

I wore a clean work shirt, Dickie pants, and Tyroleans, hoping this would be appropriate. But just in case, I tossed a rayon pantsuit and pair of sandals into the back seat. If the guys wore business suits, I was prepared to park under a dark tree and change my clothes in the car. Fortunately, work clothes seemed to be in vogue as I observed the men arriving. I waited for just the right moment to go in, but I was so nervous I couldn't seem to put one foot in front of the other.

Finally, I walked in nonchalantly and scanned the audience for a familiar face next to an empty seat. A small part of me clung to the ridiculous hope that I would hear a rousing "Hi, Lynn!" from the crowd, be taught the secret handshake, and be invited to join the executive board. But at heart, all I really wanted was to be accepted, just one of the guys.

Conversation filled the hall, then the place grew eerily quiet as all eyes looked at me. I glanced around the room, spotted an empty chair and began the long march. With my eyes riveted on the platform, I pulled out paper and pen and prepared to take notes. Just then, George Ripley called the meeting to order and a roomful of eyes shifted from me to him.

This was another first for me—I had never attended a meeting governed by formal rules. The same men who hollered all day on the job sat passively listening to the minutes of the last meeting. Motions were made and voted on, some passing unanimously, others after debate.

Brad Longley, a young bricklayer, confidently expressed his support for a decrease in benefit deductions from paychecks. Dick Smith, a longtime union man, stood and disagreed, interspersing his objections with colorful swears. The man next to him nudged him and gestured in my direction, silently asking him to hold the swears. Again, all eyes were on me.

Dick looked aggravated and mumbled a quick "Sorry."

"I don't mind," I piped up, but the easy flow of the meeting ended. I was an outsider.

Nevertheless, this was a beginning and I never missed a meeting after that. As the months went by and the men kept seeing me, they began accepting me, but not as an equal. I doubted they would ever see me as an equal. But something strange and new was happening to me inside. By being there, by sticking it out, I was developing an inner strength that surprised me. I didn't know where on earth my steely will was coming from. Sometimes I thought it was the simple routine of my life, the going to work, the rhythm of the job, the regular paycheck. There was structure in my life and I was thriving. In turn, every discouragement I faced, whether at work or at union meetings, became another challenge. All this effort for a singular goal—to make a place for myself as just another bricklayer within the ranks.

By the time the sidewalk contract was almost complete, the autumn leaves, now rusty shades of orange, red, and yellow, had fallen from the trees and gathered in the gutters where we were laying curbstone. We dressed in heavier clothing and had fewer hours of daylight in which to get the job done. I expected Domingos to announce soon that the job was finished and we'd all get laid off at once, but I learned that the end of a masonry job is a gradual process.

One by one, the workers are let go as their final tasks are complete. When I asked Domingos why some of the men weren't around anymore, he looked at me funny and said, "They work, itsa done. Whadda you think—we keepa pay 'em when they all through? Ha! Ha!"

I felt foolish for having asked, but continued anyway. "How will I know when my time is up? Will you tell me ahead of time?" Domingos' face turned bright red because he was laughing so hard. "Oh sure! I tella you about one minute ahead of time—hey, time's up!" And he held his sides and burst into laughter.

For the rest of the day, he teased me lightheartedly and joked with the men too, so I was glad to be included in these light moments. "Hey Lynn, I'ma gonna send you a letter ina mail—Dear Lynn, stay home—Ha! Ha!" He cracked himself up with his own wit. I shook my head and laughed at how much fun he was having.

During the break, Antone explained that you never know exactly when your last day will be.

"After ya been around awhile, ya take a pretty good guess, but anything can happen. Sometimes another man is out sick and ya fill in for him. Other times it's bad weather and ya get delays. Or, if the owner isn't satisfied, changes are made late in the game. That's how it works."

Listening to Antone, I began to get the picture.

"But a layoff is a payoff," he continued, "so it's good news and bad news. They gotta give ya a final paycheck when they finish with ya. So they put a check in your hand and say, 'you're all done, nice workin' with ya,' at the same time."

"Do you see the same people again on your next job?"

"No, some of the guys ya never see again. But the best bricklayers, ya run into them a lot, 'cuz they get first crack at most of the work that's out there."

Next time I saw George Ripley, he explained that some crews stick together year after year. He spoke intelligently and precisely.

"Some companies have steady work and use the same workers on every job. They attract the more skilled, dependable workers and compensate them well, but they're few and far between. Most contractors around here operate by the seat of their pants, bidding on jobs and holding their breath until they find out if they're selected."

"Do the big companies work all year round?"

"Sometimes they have steady work for several months, then nothing. They use whoever is available, good or bad, when the work comes up. It's tough on the contractor because he never knows when there'll be work or what kind of crew he'll end up with. And it's equally tough on the workers, who never know when or where the next paycheck will come from. Competition for jobs is stiff among bricklayers. Many have families to support."

With that, I had a better understanding of the importance of steady work to the family men and why they might see me as a threat. Two days after my conversation with George, my turn came up. Domingos restrained himself and didn't joke when he gave me the news.

"Sorry, Lynn, itsa your time," and he tried to let me down easy. "Here,sa you pay. You did a good job. Gooda luck to you." He patted me on the shoulder, and I thanked him and said a quick goodbye to the guys, who were still hard at work. I felt a sense of rejection, as though a boyfriend had just broken up with me, and even though none of the men had befriended me in a big way, I would miss them. As I gathered my tools and walked to my car, I thought about how much I'd learned and how much confidence I'd gained. Domingos said I did a "gooda job," and that was high praise.

I called Antone at home a few days later to ask about other jobs. His girlfriend answered and when I asked to speak to Antone, I felt a sudden chill.

"Who is this?" she asked, and I launched into a lengthy explanation. "Hmmph…well, hold on," she finally said. I probably made her suspicious with my information overload, but I didn't want to create personal problems for a fellow worker. I got used to this cold response, as I was met with it time and again when I had to call men at home.

Before I went to the next union meeting, Tim and I were eating our customary day-before-payday macaroni and cheese dinner, and I was talking nonstop about the upcoming meeting, the lack of winter bricklaying work, and the masonry book I was reading. I hadn't paid much attention to Tim and our relationship lately—we had fallen into a pattern of me talking nonstop about work and him trying to get a word in edgewise. He cut me short and I suddenly realized how aggravated he was.

"Lynn, you know what? You're becoming a brickaholic. Masonry is all you ever talk about anymore. Maybe you should take a break—go away for a few days or something to get your mind off brick. There's a whole world out there, you know." He abruptly stood up, taking his plate and noisily dumping it in the kitchen sink before heading for the yard.

His words jolted me. I mulled them over none too happily, but in the end decided he was right. Robin, the young woman I had met in the masonry course, kept in touch and invited me several times to visit her in Boston but I kept putting her off. I called her that night and asked if I could visit on Sunday. "I can't wait," she said. Sunday and Monday I'd stay at her place and take the Tuesday morning bus home.

When Tim dropped me off at the bus station on Sunday afternoon, the bitter cold and early darkness made people crabbier than usual, even with the holidays coming up. The bus driver was the crankiest of all and didn't even return my greeting. He drove the bus like a plane lifting off and I thanked my lucky stars there wasn't ice and snow on the highway. As the bus turned the corner at the Boston terminal, I spotted Robin waving excitedly. She was easy to spot, so tall and blond and easy on the eyes. I waved back and felt an instant rush of gratitude toward Tim for telling it like it was—I needed to get away from it all.

Robin and I chatted happily as we drifted toward the subway station and arrived at Harvard Square, where she lived in a small apartment with her musician boyfriend.

"I love your place," I gushed. "You're walking distance to everything."

"Yeah," she said, her shining hair falling around her face in little tendrils. "We're lucky to have it. And Kevin's playing with his rock band at a local club tonight so we have the place to ourselves."

"Super," I said, still staring at Robin's hair. How I would love that hair! So stylish. Mine was shoulder length and drab. I cut it whenever my bangs started falling in my eyes.

The evening quickly turned into something like an eighth-grade slumber party as we chatted and made spaghetti, drank Chianti, and caught up on each other's lives. Then, without missing a beat, we got in our pajamas and sat on the couch, still talking.

Robin had an enviable advantage in the bricklaying world—her father was a member of the Boston local and easily found her a job. In greater Boston, women worked in construction more frequently than in my neck of the woods. To boot, Robin was friends with a female electrician and a carpenter.

"They were starting out at the same time as me, and we compared notes as we went along. It's the same for all of us. The men don't want us there. Either they treat us like sex objects or they refuse to work with us at all."

"You said it!" I hadn't realized how lonely I was in my work, with no women to talk to. I wasn't one of the guys. How could I explain my feelings to the men or even to Tim? They had no idea. But Robin knew exactly how I felt, and I was relieved to hear about the hard time she and the other women were having. Now I knew the problem wasn't me.

My story came pouring out—replacing sidewalks with MF Construction, my struggles with the union, my quiet war with certain men, and all the other problems in my life. We laughed about searching for gloves and work clothes and swapped stories about the men who couldn't figure out what to make of us.

Clearly, Robin's boyfriend was not crazy about her choice of work and she herself was fed up with the daily obstacles.

"It's a constant struggle, you know? I used to be happy when I was a sales clerk, but since I started with the union, it seems like I'm depressed all the time. I get grief from the men at work all day, then come home and listen to more grief from Kevin—it's just not worth the hassle."

I didn't like hearing her talk this way. "You're not going to quit, are you? That's exactly what they want you to do."

"I know, but I'm tired of trying to stick it out just for the sake of principle. Let's face it—I love the money, but it's not worth the crap I take all day long. Kevin says it's only a matter of time before I get hurt—either by some jerk setting me up to have an accident or by some guy coming on to me and getting turned down—and I agree with him."

"Can't your dad help out?"

"He can't control what happens to me on the job, Lynn—you know that. It would only take one opportunity for some jerk to really do damage to me. I'm sick of worrying about that stuff all the time."

I urged Robin to reconsider, but I could see her mind was already made up. We called it a night and I curled up on the couch in a sleeping bag as Robin snuggled under the quilt in her bedroom. We got up at five-thirty and had coffee together before Robin went off to work. Kevin woke up a few hours later and made us oatmeal for breakfast. We talked about Robin, and clearly he adored her. I put up a good fight, but finally said I understood his concern for her on the job.

"She's a sitting duck, Lynn, and I don't want to answer the phone someday and hear something bad has happened to her. It's better for everyone if she quits now, before some guy gets tired of nursing a grudge and decides to do something about it."

"I hear ya, Kevin. I just hate to see the men win when they're the ones in the wrong."

"Well, like they say, it's a man's world, like it or not."

In late afternoon, I walked in the freezing cold to the subway and met Robin as her train pulled in. She looked tired but happy to see me.

"So, did you and Kevin talk about me all day?"

"Yup, and that boy is seriously hung up on you."

"Well, the feeling's mutual."

We picked up a loaf of Italian bread to go with the pot of minestrone soup Robin had heated up, and then we bundled up and walked with Kevin to his gig. Robin thought she might like to work as a waitress in that very nightclub, so she talked to the manager while Kevin set up his amplifier. Then we walked back out into the bitter cold.

Robin was excited. "He said I could start next week and most of the barmaids take home a couple hundred dollars a week. Plus, it would give Kevin and me more time together if we both worked nights. I think I'm gonna do it."

"I hate to see you give up so easy, Robin. Are you sure you're doing the right thing?"

"Yeah, I've had enough of the bullshit; and, besides, Kevin will be a lot happier too."

"Well, at least you know you can always go back to bricklaying in the future," I told her, comforted by the thought.

The streets were filled with people, mostly students, some tourists, old people, young people shopping, sightseeing, eating, rushing to and from class, everyone excited, going somewhere.

And that's how I felt too, so alive and happy to be here with my friend. I even loved the hurry everybody was in. We found a coffee shop and downed steaming mugs of hot chocolate, watching the wonder of it all through a plate-glass window. Christmas was a big deal in Harvard Square, with twinkling lights everywhere and lots of people who couldn't seem to call it a night. Eleven o'clock and the square was still alive.

"Everyone in Lakeville is in bed by nine."

She laughed and replied that Boston never slept.

Robin briefed me on the other women who had been in the masonry course with us and said not a one had stuck with it. We moved on to other subjects, including our deepening relationships with our boyfriends, when we heard a commotion outside. A local radio station broadcast the news headlines from loudspeakers on top of the Harvard Square newsstand, and tonight the news apparently was not good. The scene outdoors went from festive to shock. People were rushing from every direction toward the speakers, staring and listening intently. We followed everyone out of the coffee shop and joined the crowd around the newsstand. Several people were crying, couples clung together and others stood immobile as they absorbed the news. "…John Lennon, founding member of the Beatles, was fatally shot outside his apartment in New York City and was pronounced dead at 11:07 pm…"

Waves of shock and grief overwhelmed us as we tried to make sense of what we had heard. I loved John Lennon—an icon to my generation, a preacher of peace and love, and a musical genius whose songs touched me deeply and comforted me during the loneliest times of my teenage years. Abandoned by his parents at a young age, he had become successful against all odds, and I admired him for that.

How could anyone want to hurt such a person? Who could make sense of this? The older I got, the crazier the world got. The terrible news brought back all the painful memories of Sean's death too and, suddenly, I just wanted to be home with Tim. Robin understood my need to go, and I caught the last bus to Lakeville. Tim picked me up at the station and, after talking about John Lennon's death for a while, we rode home together in silence, lost in our own thoughts.

As often happens when someone dies, we gain a new perspective on our own lives. I slowly realized I never thought the words "safe" and "home" applied to me, but they did now. Tim and Mugsy were my family and we had a home of our own where I felt secure and content. I thought about how crazy my life had been when I first heard John Lennon's songs and where I was now on the night of his death—finally getting it together.

WELD SQUARE

My second job was a tough one in more ways than one. I think of it now as one of those pass-or-fail tests with nothing in between. For sure, the job could have done me in, but I hung on and got firsthand experience with the working guys who didn't want to work alongside women. I got really pounded, but I stuck it out, not to pave the way for women but, rather, because I loved the work and the big bucks. Is that so bad?

Anyway, here's how I got the job.

When George Ripley, the union's business agent, received a well-deserved promotion that took him to Washington, DC, George Medeiros took over. He was a handsome man who charmed the ladies, but underneath his playful exterior he knew his stuff and ran a tight ship. One of George's tasks was to keep bricklayers working by securing them jobs.

When he called with details about my new job, Tim and I had just finished dinner and were watching *60 Minutes*.

"It's George. Turn it down," I yelled to Tim.

With the telephone cradled between my ear and my right shoulder, I burrowed through the kitchen drawers, searching for pen and paper, not wanting to miss out on a single detail.

The job was located in Weld Square, a tough area known for drugs and prostitution, and George made no bones about the risks. "Listen to me, Lynn, I'm not fooling around. Lock your tool bag in the gang box, and I mean every day. And don't leave anything else in your car. Those junkies won't think twice about busting your windshield to get inside, and you can't trust the prostitutes either. You see a car pull up, you ignore the guy and keep on walking, understand? Matter of fact, you shouldn't be walking down there by yourself. You tell one of the guys to walk you back and forth from your car."

"George, don't worry, I'll be fine. I'm an ex-bartender, remember? Now give me the name of the foreman again and what time you want me to be there." I understood his concern but I wasn't as worried as he was. Once a bustling crossroads of family stores and trolley tracks, the four-block area was a prime example of urban blight. On two of the blocks, most of the storefronts were boarded, their walls covered with peeling paint and graffiti. Newspaper World, Ronnie's Cafe and the 19th Hole managed to stay open but thick steel bars encased their doors and windows as if this were a war zone.

The third block ran under a highway overpass. Hard to believe the Boy Scouts once sold Christmas trees on what was now an abandoned lot, strewn with garbage, liquor bottles, hypodermic needles, and used condoms. Situated just off an interstate highway exit, it was a popular spot for "drive-through" heroin dealing. For the prostitutes, the area was a revolving door—pick up a john at the tavern, service him in his car, use the money to buy more heroin, and repeat the process. So it went.

The area needed major rehab, and this new construction was part of the cure. Our work site was the old streetcar barn, which took up an entire block. Once a storage area for trolley cars, it looked to be in ruins, but this was deceiving. There was a lot of life in the old structure yet. Claremont Company had awarded Macomber Construction the renovation contract to convert it into a three-story senior-housing complex.

George informed me that Macomber was a large Boston outfit, and it was rare for an out-of-town firm to work in the city. Macomber could use half of their own employees but the other half had to be drawn from the New Bedford union. The most skilled masons always got winter work first, but Macomber was also required to hire one local apprentice, and that was me.

When the alarm clock rang at five the next morning, I jumped up, confident and ready to go. How far I had come since my first day on the job a year before when I buried my head under the covers and couldn't face the day. I quickly showered, dressed in thermal underwear and heavy work clothes, gulped down some coffee, and headed for work, eager to meet my new fellow workers and chalk up more experience. What a naive puppy I was!

About fifty men were standing in small groups outside the front entrance of the car barn, looking big in winter jackets and holding steaming cups of coffee. I parked and walked over to join them, keenly aware of how strange it was for them to see me, and I practiced over and over what I would say. "Hi, how ya doin'?" I mumbled to myself, trying to sound detached. MF's crews had averaged eight to twelve men and I expected the same on this job. Steve Curcio, Macomber's superintendent, was introducing himself to the bricklayers as I approached. He stood on a small platform, a tall man with short black hair and thick glasses. The men quieted down and formed a loose huddle around him as he explained the protocol for the job.

After giving the specifics, he announced, "The demolition crew is finished with their work as of today. Now it's your turn. You have one story of brick to repoint and two new stories of brick to add on by the end of May. We'll be working in bitter cold so anyone who's not up to the task should leave now."

The Boston crew exchanged guarded glances with the local union men. No one said a word. "All right then, your assigned stations are posted outside the shanty. Let's get to work." Steve put on his hardhat and headed inside the building. Although the job was bigger than anything I'd tackled before, I was ready and eager to begin. The men began to move toward the shanty, a makeshift shelter required by the union for jobs such as this. It was the size of a small bedroom and heads bobbed as everyone tried to find their name and assigned area on the list posted near the door.

A fortyish mason with dirty-blond hair and the outfit of a wannabe cowboy read the list and turned away in disgust. "You see this shit, Russell?" he said to the man standing next to him.

"What's that, Frank?"

"They tell me there's no spot for my brother Brian, but they got room for an apprentice—and a broad, at that. Somethin' ain't right here, and it stinks." He turned around and looked at me with an icy glare. Russell and several others looked in my direction with equally hostile stares.

Instead of fleeing, I pasted a big smile on my face and said, "Hi, I'm Lynn," and searched their steely faces for a glimmer of humanity. The silence was deafening and everyone could feel the tension grow. After a long pause, a few bricklayers outside of Frank's group returned my greeting but, mostly, those who weren't glaring at me just ignored me.

"The union hasn't heard the last of this, I guarantee it," Frank continued, his face flushed with anger.

"Let's go, buddy, we're on the back section, ground floor," Russell replied. As they left, Frank dropped his cigarette butt on the ground, crushed it, and gave me one last dirty look. Shaken to the core, I took a minute to regain my composure, then followed the rest of the crowd inside the building, grateful my assigned spot was not next to Frank. Maybe George should have been more concerned about my union brothers than about the neighborhood, I thought, trying to make light of a situation I didn't fully understand and that scared me to death. The old song *Mack the Knife* kept running through my mind.

As I walked to my work area, I felt the eyes of each man upon me as I passed by. I was the "girl," the enemy, the object of Frank's wrath. I put my tool bag down at my post and saw a man coming toward me with his hand outstretched.

"Hi Lynn, I'm the brick foreman, Ray Scoville. Don't worry, I won't bite." He enveloped my slightly trembling hand in a firm handshake. Good grief, was this guy really being kind? I was grateful for any nuggets of kindness thrown my way. Ray had a pleasant, weathered face, blue eyes, and neatly trimmed black hair. I felt I could talk to him.

"What was that all about? Did I take someone's job away from them?" I tried to keep my voice down.

"Not at all. Frank's been around a while and used to having things his own way. He usually works union jobs with his brother Brian, and he pitched a fit when that didn't happen here. It's just sour grapes—he'll get over it. Now let me show you what you'll be doing." Ray's professional demeanor helped me focus on the task and I paid close attention as he explained how to repoint the brick in my section of wall.

"Okay, you're gonna start over here." He pointed to a ground-level section of a crumbling brick wall. "You got a chisel? Three-eighths inch? And a hammer?" I produced them from my tool bag. "Good. All of this old crumbling mortar has to come out." He took the edge of the chisel and inserted it at a sharp angle into the joint between two bricks, then tapped the end of the chisel with the hammer and loosened a piece of mortar about one inch long. "You don't wanna hit too hard or you'll chip the brick. Just give it a little tap-tap-tap, then take out a piece no bigger than this." He held out the piece of old mortar for me to inspect.

I took the tools and tried it for myself. After a few minutes, I found it was easy and started to get a rhythm going. "Good," said Ray. "Stick to a section no bigger than three feet square for starters and put the old mortar into one of these five-gallon buckets. A laborer will come and empty it. If you have any questions, Bob Comeau here can help you. I'll be back to check on you in a bit." I thanked him and started to work. The building was so large there was a goodly amount of space between workers and that helped me relax a bit.

Bob was working several yards away from me on the left. A short, medium-built man with curly red hair and a kindly demeanor nodded when Ray mentioned his name. I watched him out of the corner of my eye, amazed at his speed and accuracy. He was "toothering" along a section of wall—cutting straight into joints with a small grinder, then using a diamond blade to make window and door openings. Even though many of the bricks had settled with age, Bob had no trouble forging through and keeping his lines straight. Impressed with his dexterity, I hoped I would get a chance to observe his technique more closely.

During break, I kept on working, afraid I might run into Frank again. As I threw a handful of old mortar chips into the bucket, a white-haired man with a big grin strolled over. "Remember me?" His blue eyes twinkled. "I was a mason tender on the MF sidewalk job—Henry Atwood's the name. You look like you could use some coffee." And he poured me a cup from his thermos.

I was so grateful for his kindness I could have kissed his feet. Instead, I thanked him and asked if he had witnessed the morning's incident. He gave me a reassuring pat on the back. "Join the club, kid. We've all had 'Frank the Crank' mad at us for something or other. The guy's a crybaby, always bitchin' about somethin'. Don't take it personal. He can hold a grudge longer than those opera gals can hold a note. Just ignore him."

Henry explained that even though Macomber could have fifty percent of their employees on this job, most of their men were tied up on other, larger projects. So, many of the workers on the car barn job were old-timers from the New Bedford union. "The old-timers are good, but they're sons of bitches—always whinin'. You could fill a fifty-gallon drum with all the false teeth in this place."

After break, I thanked him again and continued working. The bucket was filled with mortar chips by the time Ray came back to check on me. He was pleased with my progress and told me to just keep going on abutting sections of the wall. Lunchtime, I jumped in my car and made a quick run to a hot dog stand a good five minutes away. With only thirty minutes for lunch, I was pushing it but needed to get away for a while to relieve the tension. I rushed back with five minutes to spare and chipped mortar until quitting time.

Heeding George's advice, I grabbed my tool bag and headed for the shanty and the gang box, a locked metal bin for workers who didn't want to lug their tools back and forth each day. Some bricklayers used five-gallon buckets or metal boxes to haul their things; others carried canvas roll-ups encasing the tools inside, tied with a leather strap. Teddy Latch, a Belmont regular, had given me a sturdy canvas work bag emblazoned with New England Telephone on its side. Not only was it perfect for hauling my tools, but the logo made it easily recognizable when stored in a gang box.

Workers came and went from the shanty, dropping their tools off, warming up in front of the kerosene heater, then leaving for the day. As I stepped inside, my eyes were drawn to one wall plastered with naked women torn out of Playboy and similar mags. Several men including Frank sat on makeshift benches of simple wooden planks next to a rough plywood table. Sensing trouble, I decided to lug my tools home after all and turned to the door. Too late—Frank spotted me.

"She belongs on *this* wall, not the one we're working on," I heard him say as laughter broke out in the small room. I closed the door on my way out, hoping they didn't see my scarlet face as I hastily retreated.

Seeing the centerfolds fueled my insecurity about my appearance. I was known on the job as "the girl" and not only were my work skills being watched closely, but also was my body. If I gained a few pounds, I became self-conscious. Even with the Dickie work pants and heavy work shirts, I couldn't hide the fact that I was female and half considered wrapping an Ace bandage around my chest and cutting my hair short to blend in. I never wore makeup or perfume and went out of my way to wear layers of clothing that hid my curves. I wanted to be invisible, to be seen as just another guy on the job. Most of all, I wanted to keep picking up that big paycheck every week.

In the cold, away from the street lights, I noticed several addicts gathered in the vacant lot across the street, looking over their shoulders as they passed money and small glassine envelopes from their pockets into the waiting hands of others. What I saw next took my breath away—a girl I had been close friends with in grammar school—a beautiful, vibrant girl whose boyfriend got her pregnant at fifteen, then introduced her to heroin, was walking unsteadily from the lot back over to Ronnie's Cafe. I pulled my car up alongside her.

Hair hanging limply around her face, she was paper thin and one of her eyes was blackened. A deep scar ran down the left side of her cheek. She glanced at me, her pupils "pinned" from the effects of the drugs. "Hi, Claudia," I cried.

"Hey, Lynn," she slurred. "What are you doing down here?"

I told her about my work and asked if she wanted to go for coffee.

"No thanks, I gotta go, but maybe next time." Her head began to nod forward and her eyelids were closing.

"Okay, Claudia, take care, okay?" I drove away knowing that next time would never come. What had happened to her son? I wondered. Suddenly, my problems seemed small, and I resolved to focus on my job and not let Frank get to me anymore. Meanwhile, I went out of my way to be nice to the guys, still hoping for some small measure of acceptance. For a while, I even went home and baked cookies after a hard day's work and brought them in the next morning. At break time, I'd offer to get coffee for the men working near my station and soon had a new title, "the coffee girl."

One frosty morning, my VW wouldn't start, so I tried pushing it down the street to pop-start it. When that didn't work, I panicked and worked myself into a frenzy. Tim couldn't understand my neurotic behavior, but the thing was, I took great pride in never missing work and being punctual.

"Take it easy—I'll get dressed and give you a ride in my car. You'll just be a little late, that's all."

"No, I can't be late!"

"Why not?"

"I just can't, that's all!"

He shook his head as I tried again to pop-start the VW and, thank God, it worked! I roared off, obsessed about being even one minute late. How could I explain to Tim that I had to be perfect? I knew it was crazy but I was determined to show everyone that I could make it as a bricklayer. I had failed at just about everything in my life—dropping out, never finishing anything, never winning anything, never getting the compliments. Now, suddenly, I had this mountain to climb and I liked it. I was good at it. And they paid me to boot! I could only go up from here. How could I expect Tim or the guys on the job to understand what was going on with me? I hardly knew myself.

By early January, the men became more accustomed to me and I was able to concentrate more on my work. Even Frank was more civil. He came up to me one day and explained why he had been so mad—he felt I'd taken his brother's spot and he needed the money. I made an effort to be decent and not hold a grudge. Frank was still somewhat guarded around me, but the ice was beginning to break.

Now that I had finished removing the old mortar from the brick wall, it had to be replaced. One more challenge before me. I hadn't used a trowel since the women-in-construction course, but Ray and Bob were patient teachers and showed me the process step by step. I scooped up a trowel full of mortar and spread it on the wall, then picked up a brick, and buttered the end joint. Though I still wasn't laying new brick, I enjoyed using the trowel and perfecting my repointing skills. Bob shared his tricks of the trade with me, learned from years of experience, and I watched and listened with reverence and sometimes awe. As the months passed, I developed great respect for him and Ray.

Cries of "Mortar here!" rang out on the job site, the signal for the laborer to refill the mason's pan. Anyone but a New Englander would be hard pressed to make out those words, said in a monotone with the letter "r" dropped. Timing is crucial so as not to interrupt the rhythm of laying the course of brick. A few impatient masons tapped their trowels on their pans, like fathers awaiting their dawdling children. This did not reflect well on the laborers, giving the impression that they were inept. Passing blame down the line was common. Maybe it was a guy thing but I failed to understand why this simple operation was such a source of aggravation. I asked for mortar while I still had quite a bit in my pan, so the laborer had plenty of time to get to me.

The demolition crew that preceded us had gutted the building and cleared out all the debris. The before-and-after photos lining the outside wall of Steve Curcio's office trailer were testimony to the huge task before us. After the trolleys had been sold, the barn was deserted for three decades and the broken liquor bottles, graffiti, and dead pigeons, prominent in the photos, showed exactly what kind of hell-hole the place had become. At some point, the city boarded up the building, leaving it to hundreds of pigeons who buzzed in through gaping holes in the roof and built their nests inside. Unfazed by the construction, the pigeons continued to flock around us as we worked. Their droppings covered the tattered roof and fell in piles through the holes and onto the floor. I could live with them, but the birds constantly irritated most of the others.

"Get the hell outta here, you stupid birds. Get lost before I hammer ya"—words I heard fairly often throughout the day.

As I prepared my tools one morning, I noticed a few men glancing my way. I was used to being watched and didn't pay much attention, just went on laying out my tools. When I lifted my mortar pan, holy shit! A dead pigeon lay under it. I dropped the pan and screamed while they split their sides laughing. They liked this gag so much they repeated it often, always waiting a few days in order to catch me off guard. I assumed the dead pigeons were found frozen on the roof or just lying around in the dirt, but one morning as I set out my tools, I learned the truth. Old Man Barney, the labor steward, passed by my area, looking like a grizzled sea captain with a crazy look in his eyes. Everyone said he was harmless, but I didn't want him anywhere near me. I didn't feel safe in his presence.

"Hey, girlie—watch this!" Barney called over to me. A live pigeon, clutched tightly in his hands, struggled to get free. With one swift jerk, Barney twisted the pigeon's neck completely backward and the bird stopped moving, its head hanging limply. Laughing, he tossed it into my five-gallon bucket. "That'll make a nice lunch!"

I turned away, sickened. He killed many pigeons this way, always trying to get a reaction from me. I didn't want to fuel the fire so I remained silent. Most of the men were indifferent to Barney's cruelty, and some of them laughed loudly, even egging him on. Henry, bless his heart, stood up for me whenever certain men got too rough or too forward and he told Barney to knock it off. Eventually Barney got tired of the sick gag himself.

By early March our crew had erected a second story and we could get a clear view of the corruptions of Weld Square from our work stations on the third floor. A piece of life gone bad, and we could see it all. Some of the guys got off on watching the addicts, prostitutes, and johns as if they were watching a TV soap opera. But how much worse is real life than TV! The crude jokes and running commentary from my colleagues never stopped, and this bothered me. Down there were kids I had gone to school with, or knew from my old neighborhood. By the grace of God, I had escaped the prison they were in. I had found a way out, through my relationship with Tim and through my work, brick by brick. Many old friends had died before they reached their twenties, and many down below would soon be dead as well. I felt great sympathy for the quiet men on the job who had children with drug and alcohol problems, or problems themselves, and they had to listen to this stuff all day long.

I ran into Claudia every now and then and she always declined my invitations for coffee or lunch. She never asked me for money, which I would have given her, and I respected her for that. I learned that her family was a mess. She was not allowed to visit her child, who lived with his grandmother. Her two brothers were also addicted to drugs and their parents were so distraught they finally cut off contact with their children. Seeing Claudia and other old friends sinking in addiction nearly brought me to tears—the help they needed was beyond my power to give. I think I felt guilty, too, for being a survivor.

May arrived and brought beautiful weather; the crocuses and daffodils even poked out their heads in the hell of Weld Square. We were now nearly finished with the third floor. Other workers joined us in stages—first the carpenters, then the plumbers, the electricians, and finally the roofers. Even though the weather was sunny and inviting, most of the bricklayers sat alone in their trucks or cars during breaks, listening to the radio and eating lunches they'd brought from home. I began eating lunch in the parking lot with the roofers, who were closer to my age than the bricklayers. We'd turn up the radio in someone's truck and sit outside, joking and laughing so hard my sides hurt. It was great therapy for me, and I felt more confident and upbeat when I returned to my post in the afternoon. My comfort level had risen since I was no longer under constant scrutiny by the men.

But I was never far away from treachery and humiliation. After lunch one day, I needed to use the rest room, a situation I avoided as much as possible. The portable toilet on the construction site was your standard economy model—no ventilation, no flush, no sink, no paper. If you could hold your breath while inside, you might survive.

I took a deep breath, marched in and latched the door. Mission accomplished. As I buckled my belt and prepared to leave, still holding back a mighty exhale, I found the latch on the door stuck tight. I tried jiggling it again, making sure the latch was fully released. Nothing. The hinges must have jammed. It was then I heard the raucous laughter of the crew outside. Old Man Barney had placed a plank across the door and barricaded me in. A few calls of "Let her out, Barney" came through amid the laughter, but I knew that creep Barney would not let me out until he was good and ready. The man was evil.

I tried to calm myself as claustrophobia closed in. Besides the vile stench, the temperature inside the stall could fry an egg. After what seemed like hours, Barney finally opened the door and I burst out into the fresh air, trying not to vomit. After resting and working my way back to normal, I made my way back up the staging, trying heroically, I thought, to keep my emotions in check. When I passed Bob, he looked at me kindly. "You okay?"

"I'll live."

Bob looked me in the eye and said firmly, "My father always told me to do your best and forget the rest. Try to focus on your work. Ignore those meatheads and you'll be all right."

"Time will tell," I responded grimly and picked up my trowel, determined to go on. Time, in fact, did tell and at the end of May, the last brick was laid. We had created a beautiful building for senior housing, aptly named the Car Barn, a first step in the resurrection of Weld Square. I felt great pride in my new skills and amazed, I suppose, that I'd actually made it through the entire six months without crumbling. I had a better understanding now of what was going on with me. Little by little, I was becoming the master of myself, slowly but surely. Boyfriends, partying, rebellion, and other outside forces no longer ruled my life. I felt strong and directed. Wherever the union sent me next, I was ready to go.

A WALL OF CONFIDENCE

Georgeorge Medeiros pretty much determined when and where I worked, and I was back with MF Construction for the summer, doing cement work. Though I liked the company, I was eager to move on to bigger projects. MF had several jobs going at once, and I was assigned to work on building an addition onto Shaw's supermarket in North Dartmouth. The Shaw's foreman, Kenny Borges, put me strictly on "grunt work"—lifting blocks by myself and running the saw. I stayed there for a month and collapsed into bed each night from exhaustion.

I observed the best bricklayers every chance I got and marveled at their skill. The "lead man" started laying brick at the corner, beginning with a few rows, or courses, that looked like the beginning of a pyramid. At the opposite corner was another lead man doing the same thing. In between the two were "line men" who continued laying the brick courses until they met up with the lead man in the end corner. The stars in this position were called "line burners" and never lacked for work. Both the lead men and the line men started out by picking up a brick in one hand and dunking their trowel in mortar with the other. Hence the phrase, "pick and dip." Next they buttered the edges of the bricks, like frosting a cake, and laid them in the proper place.

After a section of wall was completed, the lead man pulled a string-like line horizontally along the wall to make sure it was level. He then used a level to check the wall vertically. The consistency of the mortar, the rate of absorption by the brick, and the force of gravity helped to determine the precision of the wall. If the mortar was too wet, the brick sank in and didn't sit right. If the mortar was too stiff, the brick sat too high, throwing the course off. Adjustments had to be made before the mortar set. "On the hang, give it a bang" meant the wall bulged out a bit. To correct it, you take a two-by-four board and hold it flat against the wall, banging it with the butt of a hammer. "On the batter, doesn't matter" meant the wall leaned in a bit but would even out on its own.

Hauling block and running the brick-saw day after day had become boring for me, so when Kenny told me I was being sent to a job in Newport, Rhode Island, I was delighted. One of the line men, Monty, was assigned there too and he offered to carpool with me from the MF office in Portsmouth, Rhode Island. I said yes and arranged to meet him at the office the next morning. Monty drove me in his van each way and didn't ask for gas money, so I saved a few bucks.

The first few days, he bragged about what a great bricklayer and stonemason he was, and I nodded and smiled. When I tried asking a few questions about the art of bricklaying, he quickly brought the subject back to himself and I learned nothing. On the way to work each day, other MF workers would pass us on the road, three men squeezed into the cab, some sitting in the bed of pickup trucks. I loved to hear the greetings and tooting horns as we passed and I longed to have a pickup truck of my own.

The Newport job involved building an extension onto an arcade. Monty and I were partnered up to lay twelve-inch block and I welcomed having an extra pair of hands to help me lift the block, but the staging the laborers hastily put up didn't seem safe to me. They threw it up haphazardly, without taking the time to tie it in properly. I worried about an accident as the staging swayed under the weight of the block. On the MF sidewalk job, I heard a story about an employee who slipped on black ice up on a staging, fell seven stories to the ground and died from a massive head injury. His hard hat was no protection against such trauma. Other men talked about having seen death on the job, mostly victims falling from high staging or cement block collapsing overhead and crushing them. The shaky staging I stood on now brought to mind all the horror stories I'd heard, so I was mighty careful as I walked to and fro.

Several masons from Newport who knew Monty confirmed he was a great stonemason. He had worked in the famous Newport mansions restoring marble tile and his work was superior, according to them. Monty, I discovered, was also skilled at drinking too much Portuguese wine and getting himself into fights because of his hot temper.

On the drive to work, he told me about a laborer on a Providence job who had threatened him. "That's why I carry this," he bragged, pulling a revolver from underneath his seat. I felt chills run down my spine. I was terrified of guns in general but especially in the hands of people like Monty. "Is it loaded?" I stammered.

"Ha, ha! Of course, it's loaded! How do you expect me to protect myself with an empty gun?"

"Heh, heh," I joined in weakly. As he put the gun back under his seat, I noticed it was pointed in my direction and hoped we could avoid any big bumps. On the drive home that same day, I told Monty I'd be taking my own car to work from then on so I could run errands.

"Okay, well, just let me know if you ever need a ride—I'll be happy to give you one any time."

I thanked him and made a quick dash for the safety of my own little VW.

The Portuguese flavor runs strong in New Bedford; I ran into George Medeiros at the Madeiran Feast of the Blessed Sacrament— "The Portuguese Feast"—an annual three-day bash in New Bedford's North End that drew 350,000 people from everywhere. George was cooking *carne d'espeto*—chunks of seasoned beef on a ten-foot skewer —at the barbecue pit. About fifty people at a time lined up their skewers over the intense heat. Many sprinkled beer and spices on the meat as it cooked, then put it in fresh Portuguese buns called "pops," which they ate immediately.

"Oh, hi, Lynn! Hey, I've been meaning to talk to you about the annual apprentice contest," said George, trying to speak over the crowd and looking sooty from the pit. "You should think about entering." He filled me in on the details and said the union would pay my entry fee.

"Sounds great. Sign me up."

"Wow, what an opportunity," I said later to Tim. "Now I'll see how I stack up against other apprentices and, if I do well, the men might take me more seriously."

A month later, Tim and I were on our way to the contest, held at the South Shore Mall in Braintree, south of Boston. I had pictured the contest in the remotest area of the mall, an empty store perhaps, and expected to see folding chairs for the contestants, their guests, and the business agents. Coffee and cookies afterward, maybe. The union would probably announce the winners in their local newsletters, and that would be that.

Reality hit as soon as we reached the central lobby. This was a much bigger deal than I thought. A crowd stood under a huge banner—*Massachusetts State Conference of Bricklayers and Allied Craftsmen Annual Bricklayer Contest*. On a raised platform sat Governor Michael Dukakis flanked by state dignitaries and union representatives. Five contest judges sat on the right side of the stage, pads and pens in hand.

In the center of the lobby, a large work area had been roped off and some of the contestants had already taken their positions. Family, friends, union members, and curious shoppers surrounded the area.

"C'mon, Lynn, they're getting started," I heard Tim say, but I couldn't respond, I was so stunned by the magnitude of the thing.

I heard myself saying, "Let's get out of here, Tim, I can't do this."

He put his hands on my shoulders and looked in my face. "You can do it, Lynn—take a deep breath and don't look at the crowd. C'mon now, you're gonna do fine."

"Hi, Lynn," George Medeiros called out as he walked toward us.

I gave him a look. "Why didn't you tell me this contest was such a big deal?"

"Because you wouldn't show up, am I right?"

"You're damned right."

He shrugged. "What are you worried about? You're gonna do just fine."

If I'd have had my trowel, I would have bopped him one, but it was too late to turn back—I could only go forward. I took a deep breath and went to my station, checking out the competition on the way. Twenty-eight contestants were ready to go, including two women who also seemed nervous. Several of the male contestants looked defeated already, as if they were last year's losers giving it another try. I could smell the "morning-after" liquor breath of the young apprentice in the space next to mine. We were quite a diverse group, I'd say.

Each station was equipped with a stack of four-inch-wide cement blocks, a pan of mortar, and a canvas tool bag that held a trowel, a level, a ruler, and a plumb bob—gifts to the participants.

Chuck Raso, business agent for the Boston local, tapped on the microphone and the place quieted down. After introductions and a brief speech, he read the rules: "You must build a four-foot-wide cement block panel with no limit on height, one side veneered with red brick; build three courses of brick in eight-inch-high increments. You get three hours to complete the panels and you'll be judged on speed, skill, and accuracy. Good luck to all. Begin!"

It was all happening too fast for me and the large gaping audience made me nervous as hell. I looked around frantically to see how the others were doing.

Tim realized I was in trouble and positioned himself in front of my station. "Stop looking around. Concentrate on your own work." His words made me even more nervous and I froze. Sensing my disorientation and panic, he tried a more sympathetic approach, "It's okay, Lynn. You know what to do—just concentrate."

I shut my eyes, blocking out the activity around me, and tried to gain control. Just pick up one block and get started, I told myself. One block, one block, one block. That's all you have to do right now. I grabbed a block, set it down and went to work. That one block was a beginning.

As my panel took shape, I felt the familiar rhythm of a brick-layer—lay a block, spread it with mortar, lay another. Use the level, use the line, make it straight—the formula that got me on track when I was wild and undirected gave me that same sense of steadiness and stability now. A few seconds after I lay my trowel down, Chuck was back at the microphone giving orders.

"Time's up! Put down your trowels. The judges will examine the panels and announce the winners."

I stepped away from my panel and took a quick snoop around. Others had built panels that looked to be four and a half feet high. My little panel was under three feet, but then I noticed some that were even shorter than mine.

Tim handed me a Coke, which I devoured. "You did a great job." I was so relieved it was over, I couldn't talk, but Tim said just the right things. "Come on, let's take a look around." We passed the judges, who were intently going from station to station, taking notes and talking among themselves. A booth manned by union volunteers had been set up next to the stage, where the public could try their hand at bricklaying. Many children were experimenting, girls as well as boys.

Good for them. If nothing else, they had seen three women bricklayers today. That alone was worth my showing up.

Tom McIntyre, the union's state director, took the stage. "Contestants, please return to your stations. The judges have made their decisions." Everyone scuttled back to their positions and all eyes were glued on Tom. A large trophy and three plaques sat on a table next to him. "In fourth place—John Palmieri of Brockton Local 5." The audience applauded as a thin young man in denim coveralls came forward to claim his plaque and a fifty-dollar savings bond. I cheered him on.

"In Third Place—Lynn Davidian of New Bedford Local 39."

I couldn't believe what I was hearing and looked at Tim for confirmation. His face was all smiles.

"You won! Go on up—hurry!"

Like a robot, I walked up to the podium to claim my prize, and applause rang in my ears as I returned to my station. At that moment, I spotted George making his way through the crowd to congratulate me. "Great job, Lynn," he beamed. "I knew you could do it!"

I watched the second and first place winners claim their prizes before it hit me. "Oh my God. I really won!" Tim and George laughed at my delayed reaction. A newspaper reporter asked me to return to my station for a photograph and I happily obliged. Then I posed with George for our local's next newsletter. While I was busy with my public relations, I realized that many of the contestants who didn't place had already left.

Tim, George, and I celebrated at the Ground Round restaurant in the mall, and over food and drinks the men toasted my achievement. "Next year I'm going to win first place!" I crowed—and I meant it.

Back in New Bedford, Tim and I headed for the Belmont Club to tell my dad, who quickly spread the word around the bar. Several rounds were bought in my honor before the jokes began. "Hey Lynn, I heard you were the only broad to win. What did the other two look like?"

"I got a cellar wall that's fallin' down. I'll let ya practice on it, no charge!"

"Can I get your autograph now before you get too famous?" This was their way of telling me they were happy and proud of me too.

Teddy, who had given me my tool bag, was the proudest. Back in my bartending days, we had watched a TV show about women in the armed forces and he'd laughed and said, "Women can't even do push-ups, never mind defend their country." I took the bait. Next thing he knew, I was doing push-ups on the floor next to the row of barstools. The afternoon regulars, steeped in booze and monotony, couldn't believe something was actually happening in their world. They came alive and cheered me on, even taking bets on how many I could do.

I had impressed Teddy and made a lot in tips that day too. As the regulars now inspected my plaque, passing it from person to person down the bar, Teddy bought a round and announced, "Here's to Lynn—but she owes it all to me. She never woulda won if I didn't make her do those push-ups!" We all had a good laugh at that—this crew would certainly keep me humble.

When I returned to work on Monday morning, word had reached my co-workers and a few men congratulated me, but it was not a big deal to most of them. If I won first place, they'd notice, I thought, already formulating my plan for next year. Now that I knew what the contest was about, I decided to practice building a panel in my basement. I bought cement blocks identical to those in the contest and stacked them in a corner. Instead of mortar, I mixed sand, lime, and water into a temporary paste so I could use the same blocks over and over. And I used the tools from the contest along with a kitchen timer. Every night after work, no matter how tired I was, I headed down to the basement to practice for at least an hour.

After a few weeks, I made a slight improvement in my speed and accuracy, but my stomach was in knots every night. While practicing, I pictured myself at the contest and was filled with dread. Would I freeze up again? Would I screw up and drop a block? The more I practiced, the more anxious I became. Tim noticed my tension and recalled an article he had seen in *Sports Illustrated* in which a well-known football player endorsed a book called *Relax and Win* by Lloyd B. Winter, claiming it helped him keep his focus and go on to victory.

A few days later, Tim appeared with the paperback and I devoured it. Although the book was sports oriented, its principles applied to bricklaying or any challenge. The change in my practice sessions was immediate. First, I cut down my practice schedule from five to three nights a week and incorporated the author's relaxation techniques into my routine. The techniques also helped me on the job.

In the past, I tackled challenges head on, like a wild stallion frantically trying to kick his way out of a stall. Now I was learning the mental techniques necessary to channel that energy to achieve my goal. I was no longer flailing madly but developing a sense of inner power. Months later, one practice session a week was sufficient, thanks to my new level of self-confidence.

DOWN AND UP IN FALL RIVER

*B*efore embarking on my biggest project yet, I took a kind of involuntary sabbatical. With winter approaching, work was slow and George had no assignments for me, so I began waitressing three nights a week at my dad's fish-and-chips restaurant, downstairs in the Belmont. Over the years, he had opened and closed the Whaler Restaurant several times. When it was open, the bar business increased, since the regulars could order up a meal without leaving their barstools. And downstairs patrons liked to order drinks from the upstairs bar. But the profits were small and Dad didn't really enjoy the hard work of running a restaurant as well as a bar.

I thought about asking him to let me take over the Whaler Restaurant. I knew I would need help, so I talked to one of my old neighborhood friends, Tom Malloy, who was now a city councilor. Tom was a Belmont regular and knew just about everyone in the city. When I ran the idea by him, he was all for it and assured me he could drum up lots of business for us.

Dad agreed to let us give it a try and we worked out a deal. Tom Malloy and I would take over completely and pay Dad a certain percentage of the profits. I hired Dave LaPalme, one of Tim's friends, to handle the bookkeeping, and we were set to go. We bought fish at Porky's fish market in bulk at a discount and everything else at National Wholesale. I used some of my savings as start-up money, then counted on the restaurant's receipts. Tom didn't take any pay for the first few weeks, since he hadn't contributed to the start-up.

The regular customers came in like clockwork, but no new patrons came by. By the end of the second month, things were not looking rosy. Tom had met a girl and fallen in love shortly after we opened and was spending his time with her. His promise to find new customers died and soon he was not even showing up for work himself. He would send a sister or brother down to take his place, but they didn't know the ropes. Before long, the only person not losing money on the fish-and-chips venture was Dave, the accountant, who advised us to close up shop. Tom and I agreed to turn things back over to my dad and thanked him for giving us a chance. Luckily, he did not rub our noses in our failed venture. But sometimes failure is a blessing, and giving up the restaurant freed me to build my career in masonry.

Meanwhile, I didn't see much of my family or old friends anymore. My brother Dave was on the road, working as a lighting director for famous rock bands. He rented an apartment in California but was seldom in one place for long. Steve sold jewelry on Martha's Vineyard in the summer and Fort Lauderdale in the winter. When my grandfather died, Steve fixed up the second floor of their tenement and moved in, taking care of the house and yard for Grandma, even though his work schedule frequently put him on the road. Dawn now had a little boy, William, and was putting herself through nursing school. Mark was in college and also managing a movie theater.

The only friends I saw regularly were Pam and her son, Jason, who had moved to Wareham not long after Pam graduated from college. Tim and I had moved to Lakeville around that same time. Pam's boyfriend, Donny, was a musician and spent most of the year on tour. With me working through the union and Pam working as a social worker in Hyannis, we could see each other only on weekends, so the time was precious. Even our dogs were close. When Honey came to visit, Mugsy would get lovesick and chase her all around the house.

One Sunday afternoon while we were playing with Jason in the yard, George Medeiros called to give me some big news.

"There's a large-scale wastewater treatment plant going up in Fall River and they need an apprentice, probably a two-year deal."

I hesitated, as I still occasionally worked for MF and hoped to return to them in the near future. If I took another job, they might not hire me back. I felt a bit disloyal since they gave me my first job and I really enjoyed working with the crew. I talked over my concerns with George and he felt it was in my best interest to go with Westcott, a well-established high-profile firm.

After mulling it over with Tim, I decided to take the job. The very next day, Pam got an offer to become a property manager for a Boston real estate management firm, which meant leaving social work and doubling her pay. Our close friendship was marked by a vigorous synergy; major changes in our lives seemed to take place around the same time. We felt a rush of excitement for ourselves and each other as we prepared to begin a new day.

Fall River would be my workplace for the next two years. The city's reputation was as hard-edged as New Bedford's, and the two cities shared many of the same problems, including high unemployment and high-school dropout rates. The factories fed and clothed the city—men toiled in rubber and electrical plants, and women filed into garment plants to make men's and women's suits. Fishermen, mostly Portuguese, brought in the weekly catch.

The city was picturesque, offering magnificent views from the highlands, where the notorious Lizzie Borden once lived, to the lowlands, where the immigrants and factory workers lived in neat three-deckers. Some of the tenements sat so close together that an occupant of one apartment could hold hands out the window with his neighbor next door. The gulls hung out over the Braga Bridge, and parks and ponds appeared like gifts in unlikely parts of town. Fall River also boasted some beautiful granite mills, many now operating as factory outlets. The city of hills and mills looked beautiful at night from the bridge, aglow with thousands of twinkling lights.

Immigrants still arrived regularly from mainland Portugal and the Azores and set up shop along Columbia Street. The smells of *malasadas*, sweet bread, *linguiça*, and *caçoila* wafted through the air and followed me to work. You could count on three good traffic jams a day as workers from the first, second, and third shifts drove to and from their jobs in the factories.

I was the only female in my union, Local 39, which covered a large region, from Swansea to Provincetown. Westcott Company was constructing a nine-building wastewater treatment plant on the west side of town and I was hired to fill their minority quota. As I approached the job site, whew, I could hardly believe it—this was what they meant by ground zero. Twenty acres of land lay flat and barren before me. Starting with just one brick, we would create this massive facility and I would be a part of it!

Westcott was strict in their compliance with affirmative-action laws. Joyce Brown, a company secretary, had been appointed equal opportunity officer, and she was frequently there on the job site. I was pleasantly surprised to see two other women on the site, one an apprentice electrician and the other an apprentice carpenter. I wondered if they were the same two women my friend Robin had mentioned from the Boston local. The hope I had for a more enlightened crew, however, quickly faded that first day as I set up shop on the staging. Derek Ribeiro, one of the old-timers, said loudly, "Next thing you know, they'll have monkeys doing this work." I ignored him. The job was huge and I was here to learn, and that jerk was just a distraction.

The vastness of the project and the number of workers floored me. So many people doing so many different things! We were like an invading army building on newly conquered land. I was not used to working on big complex projects and tried to hide my nervousness. Some of the men had job titles I'd never even heard of. Stanley, the brick steward, sent me up on the staging to work and I grew a little panicky up there alone. I took out my tools, took a quick look around to get my bearings, and spotted the necessary materials.

The mason tender filled my pan with mortar and I hurried over to the stack of blocks, lugging them back to my station as fast as I could. I worked hurriedly to cover up my confusion and uncertainty about the job. As I was scooting back to my station, Stanley yelled up at me, clearly irritated, "Hey—stop running up there—it's dangerous!" I slowed my pace, embarrassed, trying to ignore the staring eyes of the men as I returned to my post.

"Don't worry about him—you ever hear the story of the tortoise and the hare? Well, he thinks he's the tortoise," said a friendly man working on my right. He introduced himself as Whiskey Pete, a middle-aged bricklayer with a face creased and lined by years of weather. I would soon learn he was a hard-working, hard-drinking man and as honest as they come. Pete's brother John was my mason tender, and they worked together on most jobs.

I was getting better at pegging my co-workers as with me or against me, based on their initial reaction. Derek Ribeiro fell into the latter category, a surly man who worked on the staging to my left. On my third day of work, he let loose his feelings and repeatedly screamed, "What the hell are you doing on this job anyway? You shouldn't be here! This is no place for broads and I ain't puttin' up with it! You don't belong here—you should be home taking care of your kids!" I continued working and tried not to listen.

Derek kept at it and a few men told him to shut up and get back to work, but he paid no attention. The superintendent overheard him and made a phone call to Joyce at the main office. She wasted no time, hopped in her car, and drove a quick forty miles to the job site. I saw her arrive but didn't know why she was there. She looked like somebody's wife, standing in blouse, skirt, and heels at the bottom of the staging, listening, saying nothing. By now, Derek had been at it for close to an hour, calling me names and yelling. When she'd heard enough, Joyce tersely called him down. Derek, who was not aware of her presence, was shocked. He turned ghostly white, put down his trowel, and slowly crept down. A longtime employee, he was in good standing with the company, but this behavior was unacceptable.

Joyce took him aside and read him the riot act. She was calm but furious and very, very clear, and I could see Derek hanging his head. I wondered if he would be suspended or fired, but he climbed back up on the staging. I continued working while the rest of the crew craned their necks to see what was going on. As Derek passed me on his way back up to his post, he glared at me with contempt, "See the trouble you got me into?"

I kept my mouth shut and continued laying block. When I looked up a short time later, one of the older men on the staging gave me a respectful nod and I knew I had done the right thing.

At break time, one of the young apprentices from Boston mentioned he was taking some advanced courses in masonry.

"Oh, I'd love to do that, but I can't afford it."

"You pay your union dues, don't cha? The union will pay for your training. That's part of why you pay them."

"That's awesome!" I exclaimed, and on my lunch break I sped to New Bedford to check it out. Addie, the secretary, was not surprised to see me. I had become a pest, to be sure, a determined pest, at the union office, always asking questions or looking for new ways to advance. As usual, she sent me in to see George Medeiros and he confirmed it. At that time, however, there were not enough apprentices to fill a class.

"Well, why should that keep me from being able to learn more?" By now he knew me all too well—I was not about to give up. With reluctance, he placed me in a welding class that met three nights a week at Voke Tech, the vocational high school in New Bedford where

Tim worked. Welding, I discovered, had as much to do with masonry as cake decorating had to do with auto mechanics. I hated everything about it—the time it consumed, the sexist comments from the male students and the teacher. While I was working with a torch one night in class, I got a flash from an arc and that straw broke the camel's back. Yanking off my face shield and gloves, I walked out of the class without a word, never to return.

The next day I marched back to the union office on my break and Addie simply gestured for me to go ahead and see George. "I'm done with welding and I want a course in advanced masonry," I announced.

He put me off. "Lynn, there just aren't any courses around here right now. You'll have to wait for more apprentices to be hired."

"That could take forever." I left the office determined to find the course myself and did some research over the weekend. Hmmm. Right away I found what I wanted—a course in Plan Reading and Estimating, offered by Wentworth Institute of Technology in Boston. "Hmmm, sounds perfect." I called and asked them to send more information, then I handed George the brochure and asked for the union to foot the bill.

He looked over the material. "You're probably better off with welding. I doubt you'll ever have need for this type of course. It's mostly for men who own their own business."

"Maybe I'll own my own business someday—you never know." He rolled his eyes in exasperation and said nothing.

The thought of taking a college course with my eighth-grade education was intimidating, but I had fallen in love with the trade and longed to learn more. I gobbled down masonry books in my spare time, so I just might be a good student. The course ran on Tuesday and Thursday nights for two semesters. If I left Fall River exactly at quitting time, raced home to wash up and change, ate a sandwich in the car and drove like a maniac, I would just make it to Boston in time for class. Wentworth, here I come!

And so I went. I soon became a pro at maneuvering around Boston, darting in and out of traffic, and sometimes even finding a legal parking space. Wentworth opened my eyes to a whole new dimension of the trade. Although I was the only woman in the class, I was as respected as my fellow students, several of whom were from overseas.

The instructor was professional and the course challenging. I began to entertain thoughts of becoming a foreman someday.

However, the two-hour trip back and forth to Boston, combined with extensive homework assignments, seriously cut into my sleep time. Exhaustion caught up with me one night as I drove home from class, and I found myself three lanes off target, headed for a concrete barrier. Shaken to the core, I pulled over to a rest stop nearby to sleep before continuing on. That weekend, I did nothing but sleep and gradually I adjusted to the new schedule.

The Westcott job was going well and, as time went on, I felt more comfortable with the pace. Whiskey Pete was working next to a few highly skilled bricklayers and I wished they were next to me. Occasionally, I overheard the conversations of the best bricklayers on the wall and they talked about "the greats" of bricklaying as others might talk about the greats of baseball—Ted Murphy, Dick Thomas, and others. I was all ears listening to their stories and thought I would die to meet one of the legendary ones.

That opportunity came after work one day when I went with Whiskey Pete and his brother John to the Harborside Bar and Grill. John's girlfriend, Carol, was a bartender there and his co-workers were the beneficiaries, putting away enough drinks to sink a ship. After ordering food, I noticed a group of men from the job gathered at the end of the bar. The star of the group was the mythic Ted Murphy, a man who was capable of laying more than 1,200 bricks a day, according to Pete. Most men averaged 600 bricks and apprentices 450.

Gathering my courage, I walked over to Ted, introduced myself, and said I hoped someday to be as accomplished as he. He looked me over with a lopsided grin and a slight wobble of his head.

"Kid, you've got three strikes against you. You're not strong enough, you're not tall enough, and you're a woman."

Determined not to show how devastated I was, I muttered, "Well, you're entitled to your opinion," and backed away to rejoin my buddies. My hurt quickly turned to anger. I'll prove you wrong, you son of a bitch, I said under my breath.

"Don't listen to him, Lynn—he's plastered," said Whiskey Pete, who was well on the way to plasterville himself.

"He's a legend in his own mind. That's his downfall," John agreed.

Both Pete and John were now my close friends and helped me immeasurably on and off the job. Humble, kind hearted, decent, they made up for the creeps, and their support boosted my spirits and self-confidence. Pete's dry wit put all the upsets on the job in perspective and a little liquor fueled his comic side. We began to meet every Thursday night, joined by a few others, for dinner at the Harborside, all of us dirty and sweaty from the day's work. Pete dubbed us The Westcott Supper Club and it became a regular event. Those Thursday nights were like therapy sessions for me.

Autumn flew by and December arrived with a vengeance. The winter months tested the mettle of even the heartiest bricklayer. If the temperature reached thirty-two degrees, we worked, even though the icy gusts battering us from the ocean drove the windchill factor to below zero. Mustaches and beards turned into icicles; we all suffered rough, chapped cheeks and noses.

Getting dressed for work took forever—layers of long underwear, flannel shirts, thick pants, woolen socks, and hooded jersey jackets. I usually topped it all off with a thermal vest which left my arms free and unrestricted. The clothing never stood up for long to the relentless bash of block, mortar, and the elements, so I became a regular at the Goodwill thrift shop.

Gloves had to fit snugly so you could feel the brick as you worked. Most of the men wore thick brown gloves, but some of the old-timers wore no gloves at all. Their hands were as tough as a bull's hide and full of cracks. Handling the wet brick wore away at the skin on their fingers and they would develop pinholes, which were very painful.

I still couldn't find gloves small enough for my hands, so I used masking and electrical tape, wrapping layer after layer around my fingers. This time-consuming process wore through within hours, leaving my hands exposed. I could not keep breaking up the rhythm of my work to reapply new tape, so my hands began to look like the old-timers' hands. Yellow rubber dishwashing gloves would have worked better than tape, but I couldn't bear the housewife jokes which were sure to follow.

One Saturday, I drove all the way to New Hampshire in search of a new product, Thinsulate, made by the 3M Company. It came in insert form for boots or gloves, and I spent half my week's paycheck buying a good supply. They were better than nothing, but no matter what I wore, the bitter cold eventually got me. Involuntary shivering made it difficult for me to keep a tight grasp on my tools, and I envisioned my trowel falling thirty-two feet to the bottom, where I'd have to retrieve it and climb up again. I began doubling up on my tools, packing two of each in my bag so I would have a backup, just in case.

One afternoon we were working on the preliminary treatment building, directly over the sewerage tanks. The stench from the waste below filled the air and I wondered what hazardous chemicals were clogging my lungs. Absentmindedly, I reached back for my level and kicked it off the staging. As I watched it splash into the fetid tank, I thought of the fifty dollars it cost—not much compared with the cost of trying to retrieve it. Luckily, I had a spare level in my tool bag and quickly unpacked it, vowing to be more careful.

Already two foremen who were not producing quickly enough had been given the ax by this no-nonsense company. A third foreman, Clarence Whatmough, reputed to be top man after thirty years with the company, took over. His thick white hair and friendly green eyes earned him his nickname, the Silver Fox, and he supervised crews on multimillion-dollar projects with an understated air of profession-alism and grace. To get to the top, he believed you must start at the bottom—and that is exactly where he put me during my second year on the Westcott job.

My above-ground work was done for the time being, and I was sent into the trenches. As I descended the rusty ladder into the manhole, the smell of raw sewerage assaulted me. It was a "live" hole in which the septic waste pipe was temporarily plugged to allow for repairs. The farther down the ladder I went, the more claustrophobic I felt. Hoping I was not being set up for another prank, I inspected the retainer cap holding back the sewerage flow, alert for any sign of leakage. I started to take a deep breath to calm myself, but changed my mind as I imag-ined the airborne diseases racing into my lungs. Struggling to keep my face away from the slimy walls of the pipe, I grasped my trowel and began to build the brick inverts that were needed to channel water from pipe to pipe.

As I climbed out of the manhole at day's end, I thanked the Lord for daylight and fresh air and raced home, where I planned to spend the evening in a hot, soapy tub. Should I burn my clothing? Nah, it would be my official uniform until I was done with sewer duty, then I'd have a bonfire. In early February, when the brick inverts were complete, Clarence informed me I could begin work above ground the next day. Hallelujah, I wanted to kiss him. I settled for the look of approval on his face as he acknowledged my toughness and endurance down there. That look was almost worth serving time down below.

On the staging the next morning, I felt like a groundhog coming out of my hole after a hard winter. The daylight was a dream, but the bitter wind would not let up. Laying brick in a New England winter is no easy feat. Every step is labored as your body tries to work while battling the cold. The air stings your lungs; your frozen hands scream as you grab each new brick and your limbs tremble as you climb the staging. You live for the heat of the break. Despite all this, the preparation of the work area in winter is comforting. The staging is covered in polyurethane to form a tented work area. Propane heaters are lit a few hours before work begins, raising the temperature to a brisk thirty-five degrees, just enough to prevent the mortar from freezing. Water is splashed into the pans as they are readied for the freshly mixed mortar. Movement is slow and deliberate, so as not to rend a tear in the cocoon of plastic sheeting. The fact is, winter work is a gift for a chosen few. Eyes reflect unspoken gratitude for the chance to work through the bleak winter months.

THE WEDDING

Spring arrived with a splash in Lakeville that year, warm sunny days and eager robins and blue jays, and my thoughts turned from bricklaying to our house and garden. When could we fit in spring cleaning and what would we plant this year? We sat outside and watched Mugsy troop through the yard, sniffing the new smells of spring, oblivious to the birds and bees that hummed and buzzed around him. Wildflowers grew alongside the roads and decorated the fields, and everywhere crocuses and daffodils danced. It was a spring of surprises.

The biggest one came on a winsome day in May when Tim announced that he had a kind of surprise for me. A surprise? Sure. I like surprises. After dinner, looking a little nervous, he asked me to sit down in the living room. He had something he wanted to say.

"Do you want to marry me?" he stammered.

Marriage? I completely flipped. My insides started doing somersaults and I could not feel the ground underfoot. Marriage? I was taken by complete surprise. MARRIAGE? My mouth flew open—"What do you mean?" I know my response was truly stupid, that he might just be joking or something. It was the best I could do.

He looked puzzled and a bit hurt. "What do you mean, what do I mean?"

"Marriage? Are you proposing to me?" This response was even stupider than the first, but I was in shock. We had a world that went along in certain ways, the sun rose, the sun set, we bought groceries, we cooked, we were in bed by nine-thirty, and now Tim had turned it upside down.

"I think so." He seemed confused himself.

We both started laughing. "You serious?"

Tim, now really mixed up, didn't say anything.

Good grief, what if he changed his mind? I gathered my wits about me before opportunity passed. "Sure, I'll marry you!" I blurted out.

"Good!" And it was settled.

Marriage. To Tim. It was really a good idea, wasn't it? We were good for each other, stood by each other, we had already made a home together. It really was time to make this commitment.

We set the date for July 4, 1982, Tim's twenty-eighth birthday and the day of our annual Fourth of July celebration. Why not? This year our guests would get a party and a wedding, too! My dad offered to pay for everything and after much discussion, he agreed to rent a canopy, tables, chairs, and a portable dance floor. Wow. Just months ago, I was up on that staging in Fall River freezing my butt off, and now my thoughts were turned to dresses and hair styles and all the little details of a summer outdoor wedding. I spent hours with Mom, my sister Dawn, and Pam traipsing from store to store looking at satin dresses, taffeta dresses, just-below-the-knee dresses, and long country dresses. We leafed through magazines to check out the hair styles—short and sassy, upsweeps, shoulder-length chic, curly-heads. It was such fun!

Tim was especially amused to see me come home from the Westcott job covered with grit and grime and immediately start looking through wedding magazines full of frilly garments. It took me a while to shift gears, but I think I probably unwound in the car on the way home. Something deep inside me kept up the steady rhythm of laying brick after brick after brick. But my mind moved out of the city as the car did and came under the spell of winding roads, fields and farms, horses hanging out together behind fences. In truth, I loved both worlds, the gritty one on top of buildings and the softer one at home, doing things around the house, gardening, cooking, playing with Mugsy, and, this summer, preparing for the big event. Tim tried to get me to keep the wedding in balance; he didn't want me to get too carried away by pomp and circumstance. We had always been so casual, so unplanned, and he wanted this wedding to be truly us, the way we were. So did I.

Saturday, July 4th opened bright and full of promise for our wedding. Our wedding! Even now, I couldn't get used to the idea, but it was really happening, even as winter turned into spring, and spring into summer. Tim and his best man, Uncle Guy, took over our house in Lakeville and I had to flee to Mom's, but not before I recoiled at Uncle Guy's black eye—he was in a fight before he left New York City, but his tinted glasses hid it well.

The women gathered at Mom's house in New Bedford and turned it into a salon. Perfume, hair spray, ruffled slips, dancing shoes, beautiful gowns in the colors of summer took over the upstairs. Everything here was optimistic, voices were filled with excitement, as if something incredible were about to happen. Dawn, my maid of honor, looked lovely in her summery lavender gown. Amy, my flower girl, twirled about from mirror to mirror in white lace with a fairy ring of flowers and ribbons atop her head. Pam ordered me to "shtay shtill" through a mouthful of bobby pins as she tried to pin up my hair in a French twist before I put on my wedding gown. Yup, I was doing this up right. White, of course. A white, full-length, honest-to-goodness, absolutely beautiful wedding gown for this bricklayer.

My hair done, I wriggled into my gown and Dawn buttoned up the back. I stuck my foot in one shoe, then—but where was the other shoe? "Hey, anybody seen a white satin shoe?" Down on the floor I went to look under the bed.

"Lynn, get up before you ruin your dress!" Dawn scolded, as Amy came running into the room, clutching my lost shoe.

"I'll bet you fifty dollars your dress will be dirty before you reach the altar," Pam remarked, goading me into a more cautious mind-set. She knew I would hate to lose my hard-earned money on a bet. "You're on." I focused on staying lily white, at least for the next hour.

Everyone piled into Pam's car except me. "We'll see you there," Dawn called as they drove away. I had more grandiose plans—I was going to my wedding in style. Mark had recently bought a new car and he and Steve were going to chauffeur me.

"Steve, Mark." I called once, then twice, then ran to see if they were waiting in the car. They were in the car all right, but the car was not in the driveway. I learned later my brothers had got their signals crossed. They thought the bride was riding with Pam and the wedding party. They had already left long ago and were thirty miles away. Good grief, I was alone and had no way of getting to my own wedding!

"Oh, Jeez, what do I do now?" I was frantic. At some point, wouldn't they discover the bride was missing and come and get me? A cab from New Bedford to Lakeville would cost a small fortune. I couldn't get anyone to drive me because everybody I knew was already on their way to Lakeville.

I called Amy's grandmother and told her my sad story: "Hi, it's Lynn, and I can't get to my own wedding!" She listened with sympathy and said, yes, she'd pick me up but she'd have to use her son's car because Amy's mother had already left with the family car.

"Sure, that's great. Your son's car, whatever." Ten minutes later she drove up in a battered old Ford Pinto—not what I had planned for my grand entrance. But, heck, I was grateful for the ride and in a way the Pinto fit us better, it was authentically us.

"Sorry about all the mess on the floor." She struggled to make room for the yards of material that encased me. I gingerly flipped an oil can into the back seat and settled in snugly, looking like a small balloon. As we drove up to the house in Lakeville, nobody glanced our way. What bride would arrive in a beat-up Pinto?

"Thanks so much for the ride. Could you drive up to the front door so the guests in the backyard won't see me?" I whispered. As I bundled up my dress and climbed out, I could see a long black streak of grease running down my left sleeve, probably from the nozzle of the oil can. Now I was in a real mess. How would I get the black stain out before the ceremony?

My attendants were in the house waiting, wondering what was keeping me. "Oh, my God, look at you!" they squealed, almost in unison, gathering around and trying to erase both me and the stain. At that moment, I heard the first strains of music from the yard and Tim's sister Maureen came running in, "Lynn, it's time."

"No, I'm not ready yet!" I cried, trying to fight back panic. Every effort to hide the grease stain had failed, until Pam came to the rescue. "Let's try this." She pulled out a small bottle of Wite Out from my desk drawer and began dabbing it on the blackened spot and—voilà —you couldn't see the stain unless you stuck your nose in it. I waved my arm frantically, up and down, up and down, trying to dry the Wite Out and then, of course, I smudged the whole mess into a swirl of gray.

"It looks fine," said Dawn, haltingly but reassuringly.

"That was the easiest fifty bucks I ever made," Pam chimed in.

"Come on, Lynn, everyone's waiting!" Maureen called, making her second frantic appearance.

The guests must have thought I had second thoughts about this wedding. My maid of honor and flower girl were already marching up the garden path with no one behind them. I gathered up the train of my gown and dashed out, trying to catch up with them before they disappeared entirely. My dad stood like a sentry, waiting to walk me down the aisle, or rather, across the lawn. I took his arm and heard him whisper, "You look beautiful, dear." I was thrilled to hear praise from him, then dismayed to realize I had forgotten my bridal bouquet.

Tim stood there, looking incredibly handsome in his gray tuxedo, beaming as he watched me walk down the aisle. Suddenly the only thing that mattered to me was being with Tim. I was truly happy.

The reception was a joyful celebration for family and friends. Tim changed out of his tux at the first opportunity, but I felt like Cinderella at the ball in my white wedding gown with the gray smear, and I wanted to wear it all day. And so I did. I wore it dancing and talking with guests. I wore it while flipping burgers at the grill and traipsing through the dirt near the horseshoe pit. The day was filled with music, food, and dance; the men played horseshoes, the women chatted and tended to children. Like our usual Fourth of July parties, this wedding reception had no end. By evening, some guests had drifted away, others slept at our house.

Tim and I stayed at a nearby hotel, returning home the next morning to say goodbye to the remaining guests before leaving on our honeymoon. Mugsy had climbed into the back seat of our Corolla and used my wedding gown as a bed. It was a perfect ending—the dog sleeping blissfully on my wedding gown! We later learned that Dawn had taken the dress to the cleaners, where the proprietor held it up and gasped.

"Oh, my word. I've never seen a bridal gown in such horrendous condition," she squealed. "We can't possibly salvage this."

I hung it in the back of my closet, where it rests today.

We spent our honeymoon on a ten-day trip to Ireland, thanks to Mom. This was her generous wedding gift. Neither Tim nor I had ever crossed the Atlantic and we fell in love with the Irish countryside in all its lush and enchanting shades of green. It was a time of romance and exploration. Surprise! We even met an Irish mason in our travels. At first we were shocked at seeing entire families in the pubs but we got used to it. Pubs were more than bars, they were social clubs, an Irish tradition. Was this where Sue Bishop got the idea to send her kids to the Belmont to retrieve her drunken husband?

I spent much time inspecting the stone houses that dotted the green hills, curious about the art of stonemasonry. One home owner came out and graciously told me in great detail about how he had built the house himself, using cement and sand in place of mortar between the stones. Everywhere we found friendly people, wild scenery, poetry. But the dream was coming to an end. And when it was over, I was back in Lakeville doing the dishes, back in Fall River laying brick, but things were different now. I was Lynn Donohue, married woman, and it felt good.

GOING FOR THE GOLD

A year had passed since my third-place win in the apprentice contest and this year I planned to take home the grand prize. To that end, I had been practicing in my basement all year long, and I knew I'd be a formidable competitor. I don't know why I was obsessed by this contest. Something inside me wanted to win, wanted to triumph over every sexist swear ever hurled at me, wanted to win for the time I was locked in the porta-potty by that shit Barney, wanted to win for every day I'd gone out there freezing my butt off and wearing my hands to the bone, wanted to win for me, for Tim, for Mom and Dad, for my friends, and for all the women who struggled to make it in a man's world.

With growing excitement and trepidation, I began counting the days as Saturday, June 24, neared. Luckily, my job required such demanding physical labor, I was exhausted and able to sleep at night. Otherwise, my eyes would have been wide open all night, staring at the ceiling, waiting, waiting. On Friday I had trouble concentrating on my work. At the end of the day, several men said goodbye and good luck.

George Medeiros stopped by the job site that morning—"You're as excited as my kids the night before Christmas. You're ready, Lynn. Don't sweat it. You're gonna do fine."

I stopped at the Belmont Club after work. For months, I'd been telling Dad I hoped to win the trophy this year and wanted him to be there. Despite my painful memories from childhood and the years of estrangement, I still longed to make him proud of me and my accomplishments. If I reminded him tonight to come tomorrow, the odds were more in favor of him showing up. Luck was with me and I found him in the office, going over his inventory. After I confirmed the time and location, I made sure he knew how to get to the South Shore Mall.

Teddy and some regulars were perched at the bar, as they had been month after month, year after year, nursing their beers and watching *General Hospital*. "Hey, where ya been?" Ronny barked. "Ya got time for a beer? I'm buyin'."

I thanked him, but declined. I told him I was keeping busy with union work and living in Lakeville, so I wasn't in New Bedford as much as I used to be.

"So, to what do we owe the honor of your presence today, m'lady?" kidded Artie, mimicking an English accent.

"Oh, I just wanted to remind my dad about the bricklaying contest—it's tomorrow."

"In that case, you'd better get busy doin' push-ups or you'll be out of the runnin' in no time flat!" Teddy said with a snicker.

Laughing, I was out the door, heading home.

I picked at my dinner and skimmed my favorite book, *Relax and Win*, one last time, then spent an hour tossing and turning in bed before plunging into dreamland. The alarm went off at seven o'clock, but I'd been awake since five, the time I normally got up for work. I forced myself to lie quietly in bed and mentally prepare for the day ahead.

After a quick shower and coffee, Tim and I headed for Braintree. A complimentary breakfast was first on the agenda. As we parked and walked toward the mall entrance, I marveled at the difference in my demeanor since last year's contest. I was ready in every sense of the word. At the breakfast, I spotted the second-place winner from last year and headed over to greet him.

"Hi, Kevin. Remember me?" He looked up blankly. "I'm Lynn—I won third place last year."

"Oh, yeah."

"Are you ready to give it another shot?" I was trying to be congenial.

"This year I'm comin' in first. No problem. The guy that won last year, he's a journeyman now, so I got no competition."

I thought, *Wanna bet?* But I said aloud, "Well, good luck. I'll see you out there."

Several mason tenders were already standing at the cement mixer in the contest area, and I made a point of introducing myself in a friendly way, hoping to gain the favor of the one assigned to supply me with mortar. Tim spotted the New Bedford Local 39 banner on my station, and we walked toward it, scanning the crowd of spectators that was beginning to form but seeing no sign of my father.

The state dignitaries, union representatives, and judges assembled on the platform. As the opening ceremonies began, I shut my eyes and reviewed the techniques I had learned to help me focus and block out all distractions. As soon as I heard Chuck Raso say, "Begin!" I calmly started working. My mental cocoon protected me from being mindful of the crowd and the other contestants. The mall's air-conditioning system was in low gear and sweat was running down my face, but I didn't let it distract me.

Sarcastic comments from a group of teenagers that passed nearby seemed like they were coming from the next town. I was totally focused on building my panel. Each block and every trowel of mortar were like notes in a symphony I was composing—precise and rhythmic, coming together to create a masterpiece. I felt the same as I did in the safety of my own basement, practicing on my panel after work.

After three hours, Chuck Raso stepped up to the mike, raised his arm, and announced, "Stop!" Everyone stopped on the button. For the first time, I stepped back and surveyed my panel, already knowing it was perfect. Perfect! As I glanced around the other stations, I noted some panels were taller, but so what.

As the judges began their inspections, Tim greeted me with a warm smile and a tug on the arm, "You did great!" He had steered clear of me while I was working, as I'd requested, for he too believed in the principles in *Relax and Win*. I finished off the soda he'd brought me in a couple of gulps and marveled at the difference in me—my attitude, my performance since last year. As one of the judges passed by my station, he leaned over and whispered, "You're scoring high." A wave of excitement passed through me.

"The judges have made their decisions," Tom McIntyre announced over the loudspeaker, and the crowd went from a hum to a hush. "Fourth place goes to Tony Romano of Worcester Local 25." At first, Tony looked dejected for not placing higher but he put a smile on his face and accepted his plaque. "Third place goes to Danny O'Malley of Springfield Local 1."

Danny yelled, "Yahoo!" and ran up on the platform, drawing applause and laughter from the crowd. Just then, I spotted my father across the way and whispered the news to Tim, who said he'd seen my dad arrive an hour earlier but lost sight of him. I hoped he'd arrived in time to see me building my panel. "Second place goes to Steven Rycroft of Hyannis Local 34."

For a stinging moment, I panicked, thinking maybe I had not even placed. I waited forever for his next words.

"First-place winner is...Lynn Donohue, New Bedford Local 39!"

The crowd burst into applause and I heard men from my local calling out, "All right, Lynn!" "Good job, Lynn!" I was overjoyed, laughing, crying, taking it all in, while Tim hugged me and pointed me in the direction of the stage. I felt like Tom was awarding me a million dollars instead of a silver trophy and a two-hundred-dollar savings bond.

"Lynn Donohue is the first woman in the United States to win first place in an apprentice contest," he announced. Another burst of applause followed and I waved the trophy over my head with one hand as I left the platform. I was on top of the world!

As I floated back to my seat, everyone began congratulating me, patting me on the back, clapping for me. In my entire life, I had never felt such approval. Yet I scanned the crowd for my dad, still looking for *his* approval, and saw him coming toward me with Tim. George Medeiros reached me first and gave me a bear hug. "Congratulations, Lynn—you did it! Go pose for your pictures, then we'll celebrate." He caught up with a group of business agents and I heard him boast, "How do you like that? We have a woman in our local who can beat any man in yours!"

I was called back to the stage so I signaled Tim and Dad to wait for me. I held on to my trophy for dear life and posed for photographs. Now every business agent from every local will know who I am, I thought, and I can really begin to make a name for myself in the union.

After the photo session, Chuck Raso asked for the trophy so he could have it engraved.

"No thanks, I'll take it just the way it is," and everyone laughed. I didn't want to let go of it and the victory it symbolized. After he assured me I would get it back safely, I handed it over and made my way from the platform to Tim and my father. Tim gave me another hug and my dad awkwardly put his arm around my shoulders, gave me a brief squeeze, and quietly said, "You did a great job, dear." I had waited all my life to hear kind words like these from my father and I became choked up now as they sank in.

George, Tim, Dad, and I all went to the Ground Round to celebrate. Contestants and their families filled many of the tables and I basked in their congratulations. It was my moment and I felt like Miss America, Queen for a Day, Rocky Balboa. I have arrived, I thought, I have finally arrived.

Dad was anxious to get back to the Belmont and asked us to join him. George declined, but Tim and I jumped at the chance to share the good news with my staunchest supporters. They were thrilled, and many a round was bought in my honor. I loved the regulars here; they were like family to me, but I now saw what a self-destructive lifestyle they led. I no longer belonged here. I had outgrown the barroom life and would continue on in bricklaying to bigger and better things.

In November, the Massachusetts State Convention of Bricklayers and Allied Craftsmen took place in Hyannis on Cape Cod, a three-day affair held at Dunfey's, an elegant hotel with a golf course in back. Attendees were union reps, masons, contractors and politicians, spouses and girlfriends. This year the union paid my way in honor of my first place win in the apprentice contest.

I invited Pam to the festivities—her boyfriend Donny was on the road—and we arrived at the hotel on Friday night. The three of us shared a room, with Pam sleeping on the couch. I'm sure a few eyebrows were raised as Tim escorted us both around, dressed to kill. Tim and Donny had long ago realized we were joined at the hip as best friends and they had learned to live with it.

Over a thousand people attended the dinner, and each table was reserved for a particular union local. I was happy to see George Medeiros and Clarence Whatmough among the guests at our table. I looked around at the other tables and noticed several men I knew, including Frank Reed and Ted Murphy, who had given me such a hard time. "I'll show them a thing or two tonight," I said to Tim as we sat down at our table.

After an elaborate meal, Senator Ted Kennedy took the stage to make his keynote speech.

Immediately following, George Medeiros took the microphone and called me up to the platform. "I'd like you to meet the first and only female apprentice bricklayer to ever win first place in a state competition, not only here in Massachusetts, but anywhere in the United States—Lynn Donohue! Local 39 is proud of Lynn's determination and accomplishments. Congratulations, Lynn."

He presented me with my newly engraved trophy and everyone applauded. Holding it tight, I stepped over to have my picture taken with the senator and George. It was my night to shine, and I enjoyed the congratulations that hummed through the evening. Even Frank, the man who had mocked me, sworn at me and humiliated me, cracked a smile and shook my hand.

Ted Murphy patted me on the back, "Not bad for an apprentice." We finished at the hotel lounge and danced the night away. That night as I lay in the comfortable king-size bed, I thought about how far I'd come in my journey—but the craziest part was, I knew it was just beginning.

"Mama Said There'd Be Days Like This"

No matter how great things look one moment, adversity is never far away; it watches us, studies us, then moves in when we are looking the other way. The real enemy is hubris. You must temper it with humility because the moment you begin feeling all-powerful, watch out. There are forces out there whose job is to put you in your place.

And so the day started with such promise and with me so full of myself. I was reveling in one of those perfect moments, sitting at the kitchen counter, my hands curled around my favorite coffee mug, watching the robins as the morning sun streamed through the window. I was full of joy with all the good things that had happened in the past year. The wedding band on my finger, the trophy on the mantle, the framed photograph of the Dublin countryside all reminded me of just how blessed I was and how far I had come. I offered up a silent prayer of thanks.

Moments later, I was driving toward Cape Cod and my first day on the Falmouth Hospital expansion project. By the end of March, I figured, I'd have the 6,000 hours I needed to complete my apprenticeship. I'd also completed the Wentworth course and another course through the Chicago Technical Institute in Construction and Estimating, a two-year mail-order course, as well as the required 450 hours of extra training. The three-year apprenticeship period felt more like ten years, but I was reaching the end and moving closer to better pay and more challenging work.

Macomber Construction, the company I'd worked for at the Car Barn, had won the bid for the hospital project and the job was supposed to be completed by late spring. As I joined the group of men waiting for instruction, I saw many of the same faces I'd worked with before. Ray Scoville was once again the acting foreman and I was happy to see my old pal Bob Comeau. When I spotted cranky Frank, my smile waned, but then I recalled his civil words at the Hyannis convention and thought things might go better this time around.

I felt as if I fit right in. Many of the same Boston crew I'd seen on the Car Barn were here, too, but I hadn't spent enough time around them to remember their names. I also met many friendly Cape Verdean bricklayers from the Falmouth area. As I read through the assignments posted outside Macomber's trailer, I was thrilled to see I would be laying brick. Usually, I was put on grunt work, along with the minority workers, and didn't get to do the challenging work unless someone took sick or got fired. Even if I did get a chance to lay some brick, I was often pulled off to do the wash down, another task often delegated to minority employees. So much for equal opportunity.

Fortunately, I had more experience under my belt now than the last time I worked with this crew. Eager to get started under a blue sky and warm sun, I grabbed my tool bag and headed for my station. As I walked along the staging, I noticed that Frank and another man were at the stations right around the corner from me. I greeted Frank as I went by and earned a slight nod in return.

"Who the hell is that and what's she doing here?" I heard the other man ask.

"Nobody," Frank replied.

What a perfect station! Here on the third level of the building, over the treetops, I enjoyed a breathtaking ocean view. The wind blew softly today and the gulls sailed by like dancers. My mason tender introduced himself as Jellyroll, and I could see he'd earned the nickname by eating too many of them. He was a pleasant Cape Verdean man of such wide girth, I wondered how he made it up and down the staging. Jellyroll sang with an oldies band all over Cape Cod and invited me to come hear them.

"You'll hear me singing all day on the job, so you don't need to bring your radio."

"Great. Do you take requests?"

He laughed heartily and headed down the staging to fill my pan with mortar.

Jellyroll's physical size actually came in handy. The heavy pallets of brick had to be hauled up to the proper staging levels by hand, with ropes and pulleys, since the area was too tight to accommodate a fork lift. I dove into my work, laying out the first course of brick in record time. I loved brick veneer jobs like this one because you didn't have to build a wall of concrete block first. You simply laid the brick up against metal studs, stopping at the angle irons that helped support the weight of the brick between floors. Jellyroll was singing away in his rich baritone down below and I found myself humming along as he belted out *Under the Boardwalk and Chain Gang.*

By month's end, I had completed three floors of brickwork in my section. It was a real thrill to stand back and observe my work, knowing soon I could lay claim to having built the whole east corner by myself. Frank's sidekick, Russell Carleton, continued to spread his negative attitude among our co-workers. A heavy-set, baby-faced man, he loved to start trouble and, though I could hear his voice, I was glad I couldn't see him from my station. I would have made too easy a target for him.

Meanwhile, I started carpooling with Bob Comeau and I loved to pick his brain as we drove. Bob was a fourth-generation mason and a walking encyclopedia on the history of bricklaying. His grandfather's generation donned white shirts, bow ties, and spats while on the job, taking great pride in polishing their tools and wrapping them neatly at the end of the day. Being with Bob was a good way to begin and end the day.

In March, 1983, I reached the six-thousand-hour mark and became a journeyman. The official swearing-in would take place at the next union meeting, which happened to fall on my birthday. Bob explained the process of going from apprentice to journeyman in simple terms as we drove to work that morning. We were like teacher and student.

"When you join the union, as you know, you are issued a little red book and it goes with you to every job, kind of like a driver's license, to identify you as a bona fide union member."

"Yeah, yeah, I know. It's my bible."

Bob was all business, glancing at me frequently to be sure I was paying attention. "As you gain training and hours, the business agent keeps track of your records. Codes are designated to your work: P for plasterer, CM for cement mason, B for bricklayer, and so on. Laborers are in a totally different union than masons."

"Yup, I know all about the codes."

"When your record shows 450 training hours and 6,000 work hours within a three-year period, you are eligible to be sworn in as a journeyman. The terms journeyman and bricklayer are interchangeable. Your benefits don't change—you still have unemployment, workman's comp, and disability coverage. And you still don't get paid breaks, lunch, sick leave, or a vacation. Your rate of pay is determined by your title and the region you work in—working in Boston pays better than working in New Bedford. When you become a journeyman, you are also allowed to work as a brick foreman at a higher rate of pay, usually a dollar more per hour."

"Yup, I know." Though I was listening patiently, what I really wanted to know was this: How would my life get better as a journeyman? Bob was coming to that.

"Apprentice pay goes up in increments of ten percent as you gain more work hours. As an apprentice, you are paid fifty percent of journeyman pay. Then for every five-hundred hours you gain, your pay goes up—sixty percent, then seventy percent, and so on—until you reach a hundred percent and become an official bricklayer."

That was the part I liked the best.

On the job that day, I felt like standing at my station and yelling to everyone, "Hey! I made it! I'm a bricklayer!" but opted instead to tell the three people I knew who'd be happy for me: Jellyroll, Ray, and, of course, Bob. It was almost lunchtime when Ray came over to my station and said pleasantly, "Good work, Lynn, but we need to make a change. I want you to gain a course on your wall."

"Okay, Ray—no problem," He hurried on to the next station and I didn't get a chance to tell him about my new status.

As foreman, Ray was the person who had to make sure the job went according to the architectural blueprints. Certain benchmarks had been laid out on paper. For instance, the courses of brick had to be lined up accurately with the door and window openings. I often saw him going from station to station, a solitary figure, measuring and referring to his blueprints. I remembered a worker being told to gain a course on the Car Barn job. To do this, I seemed to recall, he used more mortar to make the spaces between the courses of brick higher.

Just to double-check, I went around the corner and asked Frank if I was correct.

"Yup—open up your bed joints, just like you said—you're a journeyman now, right, so you must know what you're doing."

"What are you helping her out for?" Russell yelled from a distance.

"Thanks, Frank." I scurried back to my station before Russell made too big a deal out of me asking for help.

I rose to the challenge, delighted that I could try something new. I started to add double the amount of mortar to the area between the courses of bricks and noticed the difference in height as soon as I finished a small section. Using my level to be sure the course was straight, I continued on in the same manner. Ray was making his rounds, inspecting each man's work, measuring it and comparing it to the blueprints.

I'll tell him about my new journeyman status when he gets over here, I thought.

Ray arrived at my station and looked stunned. "What the hell? I told you to GAIN a course, not LOSE one!" He was usually a patient man, but this time he was angry. "You just threw the whole building off by a course. Why didn't you ask Frank or someone else if you weren't sure what you were doing?"

I stood with my head down, humiliated. "I'm really sorry, Ray," I stammered, trying to think of a way to diffuse his anger.

"Sorry doesn't help now. Take it apart and then first thing tomorrow, do it over. And if you're not sure what you're doing, ASK, for Chrissake," and he walked away.

With burning cheeks and a heavy heart, I tore down the new section, and cleaned the mortar off the bricks, stacking them nearby so I could redo the section the next morning. Frank and Russell were snickering on the other side of the wall, and my humiliation turned into anger. I stomped over to Frank.

"Why didn't you tell me the right way when I asked you?"

He shrugged apathetically. "Think of it as a favor. Now you'll never forget what gain a course means." And with that he picked up his tool bag and began climbing down the staging. "You bastard," I said to myself, marching back to my station to pack up my tools. After most of the crew had driven away, I marched over to Bob Comeau's car and threw my tool bag in the back seat. I didn't cry. That's the most that could be said for the day.

During the drive home, I told Bob my story. He commiserated with a grimace. "Some guys like Frank forget where they came from.

You're not the first apprentice he's done that to, and you sure as hell won't be the last. And there's a lot of other guys on the job that think just like him. Small-minded jerks. So what you gotta do is shake it off. Go back to your station tomorrow with your head held high. Fix what you have to and go on from there. Don't let Frank or anyone else get the best of you—it's not worth it."

Tim listened sympathetically to my story and agreed with Bob.

"It sounds like the kind of stuff seniors do to freshmen in high school—making them look like fools in front of everyone else. And the weird part is, when those seniors were freshmen, they had the same crap done to them. But instead of letting it go, they opt for revenge."

"Yeah, but this isn't high school—it's my career."

"Well, some guys never grow up."

On the way to work the next day, Bob explained exactly what gain a course meant. First, grind the joints. This means putting less mortar than normal in between the brick courses and when I reach the top of my wall, I will have gained an extra course. Back I went to my station with my tail between my legs, but not as defeated as I was the day before. Now I knew exactly what to do. By lunchtime I was back on the right track, and my friend Jellyroll sang *Mama Said There'd Be Days Like This* for my benefit as he worked the rope and pulley down below. I actually smiled.

My big night arrived the following Tuesday when I was officially sworn in as a bricklayer at the union meeting. George Medeiros presented me with a certificate and everyone clapped, albeit some more fervently than others. After posing for a photograph, we walked up the street to Freestone's Restaurant—George and I and a few others—and we celebrated. Birthdays were getting good! Married on Tim's birthday, an official bricklayer on my own birthday. The Falmouth job ended shortly after the lousy Frank incident but it didn't seem such a big deal anymore, just a bump in the road. I was looking ahead.

My next assignment was closer to home. Sterling Construction of Rhode Island won the bid to build a new bus terminal next to City Hall in New Bedford. The area functioned as a parking lot, so the new terminal would be built from scratch. According to George Medeiros, it was a big-money contract and a terrific opportunity for me to work with new materials. I especially enjoyed new construction jobs and often took "before and after" photos of barren areas transformed into useful, solid buildings, which I had a part in creating. So before the job started, I snapped pictures of the sorry old parking lot. The parking meters and the old WPA lighthouse had been removed. There was nothing here except dirt and litter, and the asphalt parking surface was jackhammered up.

The bus station would shoot up square between some of the city's most beautiful old buildings—City Hall, the New Bedford Free Public Library, and the Post Office with its long marble halls and majestic columns. Bordering the project area was Pleasant Street with its luncheonettes, banks, taverns, and office buildings.

Click, click. My little Instamatic camera captured the views from every angle and I was careful to save enough exposures on the 110 film for the "after" photos. And now, I was ready to go.

On a day in early May, just after sunrise, I drove through the crowded streets of the North End to my first day of work for Sterling. The city was coming awake and the pageant of life played out before me. People who were headed to work for their first-shift jobs at the factories tossed Styrofoam cups, gum wrappers, and cigarette butts on the ground as they moved along. Older homeowners came out of their houses and tenements with brooms, sweeping the sidewalks clean again. Many of the residents had moved here from the old country and took great pride in their homes and yards. Urban gardens, Azorean-style, brought the old country to the city. These gardens boasted grape arbors and tall growing things and tangly plants and brilliant colors. The city was filled with sounds of traffic, barking dogs, and laughing children on their way to school.

Arnie Foley, the foreman, was the only person at the Sterling trailer when I arrived early. Shorter than I, he had a headful of thick, curly gray hair and a face tanned and lined from years of working in the sun. His blue eyes crinkled when he smiled and I thought, yeah, this is good. I liked him immediately. We drank coffee and chatted while we waited for the rest of the crew. Arnie was a company man with thirty years at Sterling. Salt of the earth with a wife and three grown children, this foreman had grace, and I could tell he liked my enthusiasm and willingness to learn.

Many of the arriving crew members knew me and extended greetings. I was developing a sense of belonging and enjoyed working again with men I hadn't seen since my early days as an apprentice. But there was a downside too. Russell was back like a bad nightmare, a man I had hoped was laying brick in Siberia. When the last of the crew arrived, Arnie gave us our assignments and I eagerly trooped to my station where "sound block" was to be installed, a material I had never worked with before, which filtered the noise between the buses and the neighboring restaurant. On my right was Lou Santos, the father of one of my childhood friends.

Sterling used a standard approach with their workers, an assembly-line style in which each person's work on the wall impacted the next person's. Right from the start, the pace was fast and furious. The men seemed to run on sheer tension, and instead of teamwork, there was competition; I could see it was every man for himself. The old union slogan, Brothers in the hall, screw 'em on the wall, definitely applied here.

When our materials arrived, along with our first batch of mortar, I had trouble with the sound blocks. Their shape and texture were different from anything I'd handled before and I was not used to their weight distribution. Lou showed me how to lift and place the blocks without losing my rhythm, but it took me a while to get the hang of it, and I was worried about slowing everyone else down. By the end of the day, I felt as if I'd been on the job for weeks. The pressure was emotionally draining and I needed a good hug, a bath, a beer, and a bed.

The next day things got worse. As I took my place on the line, Lou was no longer on my right—Russell was. I looked across to the parallel wall and caught Lou's eye. He shrugged, letting me know he'd been moved for reasons unknown. Okay, I thought to myself, you can handle this—just concentrate on your work. I said hello to Russell, who responded with stony silence.

I then turned to the man on my left. "Do you know if our mortar is mixed yet?"

Russell's loud voice, filled with contempt, resonated over the complex but originated directly behind my head. "Don't help her and don't answer her questions!"

I froze, my face turning shades of scarlet as the man on my left replied, "Take it easy."

"I ain't takin' nothin' easy," Russell yelled back. "I got two sons waitin' to be apprentices that can't get in the brotherhood 'cause of her. She won't be around much longer if I got anything to say about it!"

Day after day, Russell undermined and embarrassed me at every opportunity. I learned from Arnie that Lou had been moved to another section at Russell's request because he claimed he could help me get up to speed on the wall. Otherwise, I would slow the whole line down, he'd argued. Arnie did not know then that Russell's only motive was to torment me.

From the moment our materials arrived, Russell began working as fast and as hard as he could. As he labored at top speed, sweat dripped from his face and his shirt soaked through. His face was so flushed, I thought he might burst a blood vessel. Every so often, he spat out comments like "Speed it up or get off the job!" and "Keep up or get out!"

I pictured him as he must have been as a kid, the school yard bully, picking on kids too small to defend themselves and then tattling to the teacher that he'd been picked on.

A few men sided with Russell and laughed at his antics but most looked the other way, unwilling to get involved. Many knew from working with me in the past that I could hold my own and didn't expect any favors or preferential treatment. Others probably figured that expressing their opinions might endanger their paycheck so they'd better keep their thoughts to themselves. Besides, Russell was known as an expert mason and they'd have to work with him again on future jobs. Me, they weren't so sure about.

Even at union meetings, Russell worked mean and hard to make me uncomfortable. If I sat too far away for him to embarrass me with his invective, he'd stare at me with contempt and get me so distracted I wouldn't hear a word the speaker was saying. As soon as I got home each night, I took Mugsy for a walk because it helped restore my faith in normality and make me whole again. Mugsy's joy at seeing me lifted my spirits. Our schedules prevented Tim and me from seeing much of each other during the week, but on weekends I filled him with my stories. He kept urging me to talk to Arnie about Russell, but I knew that if I did, I would lose the hard-earned respect of my colleagues. Did he understand that?

But as the weeks went by, Russell's constant tirade eroded my self-confidence and affected my ability to concentrate. On one particularly bad day, the bastard "accidentally" knocked my trowel off the staging. When I climbed down to retrieve it, he looked disgustedly at me. "When you get to the sidewalk just keep going." This drew a laugh from Bruce, a man I thought was my friend, and that was it. I couldn't take anymore. I packed up my tools and began walking toward my car, my spirit broken.

Arnie saw me going and knew from the slump of my shoulders I was giving up. He put down his level and shouted, "Lynn, hold on a minute!" but I didn't stop. He ran after me, still calling my name as I reached my car and fumbled with the keys.

Grabbing my shoulders and turning me toward him, he looked me in the eye, gripped my upper arms so I couldn't turn away, and firmly barked, "Lynn, listen to me. Don't let them get to you. You've got it, kid, and they know it. Don't let them beat you!"

I held back all but a few tears. "I can't take it anymore, Arnie—it's just not worth it."

"Not worth it—not worth it? Are you tellin' me you're just gonna throw in the towel because of a few knuckleheads? What kinda bricklayer are you, anyway?" As soon as I heard him say the word bricklayer, something clicked in me. I felt like someone with amnesia who heard her name and realized who she was at last. A sense of calm enveloped me. Yes, I most certainly am a bricklayer, and no one is going to take that away from me.

"Hey Arnie, can we break?" one of the laborers called over. "Yeah, go ahead," Arnie yelled back and everyone scattered like ants. He was still gripping my arm. "Listen—this afternoon I was gonna start a few guys workin' on the east wall. Why don't I pull you and a few others after the break to lay the first course over there?" I gave him a grateful smile. "Ohmigod, yes. That would really help. Thanks for coming after me, Arnie."

"No sweat," he answered with a wink.

As promised, Arnie sent me, Lou, and three others over to a new area, strategically out of earshot of Russell and his supporters. As I passed Russell on my way over to the new section, he glared at me and taunted, "You won't be so lucky next time." I looked straight at him, paused for a moment, and kept on walking. The man could not have guessed what I was thinking—*Just you wait, you bastard, you'll be working for me someday.*

Time passed and Russell began to realize he could no longer intimidate me so he reverted to whining and complaining about other people. When the job ended three months later, I stood across the street and gazed with pride at the impressive new building I'd helped to create. Arnie's and my path never crossed again, but I kept the powerful lesson he taught me close to my heart. Hold to your own course in the face of adversity. Do not let others undermine you. Keep the faith in yourself and, most of all, courage under fire, girl.

FROM HELL TO HEAVEN

The Portuguese Feast rolled around again in early August, and I chuckled as I approached the barbecue pit where George Medeiros pulled grunt duty every year.

"Some things never change, huh, George? Is this the same *carne d'espeto* I saw you cooking two years ago or is it a new batch?"

He laughed good-naturedly, and we talked for a while about the upcoming apprentice contest. As last year's winner, I was supposed to present the trophy to the new winner at the annual conference in July, a task I looked forward to.

I planned to go to the contest and encourage the fledgling apprentices, knowing how much the support of others meant to me. I also wanted to see the winner in action so my presentation in July would be more meaningful. With those sentiments in mind, I arrived at the South Shore Mall once again, but this time there was a difference. I was no longer an apprentice but a full-fledged journeyman, and this changed everything.

Naturally, I felt compelled to speak to the two women entrants and George Medeiros looked over with amusement—"Hey, no coaching the competition." First place went to a young man from the Boston local, and as he received his trophy, smiling broadly, I felt a thrill for him as I once had for myself.

Meanwhile, with the completion of the bus terminal, I hit the road to Fall River to work for Havelock Benton, who owned a small masonry company. Because of his minority status, which satisfied the affirmative-action requirements for Fall River, Benton was awarded the contract to restore an old, abandoned, low-income housing project called Sunset Hill. Four bricklayers were needed. There were twenty buildings to renovate and I was chosen to help fill the bill.

Fall River was only about sixteen miles from home, so I didn't mind driving both ways alone in the warm summer sun, my tools and materials clanging in the back seat of my VW. My job was to build support partitions in the basement, using four-inch concrete blocks, and also to enclose the existing window openings with brick to create solid walls on the ground level.

Benton called me the night before and gave me sketchy directions to the site. His heavy Jamaican accent made it difficult for me to understand him, but the street names began to make sense. "Go round di fah connah of Broadmon, see di blinkah on Main and go tru it, mon." I realized "mon" was not part of the street name, but "man," the Jamaican expression used at the end of most sentences.

When I reached my suspected destination, I was confused beyond words. Could this be the place? I gazed hopelessly at the crumbling shells of graffiti-covered buildings, obviously abandoned for decades, surrounded by piles of litter and rubble. A motley crew of four men tossed debris out of the basement and two other guys cleaned up after them, filling a sidewalk dumpster. The men looked more like suspects in a police lineup than a demolition crew and I didn't know how I was going to fit in. A scrawny bent-over man with a deep scar across his cheek and maybe six teeth mixed mortar. Good grief, this was the place, these were the men, and this was just the beginning.

I instinctively stepped backward when a short, heavy man approached me and stared, the homeliest man I had ever seen. A devil tattoo stood out on his neck and his crooked nose looked as if it had been broken several times. He didn't look at me, he leered, giving me a thorough once-over. I desperately tried to find some feature I could focus on without distaste.

"You da bricklaya?" he said, raising an eyebrow.

"Um…yeah," I stammered, fighting the urge to turn and run. One of the dumpster workers wiped his brow, then put his hands on his hips and broke into a toothless grin, saying, "What a country!"

"Where do you want me to start?" I mumbled, hoping it would be far removed from the immediate area. No such luck. Wally, the tattooed foreman, led me to a dark, moldy section of the cellar and showed me where the partitions were to be erected. The concrete blocks were stacked in the middle of the basement floor and Wally offered to hang around and help me lift them as needed.

"No thanks, I'm all set. Guess I'll get to work now." I started laying out my tools, hoping he would take the hint and leave me alone. He looked even more repulsive in the dark basement than in the daylight, but he sucked in his stomach and puffed out his chest like a barnyard rooster trying to impress the new chick.

"Okay den, honey, I check on you latah." His broad grin gave me a close-up view of his extensive tooth decay and a strong whiff of his bad breath.

I climbed up the concrete steps and asked Benny Loc, the mason tender, to fill my mortar pan. With eyes as dead and vacant as a corpse, he looked like Robert DeNiro in *Taxi Driver*. Whatever was going on in his brain, I didn't want to know. He filled my pan, all the while muttering swears.

I thanked him and as I walked away he yelled, "What the hell are you doin' here anyway? You could get killed by one of them blackies down in the basement."

I pretended not to hear and kept on walking.

When I got home that night, I called George Medeiros and tried to describe the crew from hell. He laughed.

"They look a lot worse than they are, Lynn. Don't worry—they're harmless. They just don't get to see women up close too often, so they act stupid. But if you feel uncomfortable, you can team up with a mason in one of the other buildings."

I felt a little better after talking to George and signed off by telling him jokingly, "Well, if I do get killed in the basement, make sure you go after Benny Loc!"

Over the next two weeks, I spent long hours alone in the basement, building the partitions quickly. My goal was to get outside to work on the ground-level window openings as fast as possible. Every few hours, Wally came by to make small talk, and all I wanted was for him to make his departure. This was the first job on which I didn't take a lunch break. I was determined to finish the basement work in short order and get out of there. Tim wasn't thrilled about me staying on the job after hearing the stories about my fellow bricklayers, but I assured him I could handle it, or so I thought.

Although I had grown accustomed to most of the men, Benny Loc still scared me. He hated people in general and ranted about people he felt deserved to die. The swear words flew out of his mouth like bullets and he said he was going to string this guy up with wire, and shoot the other guy through the heart, and bash his cousin's face on the sidewalk. I felt the man should be locked up in a mental hospital. Whenever I needed mortar, I put my pan down near Benny and waited for him to fill it, then grabbed it and quickly retreated to my work area.

The only thing that kept me going was the money until the day I went to cash my paycheck and was told by the bank there were insufficient funds in the account. Benton, it seemed, had a bad habit of taking the advance funds he received from contracts back to his hometown in Jamaica and spending it on drinking, gambling, and prostitutes. I assumed he never visited the job site because he was busy on other projects. Stupid me.

The "creature crew," as I silently dubbed the demo workers, said that on payday they ran to the bank to cash their paychecks before Benton had a chance to withdraw the money. I began to follow their example, but eventually, no matter how quickly we got to the bank, the account ran dry. A few men from the local supply houses came by the job site looking for Benton, so I guess we weren't the only ones not getting paid.

George Medeiros advised me and the other bricklayers to keep on working and he would go after Benton for reimbursement. We soon learned that Benton had filed for bankruptcy and the Sunset Hill project was on hold until the lawyers slugged it out in court. With George's help, I filed the necessary paperwork and was paid in full for my time on the restoration job. How relieved I was to be away from there, far away from Benny Loc and his wild, demented rantings!

In September, George found me a job with Felouris Construction, a reputable firm that did a lot of work for the city of New Bedford. I felt like I'd gone from hell to heaven as I set off to help build the rectory of St. Killian Church in New Bedford's North End. The old, majestic granite home had been torn down to make way for a new brick structure. The parish had evolved from Irish to French and Portuguese, reflecting the population of the dense, three-decker neighborhood. They were a generous congregation who at the time could afford the best in contracting firms.

Felouris Construction was considered top of the heap and the owner's wife acted as the corporate attorney for the company. The owner maintained strict professionalism on the job. After working in that dungeon in Fall River, the New Bedford project was a breath of fresh air.

Unlike the workers on the Benton job, the men here acted as professionally as if they were working for the Pope, and the foreman, Manny Neves, set the standard with his respectful, almost courtly, demeanor in his interactions with live-in clergy members. We followed his example. No swearing, no smoking. I could get used to this, I thought.

The materials used in the project were first quality, new Belden brick and high-grade mortar, which made it easier to lay a straight course. After the Fall River fiasco, I felt I deserved a reward and found it in my masonry partner, Jack Benevides. I liked him immediately. He was an older Cape Verdean man with a gentle demeanor and lots of class. He did not so much as raise an eyebrow at being paired with a young female who was far less experienced than he, and right from the start he treated me like everyone else, with courtesy and respect.

I learned from my colleagues that Jack was a legend in the masonry business, described as "the fairest man alive" and "a guy who lays brick like he's painting the Mona Lisa." Jack worked with disadvantaged youth as a sports coach, and he and his wife, Cornelia, had been foster parents to a number of children over the years, mostly troubled teenagers. I wished I had known him during my turbulent adolescence.

Watching Jack lay brick was like taking an advanced course in masonry; it was clearly a labor of love. He was so cool and precise, I felt I was watching an artist. His giant hands were the envy of many a mason, and the fluid rhythm of his movements with trowel and brick called to mind the strokes of a champion swimmer. Unlike some experts, Jack had no big ego and was uncomfortable with praise. When I asked him questions about his technique, he answered gladly and always stopped work to lend a hand if I had trouble copying his moves. Occasionally he invited me home for lunch and I became as fond of Cornelia as I was of him.

The Felouris job ended all too soon, and I hated to say goodbye to Jack. I thanked him for all he had done for me and asked him if I could stay in touch.

"Of course, Lynn, it's been a great pleasure working with you and you are always welcome in our home. Cornelia and I are both very proud of you and wish you every success in your career."

His words were music to my ears and I greatly appreciated his fatherly supervision. Later, I asked George Medeiros to do his best to place me wherever Jack was working in the future. "Get in line, Lynn. You and everyone else wants Jack for a partner. They don't make them like him anymore."

When the annual conference rolled around again, I presented the trophy to the winning apprentice. "I attended the contest in July to check the competitors and this young man from the Boston local really stood out," I told the crowd. "He has great determination and skill." After the ceremony, I chatted with men from other locals and realized for the first time that the story of my masonry prowess had circulated beyond the boundaries of my own local.

Winter was upon us, the lean season for masonry workers. As I was getting ready to sign up at the unemployment office, George called.

"I've got winter work for you."

"You're kidding." I was astounded at my luck in being chosen to work during the worst season. Tim was happy about the extra money, but not thrilled about a busy schedule that didn't coincide with his.

We were like two ships passing in the night. As a second-shift custodian and groundskeeper at Voke Tech, Tim left for work at two in the afternoon and found me sleeping when he returned at midnight. After laying brick all day, I came home at five, showered, ate, and collapsed in bed by eight. I got up at five and left for work. The only time we saw each other fully awake was on weekends.

But we agreed that winter work was a rare gift and I jumped at the opportunity. My new employer was Anastasia Brothers, a large firm out of Boston and the low bidder on an expansion project at St. Luke's Hospital in New Bedford. Anastasia was required to hire half local union people and half their own Boston crew. The plan was to construct a large building adjacent to the hospital and attach it by way of a long corridor.

I recognized several members of the New Bedford crew and noted they were the cream of the crop. So they were hired because of their skill and I was hired because of my sex, but that was okay. It gave me the opportunity to work with the best. When I reported that first day and saw another woman on the job, it gave me a jolt. Hurray!

Sandy, twenty-eight, hailed from Taunton and served as her local's token woman, just as I did in New Bedford. Even through her thick jacket, I could see she was muscular and well suited to lifting heavy blocks. I went over to introduce myself and her response was muted. As I followed her gaze, I noticed all eyes were on us. Whoops. I had drawn added attention to the fact we were different from the others and she wasn't pleased.

After a few days on the job, something unexpected and disturbing happened. The local crew members took great pride in the fact that I worked more quickly and accurately than Sandy. After all, I had more time on the books than she did, more experience, so my advantage was perfectly normal.

The same men who had treated me like an outsider now came by my station and said, "You're shining, kid" and "You're running rings around her—keep it up!" I noticed the Boston men putting pressure on Sandy to speed up.

This no-win situation for Sandy and me was a disaster. If we were to join forces, we'd stand out as females first, bricklayers second, so we didn't. When we worked independently, the men treated us like greyhounds at the track, betting on who would finish first. By the end of my first month on the job, Sandy had disappeared. Driven out by this nasty game. I learned she had returned to her old job as a pattern cutter in a clothing factory. What a bummer it must have been for her to go back to a minimum wage. What a bummer the whole thing was. So unfair.

Drinking was the main topic of conversation on every project: who drank the most, what they liked to drink, where they drank, when they would next drink, and how they would meet up with each other to drink some more. When the men gave directions to the job site, it was always "two blocks north of Freddie's package store" or "across the street from the Hideaway Cafe."

The men who drank at lunchtime also drank in their trucks on the drive home. Many stopped in bars after work. Having grown up around the Belmont, I didn't think much about it; it was just a way of life. About half the men I worked with fell into the heavy-drinker category. They wore T-shirts that announced: *I don't have a drinking problem: I drink, I get drunk, I pass out—no problem!* They told stories of the outrageous things that happened while they were drunk, stories told and retold, always bringing gales of laughter from the crew.

The other half never touched a drop and kept their focus on the job. Some enjoyed a drink or two at social functions, but drinking was not a habit. As an apprentice and wanting to fit in, I drank along with the guys, but the time had come for me to give it up entirely. I wanted to be sharp on the job and not put myself in a position where I might be taken advantage of.

Fortunately, Tim was my boyfriend before I became a bricklayer. If I'd have been single, I would have flunked out on the dating circuit, certain that men no longer pictured me as a feminine female. They'd take one look at me and think, "dyke." The words "female bricklayer" still seemed like a contradiction in terms to most men. They couldn't grasp the concept of a heterosexual female wanting to be an expert mason. Changing the image would require many more females entering the trade, then we could join forces. But we'd have to wait for that.

The St. Luke's Hospital job was the coldest and most brutal so far. Masonry work in the winter is hell. You take a physically demanding trade, add freezing temperatures, and it's like adding insult to injury. When the weather gets below freezing on a heated job, we follow a routine: The laborers arrive at 6:00 AM to face frozen water barrels—fifty-gallon metal drums placed next to the mixer so water can be added to the sand and cement. If they aren't careful to drain the hoses the night before, the hoses freeze up and no one can work. Woe to the man who messes up on this task.

The laborers light the propane torches, which are no less than portable flame throwers, and they get the propane heater going and aim it at the barrel. Then, they break up the ice as it thaws. The full water barrels, wrapped with blanket insulation, still have ice on the top, which has to be chipped off and pulled out bare-handed because they can't get their gloves wet. The heated water is then added to the sand, cement, and lime in the mixer.

Meanwhile, the motors in the lull, mixer, and prime movers have been out in the freezing cold all night, and if even one motor doesn't start, blood pressures rise because the job is in jeopardy. The masons are supposed to be on the job at 7:00 AM in the work areas, which are heated above thirty-two degrees. The mortar is in the pans and ready to go. Also, snow and ice have to be scraped off the top course of brick.

If the tented areas are heated with kerosene heaters, the faulty ones often give off fumes that make the men nauseous, with almost flu-like symptoms. Throats and nostrils become as dry as the desert and the foreman yells, "If you don't like it, go live in the Bahamas."

As the day wears on and the outside temperature gets above freezing, the snow on the roof melts and causes dripping, sometimes stopping the brickwork completely. A bricklayer is lucky to get twenty-four hours of paid work during a week like this.

While the temperature struggles to get above freezing, the brick-layers often wait in the shanty playing cards. If conditions are right, they go up on the staging, using extreme caution because the planks are loaded with ice. Sanding them is not always sufficient because of the continuous walking back and forth. When the wind howls through, the plastic cover starts to blow off and then the workers are really exposed.

I could never stay warm during these brutal winters. The moisture from the mortar or from wetting the tubs would sometimes get my gloves wet and my fingertips would wear right down. Sometimes I wore five layers of clothes—long johns, shirts, sweater, coat, and thermal vest—but it didn't help much. Even at home, after taking a shower at night, I still couldn't get warm.

Despite all this, I was immensely grateful for winter work. And so were the guys.

On some days we were not allowed to begin work until the clerk of the works' thermometer rose to forty degrees in our heated areas. Since we arrived at seven in the morning and often sat around until eight-thirty, my father gave me a key to the Belmont Club, where I could warm up before work. It was just a short trip from the West End to the South End so I began scooting over. It wasn't long before the guys caught on to my whereabouts and invited themselves along.

"Hey Lynn, how's about a beer?" said Colin at about seven-twenty one cold January morning.

"The bar's not open yet—can't do it." After being badgered by him and a few others, I popped the caps off bottles of Budweiser and put the money on top of the cash register for my father to find later.

The news of my barroom connection spread like wildfire and I became the most popular person on the hospital job. As long as the men behaved themselves and paid for their beer, I had no objections to serving them before the bar opened. After the first few days, the thrill wore off and many returned to the canteen truck for coffee.

Three of the diehards, however, looked forward to their beer every morning and became the new regulars at the Belmont. One of these men was Brian Reed, Frank's brother, whose job I had supposedly taken on the Car Barn project. Unlike Frank, he was an easygoing guy and well liked, as well as a talented mason. When they worked on the same job, there was a certain amount of sibling rivalry, but Frank, the big brother, always stood up for Brian.

The conditions on this job were ideal for me to pick up a few new skills and practice my old ones. We worked with a different type of brick than I'd used before, slightly wider and lighter than normal. The walls I worked on were long and straight, offering perfect conditions for me to increase my speed and accuracy. I had a lot more confidence in my ability now; the tasks I was such a klutz at before were now routine and comfortable.

On each job, I tried to make things as easy as possible on my work partner since the poor guy would be teased relentlessly for having to work with a female. The least I could do was not make it worse. Some appreciated my spirit and willingness to learn, but others quickly asked the foreman to pair them with someone else. At first the rejections bothered me, like I had leprosy or something, but I eventually got used to it. The only men who unequivocally accepted me as a partner, it seemed, were those classified as minorities. Perhaps they empathized with me because they were often treated as second-class citizens themselves.

I had another gripe, too. No matter how advanced I became in my masonry skills, I was still selected to work on the wash down at the end of the day, which involved cleaning up everyone else's mess.

Once when I tried to commiserate with an older black man about the unfairness of this, he said sternly, "Pride doesn't put food on the table. You got to beat them at their own game. Never let someone else's opinion stop you from being the best you can be, no matter what the task."

I repeated the words over and over again in my mind and felt more and more empowered as I did so. I never saw the man again after the St. Luke's job, but his words still inspire me.

Toward the end of the job, I found myself working in the same area as a good friend, Jay Dias. I knew Jay from my bartending days as a soft-spoken, incredibly funny person with a generous heart.

Jay's African-American heritage helped get him into the union, a far greater injustice than the admission of women, according to many old-timers. His dark complexion—unlike the lighter-skinned Cape Verdean workers—propelled him to the top of the prejudice list, but he kept his friendly disposition in spite of the constant harassment.

We began hanging out during coffee breaks and lunch and I cracked up over his wicked descriptions of our crew. Being with Jay was therapeutic for me, like taking happy pills. Whenever I was put down, still a frequent occurrence, I thought of his comical take on that person. He had given me a valuable tool—the ability to see humor in the face of the world's madness, to keep my perspective and move on.

I wasn't successful in breaking one particular habit, and this made me wonder if the behavior was a legacy from my childhood. If a man on the job was the least bit pleasant to me, I treated him like a best friend, bending his ear like a talking head and latching on to him at break time. Any agreeable guy who worked next to me knew more about me than he probably wanted to. On the other hand, he'd often tell me about his own family, hobbies, and interests and this made for a good day. I rarely heard the guys talk about the important things with each other, as women do.

Some of these same men ignored me or acted distant at breaks or meetings if I talked to them. I felt like I was nine again, back with my older brothers. At home we were best pals, but outdoors with their friends, I was just a dopey girl who should get lost. At the job site, I often found myself standing alone while the men went off together to a restaurant or a shady spot to eat lunch. I never completely gave up hope that one day I would be invited to join them.

In a roundabout way, that winter I got what I wished for, at least for the moment. The guys complained incessantly about the Christmas parties held at the union hall, which felt like glorified union meetings with bad food. George Medeiros muttered within earshot, "These guys are never happy—I don't think I'll bother with a party next year."

I jumped up. "George, I have an idea. Listen. On the lower level of my father's bar, there's a function room with a big kitchen, which would make a terrific place for a party."

He gave me his full attention. "Oh, yeah? Sounds good. Set it up for next year with your father."

"What should I do about food, decorating, entertainment, money, and all that stuff?" I shot off.

"You're the woman—you figure it out." He walked away.

Sure enough, it was up to me to host the next Christmas party. Seeing it as my big chance to endear myself to my fellow workers, I desperately needed to do it right. I set about putting together a hearty menu—lasagna, roast beef, seafood casserole, homemade desserts—and decided on an open bar. The event was for union members only, no family. The men usually talked, ate, and went home.

But this time they'd be treated to some first-class entertainment too—I just had to figure out what would work. Dancing? No good. Only one woman at this dance. How about a church choir or Christmas sing-a-long? Nope. Too corny. Hey, what about a professional belly dancer? The dancers are beautiful, and the belly dance is about culture, not sex. Then again, sex is one of their favorite subjects so if they thought the dancer was about sex, so be it. It would be exotic, eye-catching entertainment.

I called an eager woman whose ad appeared in the yellow pages, one who said she had lots of experience. She only charged fifty dollars an hour, so she was a bargain. I booked her immediately. Dad estimated the food and liquor costs and George Medeiros promptly cut me a check. Union members received party invitations along with the monthly newsletter, and we figured about fifty people would show, based on the previous years' attendance.

I offered my friends, Bev and Pam, fifty dollars each to waitress and tend bar, and they jumped at it. Pam's mother had died the previous spring after a long battle with breast cancer and Pam wanted to stay busy over the holidays. She chose working the bar over the kitchen, figuring the tips could be turned into Christmas gifts for Jason. Bev preferred waitressing.

I dug out some decorations from storage—icicles and colorful ornaments and snowmen—and hung them from the walls and ceilings. The tables were bright with red tablecloths and candle centerpieces, which I'd rented. Bev, Pam, and I decided to wear white blouses and black skirts. When the evening arrived, I went nuts looking at my watch every few minutes. Maybe nobody would come. Maybe it would be a flop. Maybe this, maybe that, but at seven the men began to arrive.

Things were awkward at first. They looked skeptical, and it wasn't easy trying to get a bunch of tired men who had laid brick all day into a party mood. They had ambled into a new place, neatly dressed and without their wives, and now what? Thank God for alcohol. I directed them to the bar. Pam made small talk and mixed drinks while Bev served appetizers. A few of the men were surprisingly friendly, asking me about the tavern and the evening's menu. Clearly, my role as party hostess was easier for them to accept than that of fellow bricklayer.

The liquor flowed, and flowed, and before long Pam informed me we had already gone through the evening's inventory. "Yikes, let's get dinner on the table. Quick! Pam, I need you to help in the kitchen." The men loved being waited on by me and my friends, and I noticed more than a few sucked in their stomachs while flirting with my pals. The guys raved about the hot meal in contrast to the cold sandwiches and potato salad served in years past. If the way to a man's heart was through his stomach, I had won some hearts on this one. I felt warm-hearted toward them all. They really were great guys.

As I hustled in and out of the kitchen, I thought, it's going great and just wait till they see the surprise entertainment! After dinner many returned to the bar and, at this point, I ran upstairs to the Belmont and asked Dad for more beer and hard liquor.

"Sure, dear. No problem."

One of the regulars carried it down, and smiles returned to the men's faces as I restocked the coolers and Pam took her place behind the bar. Bev and I tackled the dishes while we anxiously awaited the entertainer. The entertainer! I couldn't believe I had pulled it off. What a success.

Just then, a woman who looked to be in her early sixties arrived with a tote bag and a portable cassette player. Whaaaaat? She must be the entertainer's mother, I thought, as I went to greet her. My spirits took a nose dive when she said, "I'm Almira. Where do you want me to set up my music?" This woman was indeed the belly dancer herself. She took off her coat and my eyes popped at her drooping chest and ample midsection. Was she was really going to show that belly?

Too late to do anything about it now. Let the play go on. I silently hoped the men were tipsy enough to overlook her face and body and, yes, her age. Well, Sophia Loren was sixty-something too, so scratch the age.

"Hello, fellas." She smiled revealing yellow teeth, widely gapped. "I am the lovely Almira, and you're in for a good time now!" Dressed in a harem costume that had seen better days, she popped in a cassette and began gyrating to Middle Eastern music. Layers of fat around her waist rolled in and out as she danced, and the skin wobbled below her upper arms. I looked around at the men's faces and saw shock, amusement, and distaste.

A few men hurriedly got their coats and left, looking back over their shoulders and grimacing. Several others backed away as she approached their table, and one unfortunate guy turned bright red as she sat in his lap and began pulling her veil back and forth behind his head.

"Hey, Paulie, isn't that your grandmother?" I heard one young bricklayer say to another in a stage whisper.

"No, she ain't. Looks more like your girlfriend," the second man chortled as they broke into laughter.

After the initial shock wore off, most of the men began to play along with the plump Almira, acting as though they were turned on by her feminine wiles. Gales of laughter rocked the room, and when she finished her routine, the men clapped and whistled loudly, obviously entertained in a completely different way from what I had planned. A few older Portuguese men sat in the back, shaking their heads in disbelief.

"I still got what it takes—they loved me!" The belly dancer pulled on her coat, huffing and puffing from exertion. "You wanna book me now for next year? My calendar fills up quick."

"Um…not right now, but thanks anyway." I paid her and she headed for the door. The men began to put on their coats and file out, thanking me as they left. Were they laughing with me or at me? I dunno, but the point was they were laughing happily and so was I.

I never told George about the extra $170 in liquor the men had gone through, just took the loss myself. When I returned to work at St. Luke's the next day, several men who usually ignored me exchanged greetings and later joked with me at break time.

"Did Almira make it back to the nursing home okay last night?" Manuel asked lightheartedly.

"Hey Lynn, you missing any silverware? I'll bet she stashed a few forks and knives in those rolls of fat," Billy laughed. I joked right along with them, relieved they were amused about the entertainment from hell.

George Medeiros called me at home that night and thanked me for all I had done. Everyone had fun, he said, and he wanted me to host the party again next year.

"Sure I will, but don't worry. I promise I'll audition the belly dancer next time!"

FALLING DOWN

"Come on, Mugsy!" I called out the back door as the sunrose in a pink and yellow sky. My golden retriever abandoned the rabbit he'd chased out of the garden and loped obediently into the kitchen just as I finished my coffee. Moments later, the buzz of my alarm clock startled me. I followed the sound to our bedroom, where my clock announced 5:00 AM. Jeez, I had already been up since 3:45, fully dressed and happily agitated. Today I was headed for the new Com Electric building in Wareham and my excitement was at fever pitch. It was always this way the first day of a new job.

As a bricklayer I spent much of my time doing grunt work, but on this job, I would actually be using my skills as a full-fledged mason. I would be on the line, up on the staging, working side by side with the professionals instead of down below on the brick-cutting saw or on wash down. George himself said so. Hurray!

I tiptoed into the bedroom to silence the clock. Tim rolled over, trying to tune out the sound, and I bent over and kissed him lightly. "See ya later, hon," I whispered. "Bye, Mugs, be a good boy." I patted his warm fur while he went through his morning ritual, planting several sloppy kisses on my cheek. With my tool bag in the back seat, I jumped in my car and headed for Dunkin' Donuts, where I picked up a muffin and coffee to sustain me during the thirty-minute drive. Perfect timing. I was down to the last sip as I took the Wareham exit and followed meandering, woodsy Route 28, a two-lane state highway that ran through the middle of town.

"Gateway to Cape Cod," said the sign at the Wareham town line, as if we were entering another country. The sign was aptly placed between the replicas of two lighthouses and caught the attention of tourists, but Wareham was not Cape Cod, and the locals knew it. The town was lovely and rustic in its way, with small ponds scattered here and there, but the true Cape was another fifteen miles and a bridge away. Wareham was mainly cranberry country—bogs, ponds and mobile-home parks. A section of Route 28 called "the strip" featured endless souvenir shops, rundown motels, and fast food restaurants. Tourists learned about the strip in the guidebook penned by the local Chamber of Commerce, and they loved it.

A large sign loomed up ahead on my left announcing the "New Com Electric Facility—Another Professional Job by the Luchetti Corporation." I turned off the highway and onto the site. Com Electric was the sole supplier of electricity for the entire southeast coast of Massachusetts. The job would pay well, I knew, but the chance to lay brick every day was what really excited me. With a full hour before starting time, I treated myself to a tour of the facility.

The atmosphere on this job was sure to be professional. Everything was kicked up a notch on large jobs—the quantity of materials, the expertise of the crew, and the number of supervisors and employees. Any job connected with the government followed stringent regulations, and I could tell by the OSHA and DEP signs that this one would be no exception.

The new facility was planned as one large serpentine building; the foundation had already been poured and the steel framework erected. Stacks upon stacks of bricks on pallets were lined up along the east side of the job site, and, at that moment, I wished I could complete the brickwork single-handedly. A few men began to arrive, and I quelled my excitement so as not to come off as a some kind of amateur. A few of the men I recognized, but I didn't see anyone I knew well. The remaining workers all arrived at once, parking their vehicles in rows and calling out greetings to each other as they made their way to the Luchetti trailer, a mobile office parked on site.

A strong bond develops between co-workers on a job like this, at least between some of them. You start a new job with a set of plans, a crew of people, and a pile of bricks. Each crew member plays a key role in creating a building that will live long after you are gone. It's not only mortar that holds the bricks together—it's the sweat of your brow, your skill and talent, and the determination in your heart. Just as a child is born and raised within a family, shaped by the triumphs and tragedies that happen along the way, so it is with the crew that sees a project to completion. And this building would be our baby. I looked forward to making new friends here.

The foreman stepped out of the trailer, introduced himself as Vinny Cipriani, and got right down to business. A few curious glances were thrown my way, but clearly there would be no funny business here. Vinny assigned each bricklayer to a designated area and explained what needed to be done. By the time he finished, I knew this job would be my big test; I would prove to myself and the world that I was a brick-layer. A skilled craftsman. Wow.

As I set up shop on the scaffolding along the west side of the building, I began chatting with the man next to me, an older fellow, slightly built, with a Boston Celtics leprechaun on his jacket.

"Hello there, darlin'," he said with an easy smile, holding his hand out in greeting. "They call me Fast Eddie. I may be small, but I'll lay twice the brick of any man twice my size in half the time. There's not been a tender yet who can keep up with me. Watch me closely, darlin', and you're sure to be learnin' somethin'."

I shook his hand and told him how eager I was to put my training into practice. As I worked alongside him, I could see Eddie loved to talk and had a tale to tell on every imaginable topic. Fortunately, he interspersed his stories with tips on laying brick whenever he noticed me faltering, and this helped me fine-tune my methods without feeling put down or self-conscious. This man was a gem.

We shared a mason-tender known as Foxy, a middle-aged black man just under seven feet tall, built like a Mack truck. Foxy loved the night life, and evenings he went club hopping from one disco to another, his unbuttoned polyester shirt open with a tangle of gold chains jangling around his thick neck. On the job, he smelled of stale cologne, sweat, and cigarette smoke, remnants of the night before. His bloodshot eyes were testimony to his hangovers, but he nonetheless erected staging and hauled mortar back and forth without incident.

Fast Eddie was indeed a speedy worker, and Foxy was never quick enough with the mortar to suit him. Time and again, he combined complaint with braggadocio: "Jesus, Mary, and Joseph, the mortar will be as solid as Mount Rushmore by the time ye get it here! Can't ye see I can lay circles around the lot of 'em? Step up yer pace, man, for the love o' Mike!"

Foxy didn't alter his pace, just paused an extra moment, giving Eddie a hangdog look before filling his mortar pan. Fast Eddie's nagging went in one ear and out the other so it never became fodder for a shouting match.

By the end of the first week, I hit my stride and truly enjoyed going to work each day. During the weekend, Tim and I took time to relax on the porch and catch up on each other's lives. Tim began noticing a sea change in me, and I could tell he liked it.

"Lynn, you're really changing. You seem so sure of yourself these days. You don't moan and groan all the time about whether you did this right or that right anymore. You seem to know in your heart you're doing it right."

He was correct. I felt good—the job was good for me. "Tim, I'll tell you what's different. I'm not being harassed on this job like I am on most of the others. And you know something? It's like every day is a gift, just not to be hassled. Finally I can focus and perfect my skills without feeling like I'm under a microscope. I'm accepted. I don't have to worry about the petty stuff all the time."

As I spoke, I was hearing Frank and his foul mouth and Derek and all the others who tried to make me quit. I had triumphed over those voices. Wasn't that something?

Another Monday rolled around, and I'd been on the job for three weeks. Knowing what to expect each day felt great, and I flourished in such a structured environment. At mid-morning we took a break, and I prepared to take the coffee orders, a habit I'd fallen into on nearly every job I worked. Some men liked to stay up on the staging during break, but not me. I enjoyed walking to the canteen truck, stretching my legs and getting a change of scenery.

Since there was no ladder near my spot on the wall, I swung down the side of the staging to the ground like a pro, like John Wayne dismounting from a horse in one smooth move.

Pulling pad and pencil from my shirt pocket, I headed inside the building shell and shouted, "Who wants coffee?" Hard-hats appeared in several of the unfinished window openings as various bricklayers stuck their heads inside to call out their orders. Being the "coffee girl" gave me a chance to get to know the bricklayers I wouldn't otherwise come in contact with. The men seemed more comfortable with me as waitress than bricklayer, and I took advantage of it, hoping to make myself known and someday accepted.

Being inside the building shell was exhilarating and gave me a different perspective than I had working outdoors. I could see the progress we made each day and I could picture rooms filled with busy workers inside a place I helped build.

"Large black with two sugars and a jelly doughnut," shouted Tony from the window opening on my left. "Medium regular and two glazed," called Mario, Tony's older brother. I collected bills and coins as I continued down the wall, stuffing money in my pants pocket in a jumble. Dan, a wizened mason in his late sixties, handed me a dollar and smiled. He always took a small black coffee. He was a member of a dying breed, men who reach retirement age but love laying brick and don't want to stop.

Some had bad knees, others were hunched over with bad backs. Some had gnarled hands riddled with arthritis, and others had lost parts of fingers on brick saws. Old-timers like these had an aura about them—men who had discovered the true essence of the trade. I was intrigued by their devotion and wanted it for myself someday.

When I returned with hot coffee and fresh doughnuts, it was all smiles and thanks from the crew. "Keep the change," they'd tell me, rather than watch me fumble over nickels and dimes, so I earned a little in tips by day's end. When break was over, I noticed Foxy moving staging near my station, so I backtracked and used a ladder to get back up to my spot.

Another few hours of work and the noon whistle blew. I sucked in the air of a beautiful fall day in New England and realized how hungry I was. Hard work will do that. Grabbing the edge of the staging with my right hand, I began to swing down and suddenly realized I was grasping at air. Just before lunch, Foxy had removed an anchor pin while moving a section of the staging and had forgotten to replace it. The support leg swung around, clipped my chin and sent me careening off the platform. My head bashed into the jutting edge of an unfinished section of the brick wall and it sliced my scalp. I plummeted downward, bouncing off the staging, and slammed onto the asphalt twenty-three feet below. Instinctively, I struggled to get up and heard faraway voices shouting, "It's the girl!" and "Stay down! Don't move!"

As the initial shock and pain lessened, I felt warm trickles of blood seeping out from my arm, chin, and scalp, but even laying in a heap like this, I was more concerned about my job than my injuries. I began to panic. I have to be okay or they won't let me back on the staging. I can't let this ruin my first real bricklaying job! I tried to focus my eyes on the circle of faces spinning dizzily above me.

"The ambulance is on its way, Lynn," said Carl, the steward. Eddie chimed in, "Stay right where you are and don't worry—you can sue." I heard someone say, "Your house is paid for now!" Then, as an afterthought, he asked, "Are you okay?"

"Yeah, I think so." My voice was barely audible, but I still managed to say, "Don't let anyone else take the coffee order, I'll be back," as the whine of the ambulance siren drew closer.

The EMTs loaded me onto a stretcher and into the ambulance as people yelled, "Take it easy, Lynn!" "You'll be okay, Kid, just hang tough!" "You're in good hands—they'll fix you up good as new!" Andy, the fellow I carpooled with each day, followed along as the ambulance sped toward the hospital. I had never been in an ambulance and began to panic at the realization of what had happened. Luckily, the EMT who was checking my blood pressure noticed my agitation and started to ask me questions about myself and my work. His calm demeanor helped steady my nerves by the time we reached the hospital.

The doctor in the emergency room was surprised to hear I'd got banged up by falling from staging.

"What were you doing up there?"

"Working."

He raised his eyebrows. "Well, what do you know?"

He examined me carefully and filled me in on my condition, then instructed the nurse to numb the areas in need of stitching. Once the anesthetic took effect, he began his work. Thirteen stitches for the jagged cut in my scalp, and, fortunately, he cut only a small patch of my hair. Eight stitches for my chin, ten stitches for my arm. I hurt all over, as if I'd been hit by a truck, but the x-rays showed I had no broken bones. My left arm, the one I landed on, was swollen and bruised from shoulder to wrist. The nurse applied antibacterial ointment, wrapped it in surgical dressing, and put me in a sling.

While the doctor wrote on my chart, I badgered him with questions. "Can I go to work tomorrow? Can I get back up on the staging? How soon can the stitches come out?"

He hemmed and hawed. "Your bandages must be kept clean and dry. It's important to call us if you feel dizzy or nauseous—the nurse will give you a form telling you the signs to watch for over the next twenty-four hours in case of concussion. Come back in ten days to have your stitches removed and take it easy for a while. Use good judgment in deciding when to return to your normal activities." The discharge nurse had me sign the paperwork, then handed me a prescription for painkillers and wheeled me out to the waiting room.

Andy hovered over me like a mother hen, gently helping me into his car and driving me home, admonishing me to stay in bed and rest. He said he'd given the hospital intake worker all the necessary information and I was to call Vinny when I felt better so I could begin filing suit.

I had no intention of suing, absolutely none, and it was making me angry to hear all this talk. My focus was somewhere else. One minute I was on top of the world, reveling in my mastery of the trade, and the next minute I was a helpless victim, flat on my back, my achievements undermined by this single incident. I lay in bed feeling half-alive, my head and arm throbbing, thinking, thinking. Oh, God, the irony of it all. Here I was, attracted to masonry for the money, and if I sued, I'd probably be rich enough to retire. But money was the last thing I cared about now. It was the trade I loved.

I pictured my co-workers yakking away, and their words haunted me:

"I always said the girl don't belong on the job."

"What a deal—she works three weeks, then goes on disability."

"It was bound to happen sooner or later—this is no place for broads."

"That's the last we'll ever see of her."

Their words ringing in my ears made everything clear. Though I might hurt like hell, I had to go to work the next day as though nothing had happened.

Tim was beside himself when he saw me, and his eyes filled with pain. When I told him about my decision, he thought I was delirious and tried to feed me a few painkillers. But my mind was made up. It was the only way to regain the respect I had worked so hard for.

Stiff and sore, I climbed out of bed the next morning and moved around a bit to test my capabilities.

"Don't do it, Lynn," said Tim grimacing. "You could ruin your whole future. You have to respect your body and give it a rest."

"Don't you see I have to go?" I cried. I felt like I'd been tackled by an entire football team on the outside, but inside I had a will that wouldn't surrender.

Tim shook his head as though he were dealing with a mad woman, which in a way he was. He knew the only way to keep me home was to tie me to the bed. I dressed awkwardly, having only partial use of one arm, and took a pain pill. Mugsy followed me from room to room, giving me a mournful look, obviously in full agreement with Tim. Knowing Andy would turn me down for a ride, I carefully slid behind the wheel of my car and headed for Wareham.

As I drove, I decided to ask Vinny to let me do light-duty work attaching ties to the metal framework. I couldn't lay brick with only one arm or work on wash down because my injured arm would get wet. Attaching the ties would require me to get back up on the staging, but that wasn't intimidating.

Vinny nearly fainted when I walked onto the job site.

"What are you doing here? You should be home in bed," he scolded.

Foxy rushed over, apologizing profusely for his oversight, and urged me to go home. "Jeez, I'm sorry, Lynn," he cried, the hangdog look back on his face. "I don't know how I missed that pin. I told Vinny it was all my fault. You should go home and rest."

A few of the other men expressed greetings and got back to work, assuming I had come for sympathy or paperwork to begin my lawsuit. I quietly asked Vinny to put me on tie work, and he refused. After much discussion, I reminded him he would not have to fill out any workmen's compensation forms if he let me stay. After considering that, he slowly nodded his head and said, "Okay, give it a shot, and we'll see how it goes."

He assigned me to an area several hundred feet away from my usual spot, a section of the building not ready for brick yet. A guy was already there doing tie work, which involves screwing metal brackets into a steel framework to support and anchor the brick wall itself. Gritting my teeth, I climbed the ladder to the third tier of staging, trying to appear nonchalant. The laborers working nearby nodded and returned to their own work, stealing glances my way every few minutes. They didn't know what was going on or why I was there, but they didn't want any part of it, probably in fear of having to fill out reports or be interviewed if I took another nose dive.

I began to work on attaching ties to the metal frames, clumsily, occasionally dropping one or two. The ties that escaped my grasp stayed where they fell since it was too painful for me to bend down and retrieve them. After about thirty minutes, I felt myself weakening and glanced at my watch, counting the minutes until the next break. During break, my bandages needed to be changed. I brought extra gauze and tape but couldn't do it alone, so I asked Carl, the brick steward, to help. Carl was a quiet man who kept to himself and I felt I could trust him to be discreet.

He followed me over to my car. "You look awful pale. You sure you don't want to go home?"

"No, I'm staying." I handed him some medical supplies, and he began removing the dampened gauze from my arm.

"Christ, Lynn," he stammered when he saw the damage that lay underneath. He was shaken, visibly upset, but he replaced the old gauze with new, loosely wrapping it so as not to hurt me. I thanked him and he nodded, averting his eyes. I made my way back up the staging, refreshed from the brief rest, and felt I could stick it out until lunch. Half an hour passed and I was still alive. But as I reached behind me to grab another handful of ties, I noticed George Medeiros driving his pickup truck into the job site, and I knew Carl had called him about my injuries.

George spotted Vinny and made his way over. After they talked briefly, he headed straight for my section of staging. I felt all eyes on me as he motioned for me to come down. Damn. I laid down the ties and slowly climbed down the staging, blinking back tears of frustration. With fatherly concern, George tried to convince me to go home. He explained his responsibilities and assured me if I filed a claim, my career would not be jeopardized. He listened to my objections, but his final words were, "Go home, Lynn. Sorry."

What I was about to say next would either make or break me, I knew, but I had to say it. As respectfully as possible, I explained that I had no intention of leaving the job and my decision was final. George was not used to being challenged, especially by a young petite woman who was as stubborn as an old mule. He knew he was being watched, and the men were awaiting his next move.

I could almost see the wheels turning in his head as he recalled my tenacity and the times I'd stood up to him in the past. He slowly nodded. "All right, kid, you win. Be careful now." After filling Vinny in, George walked back to his truck. He paused a moment, looked my way, and nodded once. The look of respect I saw in his eyes made my heart soar, and I smiled as he drove away.

At the next coffee break, my return to work was the focus of conversation.

"What are you, nuts?"

"I'd be home takin' it easy, waitin' for my settlement if I was you…"

"Luchetti ain't gonna feel it—their insurance will pay ya. Go for it!"

"The least ya can do is stay on the ground—it ain't gonna be a pretty sight if ya come tumblin down again."

"Okay, okay, who wants coffee?" They began calling out their orders and handing me money. My body hurt, I was limping, and I had to make two trips instead of one, but I did it myself, just like always. The rest of the day was no picnic, and I fought back the pain and weariness that invaded me as the hours passed. At long last, it was quitting time.

I carefully crept down the staging and walked to my car, thinking only about going home, taking a pain pill, and crawling into bed. Lost in thought, I suddenly realized that some of the men were talking to me as I walked by.

"Good job, Lynn."

"Take it easy, girlie—get some sleep."

"Hang in there, kiddo."

"A couple of shots of Jack Daniels will straighten you right out…"

"Put some BenGay on that shoulder—works like a charm."

One or two "see ya's" were the norm at quitting time, so this display of concern touched me. "Thanks—I'll see you tomorrow." I painfully shuttled home and soaked in a hot bath. Mugsy, ever loyal and concerned, plunked himself at the foot of my bed as I snuggled in.

The next morning, still sore but refreshed from a good sleep, I waited for Andy to pick me up. A sense of calm enveloped me, and, craziness aside, I felt I'd done the right thing in returning to work. A new respect was evident in the eyes of the men. The smiles, greetings and gentle pats on the back were better medicine for me than the pain pills.

It was tie work for me for the next week until my stitches came out, then I got the okay from Vinny to return to the line. Driving myself to work that morning, I arrived about twenty minutes ahead of the crew and surveyed the site. Why not go up? Yes, I needed to do it! I carefully climbed the staging, plunked down my tool bag at my new station, and reveled in the view, feeling as triumphant as if I had just climbed Mount Everest. Tears of gratitude and relief welled up in me. "I did it, really did it," I said to the world. "I'm back, just like I said I'd be. I can't be killed off. I'm a real mason now—it's in my blood." And then I said a few words to the invisible crew: "So you'd better move over, boys, because I'm here to stay!"

Trucks began to arrive, and I was raring to go. Fast Eddie took his place next to me, grinning from ear to ear, "Well, if it ain't herself, lookin' fresh as a spring mornin'. Now ya best be gettin' up to your old speed, darlin'—we don't want Foxy slowin' back down to the pace of a tortoise." I greeted Foxy warmly when he brought us our mortar and noticed he took extra care to check the staging regularly and seemed on top of things with the mortar.

"That's it—quitting time!" called Vinny. By this time, I had fully reclaimed my place on the line and my confidence to keep laying brick, come what may.

The weeks flew by, and the job was ending way ahead of schedule. Rumor had it that Luchetti had estimated the job's pace at 450 bricks per day because of the serpentine wall, but our average had been closer to 700. Mario, Luchetti's project manager, was ecstatic and said, "Hey, yes," when Vinny suggested a clamboil for the crew in acknowledgment of their hard work.

When Vinny made the announcement, he was nearly knocked over with applause and cheers. "I'll dig the clams," said Andy, who lived on the water and loved to go a-clammin'. Vinny said not to worry, he'd take care of the rest. Excitement peaked among the crew, since they were not often recognized for their efforts. This was a rare company event. Friday noon, we gathered at Vinny's trailer at the work site and everyone seemed festive and carefree. Vinny had arranged for a Portuguese-style clamboil, a variation of the New England version, in which the clams were steamed in beer (instead of water) inside large black enamel pots along with potatoes, onions, hot dogs, pork sausage, corn on the cob, *linguiça*, *chouriço* and haddock or cod wrapped in cheesecloth, then served with warm Portuguese rolls called *pops*.

Tables and benches were brought in for the occasion and we stood around the buffet table, trying to form a line, mouths watering from the sweet smells wafting from the pots. A row of large coolers held cold cans of beer, which were going fast.

Mario went from table to table, beer in hand, patting men on the back. "Hey, ya did good. Ya did great. You guys are great workers, never saw such a team."

I looked over and thought, oh, wow, this man has had one too many beers, and I sat down next to Fast Eddie and Sal, who were having a contest, seeing who could shuck their clams the quickest.

"Now this is what I call a clam boil," said Tony, his mouth stuffed with *linguiça*.

"Yea, this is the kinda job I could get used to," quipped Andy, pulling clams out of his broth and dunking them into his dish of melted butter.

Tradesmen are never told how good they are, though these skilled craftspeople are master builders. Across America, skyscrapers, hospitals, and universities are a testament to their skill and bravery. Seeing how honored they felt by a simple clam boil at a job site in Wareham nearly brought me to tears.

But I should have read the signs. Whenever I became the least bit complacent or celebratory, I was brought down again. And, of course, I hit bottom there and then at the clam boil.

When the drunken Mario reached our table, he sat across from me, knocking over Fast Eddie's clam broth as he set his beer down. The men ignored his boorishness and just continued to eat as if he were not there. When I thanked Mario for the great meal, he looked back with a sinister leer that made my skin crawl. I could tell I was in for it.

"I take care of my crew—that's the kinda guy I am," he bragged. "You fellas did a good job, but if I was still on the line, I coulda finished it even sooner. I'm one of the fastest masons out there. Just because I don't work with the tools anymore don't mean I can't still lay brick better than anybody." He fixed his blurry gaze on me and leaned across the table, his repugnant beer breath filling my face.

"Come on, girlie, let's go up on the staging, and I'll show you how it's done. I can run circles around these guys," he slurred.

After all I'd been through to earn the respect of my co-workers, Mario was messing it up by singling me out and pulling his macho routine to impress me. Telling him off would poison me with the company forever after, but remaining mute was giving me an ulcer. I struggled to keep my mouth shut. Conversation stopped and all eyes were on us. Disgusted, several men tried to divert him.

"Come on, Mario, let's get a cup a coffee," said Tony.

His head wobbled as he tried to focus on Tony. "Oh, for chrissake, take it easy, I'm just having a little fun."

Andy cut in, "Hey Mario, I heard you were on a big job in Boston yesterday."

"Yeah, the airport job—it's twice the size of this one. You guys ain't ready for a job that size."

I saw my chance and stood up. "Well, I guess I'll head out now—see you guys on Monday." I dumped my plate of empty clamshells into a trash barrel and made a quick exit. Just driving down the road, going nowhere.

GREAT LEAP FORWARD

During my three years as an apprentice, I spent lots of time doing grunt work—running the saw, chipping mortar from old bricks, washing down the wall, and other tedious, sometimes dirty tasks. This was to be expected. Apprentices always started at the bottom, but I hoped I'd be laying block and brick in the second half of my apprenticeship. But guess what? Most of the time, I was still doing grunt work.

So, okay, that's the reality of the job, I can accept it, I told myself. Things would change when I graduated from my apprenticeship and became a bona fide bricklayer, then the grunt work would all be behind me. But, no. I got a few great opportunities to work on the wall, but I was still low man on the totem pole. I observed the experts constantly but how could I ever hope to match their skills if the opportunity never came? Masonry, like many crafts, requires practice, practice, practice, and I was like a hungry kid. I just wasn't getting enough to eat.

Outside of work, something else was going on, but I had no idea yet where it would lead. I only knew I wanted to move on and up. The old romance novels I once devoured had been replaced by—yes, technical masonry manuals, estimating and planning textbooks, and motivational best sellers. I was like a giant sponge absorbing every word and hungering for more.

The first time I read *The Power of Positive Thinking* by Norman Vincent Peale, my heart leaped. Good grief, this guy was saying that I, Lynn Donohue, had wonderful talents and abilities within me, just waiting to be discovered. Having lived most of my life thinking of myself as stupid, worthless, and unlovable, he planted seeds of hope in my mind and heart. Many of my first motivational paperbacks were dog-eared, devoured many times over.

My practice area in the basement showed my determination was for real. I had built my practice wall so many times, using the same blocks and bricks, that their edges were now chipped, their surfaces eroded. I laid flagstone and brick into concrete on our front and rear walkways, back porch, front steps, and rear patio. "If you don't stop," Tim cautioned me, "we won't have any grass left in our yard." I didn't stop.

At that time I was working on the town hall in Fairhaven and delighted to be working with my old pal Jack Benevides again. After work one day, I began chatting, telling him about our receding lawn.

He laughed, then looked pensive for a moment. "You know, if it's practice you want, I sometimes do side work on weekends. Maybe you'd be interested in helping me out."

I jumped at the chance. There was no better teacher than Jack, and working a small job, away from the distractions and scrutiny of the normal job site, sounded like heaven.

"I'm laying a brick patio for my brother-in-law on Saturday," said Jack. "The pay isn't great, but you'll gain lots of experience. You're welcome to come along."

"Are you kidding? I'd love to!" I agreed to meet him at five-thirty on Saturday morning. "Do you have to tell the union about side jobs?"

"As long as you confine the work to small homeowner projects, the union looks the other way," he explained.

Working with Jack was a dream. Without the pressure that plagued me on union jobs, I was able to let my guard down and concentrate. Suddenly I was a privileged pupil with my own private tutor and could move ahead by leaps and bounds. Jack's kind and patient manner made it easy for me to hit him with questions and try new methods without fear of ridicule. This was the education I wanted, and I got two in one: Jack was not just teaching me skills, he was teaching me teamwork and cooperation between partners. My heart sang as we worked together.

We did side jobs from then on, and before long we fit together like hand in glove.

"Great job!" he'd say.

"Not too bad yourself," I'd reply. The finished products of our labors thrilled me. Within months, I learned to pull my weight on small jobs and began to branch out and work with other men as well. The principles of estimating and planning, which I'd learned in the course at Wentworth, became real to me. I was gearing up for some big changes.

Meanwhile, I drove fellow workers crazy by asking a million questions about every detail of every job. I couldn't help it—I had to know.

"Joe, how do you find side work? How do you know what type of brick to use?"

"Harry, where do you buy the materials? How do you pay for them?"

"Keith, what type of measurements do you take? What if it rains?"

"Bob, how can you be sure the customer will pay when you finish? What if they don't like your work? What if you don't like your own work?" And on and on. On one small patio job I did with Bob Comeau, I asked so many questions my voice was hoarse by lunchtime.

"Jesus, Lynn," Bob complained good-naturedly. "I never realized how complicated this work was until you hit me with all these questions. I liked it better when I just did it and didn't think about how."

Working side jobs became my secret weapon to increase my skills and confidence, and I loved the extra money, too. Side jobs, I learned, were small-scale models of big jobs with big contracts, and I was able to observe the entire process. And, wow, what a process it was. You take the customer's idea and the measurements, create a design, put it on paper, decide on materials, get the best prices, find a partner, deliver the supplies, prepare the area, build the structure, get the customer's approval, and, finally, get paid.

One Friday night, I knew I could find Bob Comeau and his wife, Bella, at The Blue Point Restaurant, enjoying their weekly ritual of fish and chips, then heading home to watch *Jeopardy*. Sure enough, I walked in just as they sat down in their favorite booth against the far wall. "Sorry to bother you, Bob, but I just wanted to ask you something."

"Sure, kid—hey, have you had supper? No? Well, come on, sit down and join us."

Bella chimed in, "Yes, please, Lynn, sit down. The seafood here is out of this world."

"Okay, thanks, I will."

We ordered the house specialty, fish and chips, and minutes later, our waitress appeared with plates piled high. "Soda coming up," said the waitress as she hustled off. I doused my plate with ketchup as Bella gently sprinkled her chips and Bob's with vinegar and Bob topped his and Bella's fish with tartar sauce. Was this love or what? A fond smile passed between them, and I hoped Tim and I would be as loving and comfortable after twenty-five years of marriage as they were.

Our plates nearly empty, Bob leaned forward, put his elbows on the table, and looked at me curiously. "So what's on your mind, Lynn?"

I picked up the salt shaker and began playing nervously with it, then turned to Bob. "Remember that side job you told me about, the one you turned down because you were already booked up?"

"Oh, you mean the patio and bulkhead in the West End?"

"Yeah. Well, if they haven't found anyone to do it yet, what do you think about me bidding on it myself? Do you think I could handle it?"

Bella and Bob exchanged a glance that spoke volumes. Bella's eyes seemed to say, Go easy, Bob, dear, don't burst her bubble, but don't let her get in over her head either, and Bob's eyes told her, Don't worry, sweetheart, I won't steer her wrong.

Bob drank the last of his soda, thought for a minute, and then said with a wink, "You'll never know until you try, will you? And knowing you, no matter what I think, you're gonna do it anyway. But just for the record, yes, I think you're ready and you have my blessing." Bella seemed happy with his answer.

While Bob picked up the tab, I walked with Bella out to their car, and she turned and gave me a quick hug.

"You'll do just fine, and if you run into trouble, Bob will be happy to help." At that moment, Bob came over to open the door for Bella.

"Well, if I get the job, I'll treat you two next time."

"It's a deal."

As I pulled up behind them at the traffic light, I could see Bella sitting close and resting her head on Bob's shoulder as he drove. Now that's the way it's supposed to be.

I called the number Bob had given me the next morning, and an hour later I was in the customer's backyard looking things over. Two hours later I picked up Whiskey Pete from his neighborhood tavern, and he helped me draw the design and price the materials.

"You're hired," said the customer in response to the price, and Pete and I went to buy the materials. We began the project, and by Sunday night we'd built a small back porch with basement-entry framework to support a cellar bulkhead. I paid Pete $450 for labor, $249 for materials, and after that I had $800 left over. I couldn't believe it!

After dropping Pete off at his tavern, I went straight to Sears and bought myself a gigantic Sony television set. Call it instant gratification—you do the work, you get rewarded. Tim rolled his eyes and shook his head when he saw me drive up with this big hulk in the back of the car, but after he heard about my profit, he changed his tune. We sat down to watch the new TV, and I promptly fell asleep.

The next morning, I hustled off to work at the town hall, eager to tell Jack Benevides about my weekend. He listened with twinkling eyes as I told him every detail of the job and laughed about the Sony TV. "From now on, you watch. I'm going to be busy every weekend, I'm going to…"

Jack found an opening and jumped in. "Oh no, I've created a Frankenstein. Sounds great, Lynn. You can handle the work, no problem. But remember, the reputation you build is just as important as the walls you build."

"Uhhhhh…What are you saying?"

Jack laid it out for me in one long sentence. "Word of mouth can make you or break you. When you commit yourself to doing a side job, no matter how small, always be sure to plan it out right—your design, the materials, how much time it will take, who you hire as a helper—so you never have a dissatisfied customer—that's not to say things won't go wrong once in a while, but if they do, be the first to apologize, even if it's not your fault, and people will know they can count on you."

"Yeah, you're right. I usually leap first, look later."

Jack was the kindly father I never had, and his gentle lessons helped immensely. "When I started out on side work," he said, scratching his head as if pulling out old memories, "I was excited, just like you. I took on so much weekend and night work I was too tired to give 100 percent to my daytime job. But my first obligation was to the union; they took me in, trained me, and gave me opportunities to learn. If I wasn't in shape on the day job, I could mess up and cause problems for somebody else. So I had to learn the hard way to balance the two, but once I did, everything was fine.

"And, oh yeah, don't forget to leave time to be with Tim, or you might end up in divorce court."

I was undaunted. "What do you think, Jack? After doing a few more side jobs of my own, I think I'll be ready to take on a foreman position on a small-scale union job. Anyway, I'm going to talk to George Medeiros about it."

"Well, ummm. You never know unless you try."

George Medeiros knew better than anyone how determined I was to become a better tradeswoman, but when I asked about becoming a foreman, he groaned.

"No matter what I do for you, it's never good enough," he teased. "First, you wanna be an apprentice. Then you wanna win the apprentice contest. Then you wanna be a bricklayer. Then you wanna do side work. Now you wanna be a foreman. Next you're gonna want my job!"

"Don't give me any ideas."

"I don't have to give you ideas, you got plenty enough already."

In reality, George agreed that being a foreman was the next step up for me and he said he'd keep his eyes open for a suitable position. I called him every few days to see how things were looking.

"Nothing yet, but I'm still on it."

He was. He called regularly and informed me of the many jobs he'd looked into, but the final result was always "Thanks, but no thanks" when it came to appointing a woman as foreman. No one wanted to take the risk. I couldn't really blame the contractors. The men might resent a female boss, which could lead to serious problems on the job. Then liability issues could clobber them. A company's reputation was at stake here, and if the job was not done well, or on time, because of internal issues, they would pay dearly. Considering my past history with men in the trade, problems were bound to arise. If I were a guy, I probably wouldn't hire me either.

After six months of slogging it out, George Medeiros called me to his union office and admitted defeat. "Lynn, I know and you know that I could put pressure on contractors to take you on, but consider what could happen. Some of these guys won't like working for a woman. You start bossing them around, they may mess things up on purpose and blame it on you, or they may refuse to work with you at all. It could be a mess. You're probably better off just forgetting about it."

My life as a tradeswoman passed before my eyes as I stood there like a schoolgirl, learning I'd failed the final exam. I was sick to death of being in a man's world that just wouldn't let women in. My building tools, all those beautiful bricks and blocks, were formed in molds, but there was no mold that fit me as a female mason.

The men on the job liked women all right, as long as they were wives, girlfriends, mothers, or daughters. Barmaids, waitresses, and secretaries were okay, too. Some of the men thought of me as an underdog, a dreamer who needed protection. Others regarded me as a threat, a disgrace, a troublemaker bent on breaking their sacred traditions. No doubt about it, my ability to do "men's work" with skill and verve bruised their egos.

From the beginning of this journey, all I wanted was to make a living, practicing a trade I loved. I wanted to be able to say I helped build that library, that hospital, that school. I wanted all of my co-workers to be like the terrific men on the job who treated me as an equal, who held normal conversations with me, who joked with me and were happy for me when I achieved a new goal. But most of the guys saw me as an alien intruder. I could not bust those walls.

"So what do I do now, George?" My face sank in disappointment.

George did not look half as grim as I did. "Well, as I see it, you have two choices. One, you keep doing what you're doing—working union jobs during the week and doing your own jobs on the side. Or two, you start your own business."

Start my own business? My ears pricked up like a Doberman pinscher's. No way am I ready for that, was my first thought. My bad experience as a restaurant entrepreneur still stung, and I wasn't eager to go that way again. And yet...

"Remember the day someone told me I didn't need to take that course at Wentworth because I'd never own my own business?"

"Well, it wouldn't be the first time you've made us union guys eat our words."

"I guess I'll stick with what I'm doing for now and think about it some more." Though I was in a black cloud of despair when I left his office, there was just a thread of hope under those dark skies. The seed had been planted.

When the restoration job ended, George didn't have any new work lined up for me, so Tim and I decided to vacation in Maine. Pam agreed to look after Mugsy and keep an eye on the house while we were away. We packed my old Datsun mini pickup to the gills with sleeping bags, pillows, and camping gear as we set off at a leisurely pace, driving on back roads along the rugged coast. The farther we got from home, the more relaxed I felt.

Outside Bar Harbor we found a low weekly rate at a hotel and moved in. Free spirits for a week! During the day, we reveled in the colors of a New England fall and browsed in the local antique and book shops. We bought apples by the roadside, watched farmers bring the hay in, and fell in love with the old wooden clapboard houses adorned with wraparound porches and big yards. When Friday rolled around, my career worries had diminished, and Tim and I were like honeymooners, enjoying the gift of time and each other's company—a true luxury. Would we always be working our butts off and never have time for each other?

As we browsed in a used bookstore on Saturday morning, I came across a moldy old paperback called *Think and Be Rich*, by Napoleon Hill. I thumbed through it with great interest, then wanted to devour it all the way through.

"Look, Tim, check this out."

"Anyone with a name like Napoleon must know what he's talking about," he said, flipping through the pages. We bought the book for fifty cents and headed for the beach. As Tim walked the beaches and dunes, I found a flat rock, pulled out my book, and slipped off to paradise.

Mr. Hill was clear and direct: set goals and speak affirmations aloud every day to reinforce them. Although the book was written in 1925, it seemed contemporary, and it spoke loudly to me now. I was buried in chapter 4 when Tim returned and I barely acknowledged his presence. "This book is incredible!" I said later at lunch.

Tim knew we were in for a long gab session, and he was willing to go along. This was one of his most endearing qualities, to take my quest seriously and truly empathize. How many women get that?

In order to be successful, said the author, you must set a concrete goal and depend only on yourself to achieve it—this was the book's primal message, and I read it from cover to cover twice by the time we arrived home on Sunday night. Tim drove the whole way home, going crazy with me saying every few minutes, "Listen to this!" and "Listen to that!" and "Oh, wow!" and "This is great!" Poor guy, he had no choice, he was in the driver's seat. Though I had read tons of other motivational books, this one was teaching me how to achieve success step by step, brick by brick. I was becoming the ancient Mr. Hill's most ardent student.

As soon as we arrived home, I hurried to the kitchen and grabbed paper and pen. Mugsy followed me around, expecting hugs and kisses, but I had something important to do and had to do it NOW. Poor Mugsy then trotted after Tim, hoping to get some attention from him, which he did. All the way home I'd thought about my goal and was desperate to write it down.

My handwriting was steady and firm. "Five years from today, I will have $100,000 profit in the bank and be the best mason contractor in southeastern Massachusetts. I will be fair and honest toward my employees and always treat them with respect." The more I looked at the written words, the more real they became. I read them aloud, quietly at first, then more emphatically. Mugsy looked at me with tilted head, trying to figure out who I was talking to.

"Sounds good to me," said Tim, his hands full of sleeping bags and suitcases.

I put the paper in my top drawer, where I would see it every morning when I got dressed. Mr. Hill suggested that you repeat the goal out loud several times a day, and I planned to do exactly that.

Good old Napoleon Hill was a genius. His book not only inspired me to set a goal but also challenged me to think about starting my own business. It wouldn't be for a while, but I knew beyond a shadow of a doubt it was in my future. That winter, I stayed busy with indoor side jobs, and as my confidence grew, I took on larger jobs, relying on a few union men to help me out—Whiskey Pete, Bob Lynch, and Jay Dias.

Taking on bigger projects was not as difficult and harrowing as I'd imagined. The basic elements were the same, except for one thing, the profit margin. On side jobs where I used two or three men, my profit after expenses averaged $2,000. That was a chunk of money.

Every day I repeated my goal to have $100,000 in the bank after five years. I repeated it to Mugsy, repeated it to the walls, repeated it to the invisible crowds before me, repeated it to myself. For the most part, I tried to spare Tim. And you know? I discovered the power of writing something down and speaking it to the world is great. The world could not hear me, of course. The one who was hearing this was me, deep inside. And so this little affirmation gave me the discipline to put my side job profits into a savings account, and before long I had $10,000 saved up.

A few union workers regularly took on side work and, as their businesses grew into bigger jobs and more men, they had company names painted on their trucks, announcing themselves as legitimate business operators. Now that I had about twenty side jobs under my belt and used two or three men, I thought it was time for a company name and a new truck.

ARGUS

S pring arrived and union work was plentiful again. Though I tried to concentrate on my work, for the first time I was losing focus. My mind raced day and night with thoughts of starting my own small business, not just the work but the way I wanted to do things. Ethics would be an important part of the deal, thanks to the example set for me by men like Jack Benevides and Bob Comeau. If I took on bigger jobs, I resolved they'd always be union sanctioned. Never would I be a scab that cheated the union. I'd pay my helpers union wages and say no to work that was nonunion, no matter what.

I also planned on treating my helpers with respect. I was a survivor of those wars and knew firsthand how it felt to be disrespected and ostracized. This was not going to happen to anyone who worked with me or for me. I would not tolerate rude behavior. Many of the foremen I'd worked for ran their crews like drill sergeants, belittling and hollering at their charges, thinking this was the way they would get cooperation. What they got was men who felt contempt for them. I planned to use a team approach with my helpers, with everyone supporting each other through the highs and lows of the workday.

I loved thinking about what I would call my business, sort of like choosing a name for my baby. Should it be Lynn's Masonry? Donohue Bricklaying? LD Construction? Or were these names too boastful? One night while cleaning out a closet, I found an old New York City telephone book and on a hunch decided to flip through the yellow pages for ideas. I noticed many businesses chose names that started with the letter A, no doubt so they would be listed first. Everyone, it seemed, had a business called AA this or AAA that, so I ruled that out right away. I wanted something different, a little offbeat.

As I leafed through the Ps, a company called Argus Printing leaped out at me. Argus! I liked the name and dug out my dictionary. In Greek mythology, Argus was a giant with 100 eyes, slain by Hermes. Argus also meant a watchful person, a guardian. Except for the slaying part, I thought Argus was a great name. Argus was trustworthy and dependable, fair and square, strong and brave. Argus was me! The name fit but I was quaking in my boots because, good grief, I was taking the next step. When you name a thing, it becomes real. Did Mr. Hill say that? Oh, dear God, it was me saying that! In case I had any doubts, Tim noted that our 35mm camera was an Argus, and I took that as a good omen. And so my company, Argus Construction, was born.

On weekdays, I finished work by three, leaving me with two hours to do my personal business, which I had plenty of these days. My first step was to hire an accountant and I put in a call to Dave LaPalme, Tim's friend from the Greater New Bedford Track Club, the poor guy who'd kept the books when I flunked restaurant management. Dave wasn't too keen on Argus either but he took me on as a client, got me a tax identification number, and I opened a business checking account, depositing two thousand dollars of my side-job profits for start-up funds.

Next step was to open accounts in the Argus name with the stores where I'd be purchasing materials. This was easy enough since the store owners already knew me as a customer who paid in advance. Opening an account at the rental shop, my source for cement mixers, drills, and other machinery, was another story.

"Fill out this credit application," they said.

I took the three-page document over to Dave and the deed was done. I got my credit.

Next I blew into a printing company in New Bedford's North End and ordered business cards and stationery. I knew the place because Jack Benevides' nephew worked here and I thought he could help. He helped me pick out a design.

When I picked up the order, the sight of my business card rendered me speechless. In bold white letters, the name of the company, Argus Construction, stood out against a red-brick background and looked, well, incredibly professional. My own name was printed in the lower left-hand corner with the word *President* underneath, and that looked pretty impressive too. My knees began to tremble—my moment of truth had arrived. I sat in my car for ten minutes, staring at the boxes of cards and stationery and thinking, Oh my God, that's *my* name on the card, I'm the president of a company! I marveled at the concept of myself as the owner of a small business and was terrified by it. This president was scared to death.

I kept George Medeiros informed of my business venture every step of the way and continued to drive him crazy with questions. Over the years, we had grown close in a father-daughter kind of way. He was proud of me, exasperated by me, and at other times thought I was just plain nuts. He was my confidant, my mentor, and my friend.

"I can't win," he complained in jest. "No matter what you do, it ends up making more work for me. I'm gonna buy myself a set of earplugs so I can get some peace and quiet when you're around."

"Go ahead—I'll just write the questions down on paper for you then," I kidded back. He shook his head in mock frustration, but his face told me he was pleased with my new direction.

George was always helpful in showing me the way. When I was ready to take on bigger side jobs, he recommended I buy my own equipment rather than continue renting. It was more cost effective. He made an extensive list of items I'd need and estimated their cost: cement mixer, mortar tubs and pans, staging, planks, and a truck to haul everything in. I took his list home and added up the figures—$29,753! Was he kidding? Where was I going to get that kind of money?

Though it was late, I called him at home. "Where the heck am I supposed to get thirty thousand dollars?"

"That's what banks are for."

"But I don't have any collateral except my house, and I can't risk that."

"Don't give up that easily, Lynn. Just go to the bank tomorrow on your lunch break and see what they say."

"Good idea."

"I always have good ideas. That's why I'm the business agent and you're not."

Whenever I contemplated a new venture, I leafed through my ratty copy of *Think and Grow Rich*, picking out paragraphs here and there for inspiration. Today one particular sentence caught my eye: "Obstacles are what you see when you take your eyes off your goal." How true, how true. I repeated it a few times. Just what I need to know when I face that big, blank-faced, concrete bank.

I had a long history with my family bank, so in some ways, it was an old friend. But I had never asked this old friend for any favors before. When I was eight, my grandparents brought me here to open a savings account in my name, depositing a $5 bill to get me started. I put birthday money into the account for a few years, but when I was twelve, I withdrew my full savings of $32.76 and spent it all on records. My parents had their accounts here, and it became my bank too. A helpful woman at the customer service desk explained my loan options.

If I chose not to use my house as collateral, my only other option was to take out a secured loan against an existing account. Hmmm. The only person I knew with that much money in the bank was my father, since he kept the Belmont Club accounts here. If nothing else, Dad was always willing to help me financially, so I paid him a visit and explained my predicament, playing down the fact that his account could be seized if I reneged on my loan. Of course, I knew there was no chance of that, but how could *he* be sure? Faith is a wonderful thing. He returned to the bank with me to sign the required papers. Thanks, Dad.

My feelings toward my dad had changed over the years. As I grew older, I began to understand where some of his demons came from. Many of Dad's bad choices in life stemmed from his drinking and poor judgment. Drink poisoned his system, his relationships, and his life; he was a slave to it.

In the end, life did not work out well for him. His liaison with Sylvia was brief. He dumped her and began an affair with one of the Malloy girls thirty years his junior. Yes, my age—I had played with her as a child! I liked her a lot but it was strange to think of her as my stepmother. But Margaret had her problems too. She worked as a barmaid at the Belmont and was married with three young children. A heavy drinker herself, she was given to bouts of depression. She ended up divorcing her husband and marrying my father. Maybe they had a chance for a little domestic bliss for a while, but I doubted it.

Visiting Dad in his new house near the Belmont with his new wife was strange. He was kinder and more involved with Margaret's kids than he had ever been with us, and I felt resentful, though I didn't mean to. Anyway, domestic bliss was not in the cards for them. Dad had recently discovered that Margaret was having an affair with Dennis, his loyal, longtime bartender, the brave guy who had broken up the bar fight with the Sidewinders years ago. Dennis was Dad's most trusted employee and had been managing the Belmont for over twenty years. Lots of hearts were broken as a result.

Dad kept his feelings buried as usual but he was deeply hurt. He fired Dennis, divorced Margaret, and a year later, she went to AA and sobered up. Dad and I never discussed any of this; we talked only about superficial things. The most he would say was, "What goes around, comes around," and it certainly did in his case. He must have been terribly lonely for much of his life, unable to reflect or share with anyone the sadness in his heart, which no doubt went back a long way—the early death of his father, a mother so mean and distant that she terrified her own grandchildren. I felt bad that he had thrown away so many chances at happiness because of his romance with the bottle.

Three days after we signed the loan papers, I picked up the bank check and felt woozy to see it made out to me for thirty-four thousand dollars. I had never seen that much money. For a moment, I wished they'd give it to me in cash, so I could see it and feel it before it went into my business account. Nahhhh...too silly for words. And, yet, thirty-four thousand dollars was only a third of what I planned to have in five years. I needed to get used to the feel of that kind of money.

I wrote my first check for a down payment on a brand-new GMC pickup truck with running lights, just like the ones I'd looked at with such longing at union meetings and job sites. It was a beauty. Dark blue with white and navy pinstripes, and that new-car smell inside the cab. I went sailing over to Pam's and she and Jason came running out.

"Do you believe it?" My face was lit up like a Christmas tree and so was hers.

"I don't believe it. You finally got your new truck!"

"Come on, get in."

Pam, Jason, and I spent all day Saturday tooting from one friend's house to another and covering all family members in between. We pushed buttons to demonstrate how the windows went flying up and down, we clicked knobs, we tested the air conditioner and heater and squealed when they kicked into gear. My excitement made everybody smile, and as I drove off, I felt I was driving right into the future.

My return to earth came soon enough when I totaled up the amount I had left in my business account for equipment. I'd have to spend wisely to get my money's worth. I picked up the *Want Advertiser* and made some calls to inquire about used items. Lady Luck must have been with me because an elderly mason who was retiring after sixty years asked me to come out and take a look at his stuff. I drove straight to Taunton, about twenty miles away, expecting to find a few rusty artifacts, and found myself a treasure chest instead.

What good condition his equipment was in! His white hair and weathered face came with a kind heart and we hit it off immediately, chatting for over an hour about our love of the art and craft of masonry. He was intrigued by my story of becoming a mason and especially liked my ideas on how I wanted to run my business. I told him everything. In addition to my life history, he got the scoop on my perspective business, and he liked what I had to say.

"Honesty and respect are dying out in today's world. I hate to give up masonry, but I'm seventy-eight and the arthritis has got the best of me now. My wife, God rest her soul, has been gone for three years, so my business has been my only companion."

Although his ad listed the equipment for a bulk price of five thousand dollars, his price went down to four thousand dollars for me.

"I know I can get more for it, but I'd like to see it go to someone who will appreciate it. I don't have any children of my own, you know, but if I did, I would hope for a daughter just like you."

I got a little choked up as I gratefully agreed to his price and wrote him a check. He helped me load my truck bed.

As I prepared to leave, he reminded me again, "Just call me if you have problems with the equipment, but I don't think you will. I prided myself in keeping it in tip-top shape. And if you're up this way, stop in and see me, would you? I'd like to hear about how your business is going."

I thanked him warmly and promised to drop by again. All the way home I thought about that kind man. How good it was that my first equipment came from someone who loved the trade as much as I did.

The final item on my shopping list was a desk, a quest that began and ended at U.S. Furniture, just down the street from my grandparents' house in New Bedford's South End. The modern styles were sleek and sophisticated, but I knew as soon as I set eyes on it which one was for me—an old-fashioned desk made of beautiful dark cherry and adorned with polished brass handles. This desk represents what I want my company to be like—sturdy, top quality, and commanding respect. With the money I saved on the masonry equipment, I could afford the desk and a high-back leather chair. I was ready to go.

Well, almost. Where was I going to put all this stuff? When Tim married me, I don't think this is what he had in mind. Now here he was, helping me clean out the garage to make room for a cement mixer and other bulky machinery. Most of the old stuff in the garage ended up on the roadside in front of our house with a big sign that said Free.

"Do you think we should hang onto this broken eight-track cassette player and these old eight-track tapes?" Tim asked as he uncovered a shoe box piled high with the things.

"Hmmm, I'm not sure. What's on them?"

In A Gadda Da Vida by Iron Butterfly, Tim read with a laugh, *Smoke on the Water* by Deep Purple, *The Best of the Bee Gees...*

"Okay, okay, I can't take anymore." I covered my ears. "We'll be lucky if we can get somebody to take them away, free or not." Tim carried the tape player and old tapes out to the street, singing *I Gotta Get a Message to You* in a high falsetto as he passed by.

"Keep it up and you'll be sleeping in this nice, clean garage tonight," I teased. Clearing out the garage to make room for the new equipment was more fun than we'd counted on. We were excited by all that was happening. I was taking control of my future and Tim was right there beside me.

Our driveway was fairly wide, so I could park my new truck easily. But where, oh, where could I put my new desk? We put our heads together and decided to convert our screened front porch into a small office. If we worked fast, we could get the job done by the following Monday, the delivery date for the desk and chair. My dad's friend Bob Cruz, the handyman at the Belmont Club, became a saint in our eyes when he agreed to Sheetrock our porch and add a bay window by Friday. My job was to replace the floor, so I hurried off to my brick supplier and picked out a beautiful Italian tile in glazed gold.

I wanted the floor to be a showcase for my masonry skills, so I decided on a classic running-bond pattern and laid the tile in with chocolate-colored mortar. The result was beautiful, and when the desk and chair arrived, I was swept away. Finally, with a little money remaining from the loan, I bought a used file cabinet, a typewriter, and some basic office supplies. Now I was really ready to go.

Well, almost ready. What I needed now was easy, I told myself—enough side work to cover my loan payments and some good men to help. I still spoke my goal aloud every morning and repeated it as I drove around in my truck—I informed the wind, the trees, the people in the street who paid no attention—"In five years, I will have $100,000 profit in the bank. What do you think of that?" And then I listed the steps I'd take to get me there. Meanwhile, I was $34,000 in debt! Whenever I experienced a moment of panic, the terrifying fear of my business failing, I just repeated my goal all over again. Gradually I began to really believe it.

Meanwhile, George Medeiros found me a new bricklaying job in Boston, a large-scale project subbed out by Anastasia Brothers, the firm I'd worked for on the St. Luke's Hospital project in New Bedford. Anastasia needed ten bricklayers and, as usual, 50 percent had to come from the Boston union local and the rest from Anastasia's regular workers. I was thrilled they chose to rehire me and, for the first time, I began to feel like a "company man," a benchmark most masons strive for. For a bricklayer, working regularly for a firm that offers close to year-round employment brings financial security, a familiar crew, and prestige within the brotherhood.

The job itself, the building of an upscale shopping center in the historic Boston landmark Faneuil Hall, circa 1742, promised to be exciting and educational. The great condition of the building's original brickwork was a silent testament to the expert skills of the eighteenth-century masons who constructed it. The timelessness of masonry amazed me. If a bricklayer from the days of the ancient pyramids met a bricklayer from the twentieth century, they would be able to compare notes and find their basic skills, tools, and materials had not changed.

The interior of Faneuil Hall had been converted into an open-air market lined with food stands that sent delicious smells wafting through the air. Greenhouse-style glass enclosures had been added lengthwise to the sides of the main building, where numerous vendors with pushcarts set up shop. The top floor of the original structure was now used as a function hall for corporate events, and a glorious rotunda stood in the center of the building, its domed ceiling beautifully tiled in mosaic designs. There was even an underground level with rest rooms, storage areas, and a few taverns.

Two similar buildings containing shops and restaurants stood on either side of the main building.

I was in heaven. Even the streets and sidewalks around Faneuil Hall were paved with brick and cobblestone, and I imagined how laborious the work must have been for the masons who left it as their legacy. The idea that my work here would be viewed by people hundreds of years from now left me awestruck. Would they picture me in the same way I pictured the original Faneuil Hall masons? History had been my least favorite subject in school, but now that I was making history, the subject was positively riveting.

The structure I was assigned to work on was an arc-shaped brick building that would become the east side of Faneuil Hall. Starting fifty yards away from the end of a side building, it would arc around the existing Faneuil Hall and end fifty yards away from the other side building. The new two-story-high facility had been designed by the architect to resemble the historic style of the original building. Even the type of brick selected looked convincingly authentic.

Frank Reed's brother Brian was selected as the brick foreman, and he said yes to letting me carpool back and forth to Boston with him. As foreman, Brian was given a company truck, so neither of us had to buy gas. Brian never drank on the job but was usually hung over from his nightly binges on our morning commutes. I was amazed that so many masons like Brian were such great bricklayers despite being heavy drinkers. After some fresh air, hard work, and several cups of black coffee, he laid more brick by mid-morning than those who started out sober. I stood in awe of this highly skilled man.

When Brian was out sick one day, I took the bus to Boston, then hopped the subway to the job site. After work, to my surprise, I found a roomy bench section on the crowded subway train all to myself. It took me a few minutes to realize that my filthy appearance had driven people away. They probably thought I'd been living on the streets. Thankfully, Brian was back at work the next day.

I still devoured books related to construction and business. Next to my side of the bed, a small library was growing topsy-turvy: masonry techniques, contract estimating, small business ownership, architecture, and general contracting, among others. I read trade books at the dinner table, in the bathroom, in bed at night, and even on my commutes with Brian. The first time I opened a book as we drove, I asked Brian if he minded.

"Are you kidding? If it keeps you quiet, I'm all for it," he quipped. Trouble was, the more I read, the more questions I asked him, and he'd turn silent if he had an especially painful hangover. Undaunted, I'd mark the page and quiz him on the way home.

By the end of my first week, I was in love with everything about the new job. Boston was bustling and I liked working in such a high-energy environment. Another great perk was Sara, a female apprentice from the Boston local who ran the brick saw. An eye-catching blonde with a ditsy personality, she said she wanted to be a mason "to make the big bucks!" She had an odd laugh, a kind of "hee-hee" whistle as though she were inhaling air through a harmonica. The men thought it was hilarious and spent much time cracking jokes just to hear that sound again. But two weeks later, Sara was transferred to another Anastasia project and we missed her daily dose of humor. She and I had worked in different areas, so we never got a chance to really talk. Had her experiences been similar to mine? An opportunity missed.

My work area would have scared the hell out of most normal human beings, and so it did me. I was perched on staging that hung just feet away from the busy Route 93 expressway near downtown Boston. I tried not to look down or behind me. I could almost reach out and touch the cars whizzing by me, and the effect was dizzying. With no safety nets below, we were careful not to invite disaster by dropping bricks and tools or by losing our footing. Working on that staging was challenging, and we marveled at our growing ability to maneuver on such a precarious perch.

Because Anastasia's crew lived and worked in a world of big-city diversity, they paid no heed to my being a female mason. How enjoyable it was to work without confronting those good-old-boy attitudes. To top it all off, the wages were fantastic! The Boston rate was higher than New Bedford's, so every week I was grossing $1,000 on average. If I could keep this up and make a profit from my side jobs, my $100,000 goal would become closer to reality.

The Faneuil Hall job was a giant step careerwise. Tim was happy about it too and we talked about the possibility of my working year-round with Anastasia Brothers. With steady brickwork for forty-eight weeks, I could net $38,000 after taxes, we guessed. Combined with Tim's salary, we could easily pay household expenses, and side jobs would give us the dessert—vacations, home improvements, and the Fourth of July party. "Maybe we can even buy shish kebab instead of hot dogs this year," Tim joked.

But my confidence was short-lived. Right up the road was a disaster waiting to happen. While working on the Faneuil Hall project, I received a phone call from a man named Fred. He noted that I'd built a brick fireplace for his cousin, who referred me to him. He owned land in Rochester, a nearby farming town newly discovered by Boston yuppies escaping the rat race. In an effort to save money, Fred planned to build his home by acting as his own general contractor and subbing out the work to local contractors.

"The basement walls are already in," he said over the phone, "all you need to do is pour a concrete floor. And, oh yeah, I'd also like a small fireplace in the first-floor living room." I agreed to look at the site and get back to him the next day with a price. I had never poured a basement floor before; this was work normally done by cement masons, who belonged to the same union but did not lay brick.

After checking out the site, I called Barry, a cement mason I'd met on the Westcott job, and asked what he'd charge for the use of two men for three days. I added in my own estimate for the fireplace, factored in a profit, and called Fred back with my bid.

"Sounds fine to me. Can you start right away?" I agreed to build the fireplace weeknights and pour the basement floor the following Saturday. The fireplace was no problem; Jack Benevides helped, and we had it done in no time. Fred paid me when we finished on Thursday, so I paid Jack and pocketed the rest.

On Saturday morning, Fred met Barry and me at the site at seven and we talked over the day's plan. I figured I'd hang around and watch Barry and his crew pour the floor so maybe I could handle it myself the next time.

Fred was a nice enough fellow, but he didn't know much about construction, and he did things oddly, out of normal sequence. Though no walls were completed yet, he had put in shrubs and mulch out front and installed a few windows in the first-floor framework. You got a great breeze through the open wall framing, but the windows were shut tight. Though the fireplace looked fine, nothing was around it but plywood flooring and sawhorses. Well, it's his house, I guess he can build it any way he wants to, I thought.

Just then, I heard the rumble of a cement truck coming down the road.

"Hey, Fred. Where do you want them to back the truck in?" I did not want to disturb the landscaping already in place.

"Right between those two trees," Fred said as he pointed. "That's where the other truck backed in with the cement for the basement walls."

"Okay." Signaling for the driver to back the truck up exactly where Fred indicated, I stood where he could see me in his rearview mirror, directing him toward the house's framework. The driver's partner jumped out of the truck and assembled the chute, pointing it into the cellar where the newly mixed cement was to be poured.

I felt uneasy when I looked at the cement truck—something was odd about the angle of the truck—it seemed cockeyed or something. As I took a step forward for a closer look, the right rear tire sank about three feet into the ground. Then, very slowly, like a huge elephant trying to lie down, the cement truck tipped over on its side. A groaning metallic sound like that of the Titanic hitting the iceberg grew louder as the mixing drum, filled with fourteen thousand pounds of wet cement, separated from its frame, turning the cab of the truck sideways and elevating it ten feet above the ground. Fred and I stared in complete shock.

The chute man ran to the truck's cab, yelling, "Joe! Are you all right?" He didn't wait for an answer, just climbed up the overturned front tires and hoisted himself atop the passenger-side cab door, which was now parallel with the ground. I snapped into gear and ran to help.

"Joe, are you hurt?" he called in through the open side window, balancing on his bent arms as he peered inside.

I heard a muted reply and breathed a sigh of relief that Joe was responsive. "Joe—shut off the ignition. Now grab my arm and I'll hoist you up through the window." The air was tense.

"Oh my God, is he all right?" I yelled up to Joe's partner, wide-eyed with alarm.

"Stay back—everybody stay back," came the terse reply.

I turned and saw there was indeed an "everybody" in the form of curious and alarmed neighbors who had gathered on the street. "My wife is calling the fire department!" one man screamed. I was literally propelled into an otherworldly state of consciousness and it took time to sort things out. The confusing comments about the ignition, the call to stay back, and the S.O.S. to the fire department became clear as I realized with sickening dread that the truck was, of course, full of gasoline.

Fred was running all over like a crazy man, waving his arms and yelling, "Oh shit! Somebody do something!" to no one in particular as he viewed the disaster on his front lawn. The wail of sirens grew louder as several fire trucks, police cars, and an ambulance arrived at the scene. A tangle of thoughts ran through my brain as I tried to comprehend it all. How did this happen? Is the driver hurt? Will the truck explode? I have no insurance! Will I get arrested? Oh my God, this is horrible! What should I do? Will this be on TV? I feel like I'm gonna faint!

All at once, a crew of firemen, policemen, and EMTs were moving in all directions on the lot, talking on two-way radios, unwinding hoses, breaking up the spectators, and getting things under control. Joe, thank God, was standing in the street, talking to an EMT, looking dazed, but unharmed. A fireman was on the radio calling for tow trucks. A policeman who was listening to Fred's tirade and making notes came over to me and said, "Are you Lynn Donohue?"

"Yes, unfortunately." I was still stunned by the whole fiasco. "I'll need to get some information from you," he said efficiently, and I tried to focus on answering his questions.

The firemen had to cut open the truck's drum with power equipment and drain out the heavy wet cement into disposal trucks before the tow trucks could right the overturned cement truck.

I learned from a fireman that a septic system had been installed the week after the basement walls were poured, a fact that Fred had never mentioned to me. I didn't have to ask where.

Fred was on a rampage, raving at anyone who would listen, blaming me and the truck company for the whole mess.

"I'll see you in court!" he yelled to me as I got into my truck and slowly drove away. There was nothing else I could do here, and I just wanted to go home.

I walked in grimfaced and worn. Tim thought for a moment I was joking, but when I stared to cry as I related the awful details, he became quiet and subdued. "Well, the most important thing is that nobody got hurt. We better call our insurance man for advice." The company referred us to a local attorney, which we took as a very bad sign.

Attorney Halloran gathered the facts and took a "wait-and-see" attitude, which didn't make me feel any better. I was devastated, fearful of losing not only my work reputation but also my home, if I were sued.

I had a generic "contract" with Fred, written up on a pad from the local office-supply store, a staple item for my side jobs. What I didn't have was proof, other than my word, that Fred had not told me about the septic system but had directed me to have the driver go right over it. Fred, of course, claimed the exact opposite.

An old Lee Michaels song called *The Sue You, Sue Me Blues* came to mind as attorney Halloran explained the legal food chain at our second meeting. Here's how it went: the town of Rochester sued Fred, the cement company, and me for emergency services and environmental damages. Fred sued me and the cement company for negligence and damages. The cement company sued Fred and me for those same two things.

Over the next few months, I went to court several times and ultimately was found liable for most of the costs. However, since I didn't have insurance and Argus's net worth was very little at that point, all parties agreed not to pursue the matter, as it would cost them more in legal fees than they could recoup from me. Halloran advised me to countersue Fred and the cement company, but I decided against it. I never wanted to see the inside of a courthouse again.

I immediately went to see Mark O'Neil to purchase business insurance after the cement truck disaster. Mark was a cousin of our late friend Sean, and I could be honest about the legal mess I was in. "Well, you haven't thrown me out of your office yet, so that's a good sign."

He laughed and told me a few anecdotes about disasters a lot worse than mine and it made me feel better. Mark put a policy together and I paid for the first year in full, not wanting to take any chances on missing a monthly payment. I couldn't risk being uninsured even for a short time.

I was glad to be working in Boston because news of the cement disaster spread like wildfire throughout my own New Bedford local. I tried to keep quiet about it, only telling a few trusted friends like Jack Benevides and Bob Comeau. George Medeiros thought the union gossip, with me as scapegoat, was spread mainly by the cement truck company because they wanted to make sure no one pointed the finger at them. Frank Reed, who lived in Rochester, also heard about it at the local coffee shop and gave his brother Brian a clipping from the weekly Rochester paper to pass along to me. Good old Frank—always looking out for my best interests. The article was fairly unbiased, but I could imagine people blaming me since I was a woman trying to do a man's job. Keeping busy at Faneuil Hall helped me to distance myself from the talk, not only physically but emotionally as well. I would survive.

THE CREW

O nce the dust from the Rochester incident settled, I took on a few more side jobs but stuck to the simple ones that didn't require unfamiliar equipment or procedures. I was bored and ready again for a new challenge, but I was still cement-shy with Argus. Instead, I tried to persuade Brian to put me on more interesting tasks at Faneuil Hall. Some of the old-timers were constructing enormous round columns to support the walkway extensions on the second floor. Great precision was required to achieve a perfectly rounded appearance, and I wanted to try my hand at it.

"Come on, Brian—you know I'm a fast learner, and I want to bring my grandchildren here someday and tell them how I helped build those beautiful columns. Come on, give me a chance," I prodded him on the way to work.

He clutched his aching head with one hand and drove with the other, flinching every time my voice rose, intensifying his hangover pain. "Awright already, I give up—just stop talkin', would ya?"

I tried to keep my excitement in check so he wouldn't change his mind, and the next day I started on the columns and the hours flew by. The painstaking work took my full concentration. By the end of the day I had the rhythm and just wanted to keep going. Watching the old-timers lay the columns was like watching Michaelangelo sculpt *David*, then trying to imitate it. Though it took rigorous practice to imitate the masters, once I had the rhythm and the steps, I gradually improved.

At the end of my fifth day, one of the old pros looked at my work and said, "Not bad, not bad at all. You do pretty good work, for a girl."

I felt ten feet tall. "Thank you," I beamed.

Faneuil Hall and my small side jobs were just about right for this time in my life, which I dubbed the post-cement-disaster era. I still yearned to be a foreman and take on bigger side jobs, but I opted for stability, recovery, and sanity, which was rather unusual for me. In fact, I was very content.

On Thursday night when I arrived home, Tim's first words were urgent. "Call George Medeiros now."

"What's up?"

"I'm not sure, but he sounded pretty excited."

George was upbeat but reticent about the details, except to say he knew of a job that involved work for the Paul Cleary Company and he wanted me to look over the plans after work the next day. I prodded him for more information, but no luck on that. When I walked into the union hall, George was on the phone and motioned for me to sit down. He promptly hung up and greeted me with a smile.

"What's up? You look like the cat that ate the canary."

"And so will you, after I tell you the news. The Cleary Company is general contractor on an Osco Drug store job in Somerville, not far from where you're working now in Boston. It's new construction and the masonry company they had lined up just backed out. I don't have anybody else available right now, so I thought of you."

"New construction? That sounds like a big job."

"Well, it's bigger than your normal side jobs." He grabbed a roll of blueprints from behind his desk. "About thirty-three thousand brick and three thousand block."

I shook my head. "George, that's way out of my league."

He knew I had been hit hard by the cement disaster, and I figured he was trying to bring me back to my old brash self. I believed he had faith in me, that I could do this job. Still I hesitated.

Again, he spoke like father to daughter. "Well, you've been talking about starting your own business and you have to begin somewhere, right? I think you can handle it. Lynn, listen—take the plans home and look them over this weekend. If you don't think you're ready, I understand. But chances like this don't come along every day."

"Okay, I'll think about it—can I let you know on Monday?"

"No later. I have to let them know so they'll have time to get another contractor if you turn it down."

I thanked him and left the office. When I looked back, he was still grinning and I had the uncanny feeling he knew something I didn't.

"Oh, my God," I said that evening to Tim as I scoped out the Osco plans, "this would be a monster job for me! I'm not sure I'm ready, and besides, I need a bigger crew and a lot more equipment, and..."

Tim took a quick look at the plans and listened to my objections without saying anything. Finally he spoke tentatively, though he must have felt some conflict himself. I could read his thoughts—Well, the money would be good but, ahhhh, Lynn would eat and sleep the job and I would have to listen to the point of going mad, since she never keeps anything to herself...

Finally, Tim spoke up.

"Well, why don't you put in a bid anyway? You've got nothing to lose. If they don't pick you, at least you'll get some experience with the bid process. And if they do, well, you can always decline if you think it's too much."

What a great idea! I went into action, spending the rest of the weekend on the phone and paying visits to Jack, Bob, and Brian, barraging them with questions and concerns. By Sunday night, I arrived at a price of $49,500 and sent off an amateurish proposal to the Cleary Company. I was proud I had submitted a bid—that was something. It meant I was pulling myself up out of the cement. But I had no expectations, not really.

Brian was under the weather on the way to work the next day, recovering from a particularly bad hangover, and he squirmed when I told him about my proposal. "You know what your problem is? You've got more balls than brains!" He was sick of the whole subject, so I dropped it and after two weeks, forgot about it myself.

Tim and I had some big plans the following Monday, unusual for us on a work night. We were going out to dinner, then to the movies and home by my bedtime, eight o'clock. But all this changed when I returned from work and Tim met me on the porch. His mood was definitely up. "There's a message on the answering machine from Cleary."

"Oh. What? Cleary? What did they say?" My heart was pounding.

"Come in and listen for yourself."

I rushed in and pressed play—"Lynn, this is Paul Cleary. I received your proposal for the Osco job in Somerville. You were low bidder and we want to sign you up. I'll send you a contract by the end of the week. The masonry is scheduled to begin the third week of May. If you have any questions, you can reach me at 555-3304."

I looked at Tim in disbelief.

"Breathe, Lynn, breathe," he joked. "Congratulations—are you gonna do it?"

"Oh, my God!" I kept repeating.

"Come on, let's go to the movies anyway and we can talk about it on the way."

I washed up, changed, and hopped in the truck.

"Forget it—there's no way I can do it! I'm in a great position with Anastasia right now and, jeez, it would be dumb of me to give that up for this one job. The guys I work with, so many went off on their own and didn't make it. Brian tried having his own business and told me it was a bust. He gave it up after the first year. And what if I screw something up and then don't get paid? How will I pay my guys? Wait a minute…I don't even have any guys!"

On and on I rambled as Tim listened, agreeing on some points and challenging others. I was too distracted to go to the movies, so we settled for pizza and bed. I lay awake all night, agonizing over the pros and cons of climbing this new Everest when I wasn't an experienced climber.

The next morning, Brian picked me up as usual and I told him about Cleary's offer. I rattled on and on about my doubts and fears, speaking so fast I was leaving him behind.

"Jeez, Lynn—don't your batteries ever wear out?" Right then and there, he washed two Excedrin down with a swig of black coffee. "You're worse than the Energizer bunny."

Poor Brian listened to me babble about the Cleary job for three more days, offering advice intermittently. Finally, on Friday, he stopped me cold. "Lynn—you been drivin' me crazy all week askin' me what I think. You really wanna know?"

"Yup." I suddenly shrank in the seat and kept quiet.

"I think if you don't hurry up and make up your mind, I'll decide for you and fire you on the Faneuil Hall project. That's my job, remember?"

That did it. I resolved right then to take the leap. "Okay, I get the message. I'll go for it."

"Good! We'll be at the job in five minutes. You think you could manage to give my ears a rest until then?"

"Yeah," I shot back and I managed to keep my trap shut all the way to Faneuil Hall.

For the rest of the day, I tried to contain my excitement and concentrate on my work. "You're awful quiet today, Lynn," my mason tender observed. "You sick or somethin'?"

"Oh, what...no, I'm fine," I assured him and did my best to act normal, but once I was back in the truck with Brian heading home, I was bursting at the seams all over again.

"How can I be ready to start the job in only three short weeks? Where would I get the start-up money for materials? Should I rent the big equipment in New Bedford or Somerville? How do I handle payroll? What about taxes? Do I need extra insurance because of the size of the job? Where would I store the brick and block? What if I stored it at the site and it got stolen?"

Brian rolled his eyes, shook his head from side to side, and whined good-naturedly, "Will you give it a rest already? You don't have to figure it all out right this minute in the middle of rush-hour traffic, do ya? Call George Medeiros when you get home and he'll help you out with all that stuff. That's what he gets paid for, remember? Man, oh, man, am I glad I'm not married to you—I'd be in the nuthouse by now!"

I ran into the house and told Tim I'd decided YES.

"Yeah, go for it!" he shouted, making a fist.

Cleary's contract had arrived in the mail that day, so I read it through three times and spent the evening composing lists: Prep for Osco job, Questions for George, and so on. I estimated I'd need about twenty-nine grand for start-up materials, rental equipment, and payroll.

George was my cheerleader. "You're gonna do just fine," he said over bacon, eggs and homefries at the Sunrise Diner the next morning. "And remember, if Argus doesn't work out, you can always go back to union work, so no matter what, you can't lose."

He suggested I return to the bank and, if my father agreed, add on to the loan I already had. Then, as soon as I got reimbursed by Cleary, I could pay the bank back in full for the extra twenty-nine thousand dollars.

"Fine with me," said Dad, with growing faith in me. I was always on time with my monthly installment payments, so he was okay with me going a step further. I thanked him profusely and left. I still don't think he knew how much he was risking, but his new faith in me meant something. It was very healing.

The following week I made commitments to buy materials, put deposits on rental equipment, and arrange for deliveries to the job site in Somerville. Lakeville suppliers always gave me standard discounts, but delivery charges to the Boston area became prohibitive. I found out I was better off using Boston-area vendors and, looking ahead, I figured I should establish Boston accounts anyway.

George Medeiros informed me that, even though I planned to use only two bricklayers besides myself, I was required to hire one man from the Boston local to meet the 50 percent quota. I intended to do everything by the book, so I made an appointment with Chuck Raso, the Boston business agent who had given out the trophies at the apprentice contest. Anxiety over dealing with the big boys in Boston drove me to JC Penney, where I bought a light-blue business suit, white blouse, nylons, and heels. I scrubbed the dirt and grit from my fingernails, put my hair up in a French twist, dressed in my new power suit, and went to the meeting, knees trembling.

I met Chuck at the union office in Charlestown, not far from the famous Charlestown Shipyard, and he immediately put me at ease as we chatted about my fledgling business. He was not merely interested in my tale; he was also supportive and appreciated me coming to him to sign up a local bricklayer. None was available, however, so he said to go ahead and use two of my own men. I left his office with confidence, until it hit me that I didn't have even one bricklayer, never mind two!

I needed a few men who were great bricklayers, but not on top of the heap just yet—I wasn't established enough to lure the big fish like Jack Benevides and Ted Murphy. And, anyway, they seemed happy working locally and, being older, might not want to travel out of the area. Whiskey Pete was my first choice for Argus. Despite his drinking, he was a topnotch mason with a good attitude, unhampered by a big ego. Friendly and easygoing, he had been a close friend since my apprenticeship days. Attitude is as important as mastery of the craft in my book.

My second choice was Bob Lynch, a laborer I met on the St. Luke's Hospital job. Bob was like Pete, minus the drinking problem. If I can get them on this job, I figured I had a chance of making a good first impression as a union subcontractor. I was filled with fear.

Pete and I were like family, so I was comfortable calling him with my proposition. "Sure, Lynn, sure. Hey—why don't you come down to the bar and have a few drinks with me to celebrate your first big job?"

I politely declined and told him I'd be in touch when I had further details. Whew! One down and one to go. I flipped through the phone book searching for Bob Lynch's number.

I didn't know Bob that well, so this one would be harder. I picked up the phone, then hung up, picked it up again, put it down, then I thought I'd better track him down in person. Bob was the labor steward on the St. Luke's Hospital job, and the steward is always the last to leave, so I took a chance and went to the site. A year had passed since I'd left that job, and two more buildings were now up and running.

I arrived at the site and located him picking up wood scraps in the new cafeteria. On the way, I tried out different approaches. "Hi, Bob—remember me? The girl? Well, I have no money, no contracting experience, I flubbed a job with a cement truck and became a laughingstock, and I want you to quit working here and come work for me on the other side of Boston on the first big job I've ever tackled as a businesswoman. Oh yeah, and the other mason I hired has a blood-alcohol level that's off the charts. What do you say?"

Somehow, I didn't think that speech would inspire him to give his two-week notice, so I decided to wing it.

Bob was surprised to see me and we chatted about a side job we had worked on together and my recent work at Faneuil Hall before we got down to business. Finally, I decided to just jump in with both feet—the worst that could happen was he'd say no. I launched into a brief description of the Cleary job and all the preparations I'd made to date. Bob listened politely, his hazel eyes twinkling at my enthusiasm.

As I wound up my sales pitch, Bob was quiet and thoughtful. "Well, Lynn, I'll be havin' to give this one some thought."

I planned to shake his hand and ask him to call me when he reached a decision. What I did instead astonished even me. "Please, Bob, I'm begging you, please, please work with me. I just know it will be great and there's no way I can do it without you!" At that moment, I realized just how much I really wanted my own company. Bob said again he really needed to think it over and he'd call me.

The next day the work at Faneuil Hall seemed to drag on forever. On my lunch break I called Tim to see if Bob had responded, but nothing yet. As soon as Brian dropped me off, I ran into the house and saw the blinking light. The guys didn't like talking to answering machines, so I often heard a beep, then silence, another beep, then the phone went dead. I hoped that wouldn't be the case now. I pressed the button tentatively. Beep, a brief pause, then a voice: "This is Bob. Give me a call at 555-3215. Thank you."

With trembling hands, I dialed his number, mumbling all the while, "Please say yes, say yes, please, please, please." Bob answered and we exchanged greetings, but his voice didn't give me a clue what to expect. He was a kind of Jimmy Stewart type and spoke with a slow drawl. "Well, I'll be puttin' in another two weeks at St. Luke's, but after that I'll be open. So...what the heck...I'll do it."

"Oh, my God, oh, thank you so much, Bob, you won't be sorry!" I gushed, overjoyed at his decision. I must have sounded like a high-school cheerleader.

"By the way, did ya know I have family in Somerville? And I've not seen them for a while."

"Hey, great. I'd love to meet them and I'll take you all out for dinner."

Bob tittered. "That's very kind, but we're eleven brothers and sisters. Throw in the families and there's well over fifty of us!"

"Ya know, it doesn't matter. I'm flying so high you said YES, you can bring them all!"

Now that I had all the pieces—a crew, a contract, start-up money, materials, and rental equipment—it was time to give my notice to Anastasia Brothers. Brian, of course, already knew about my decision, and so did George Medeiros, so I only needed to notify Anastasia's project manager, who hand-delivered our paychecks each week. After that, I felt comfortable telling the guys at Faneuil Hall, and they all wished me luck. I arrived with boxes of Dunkin' Donuts on my last day to thank everyone for making the Boston job such a great experience for me. Then I said goodbye and plunged into the unknown.

The new job began on Monday. I was so crazy with excitement and anxiety, I hardly slept on Friday and Saturday nights, but on Sunday I slept from sheer exhaustion. Monday morning at 4:45AM, I picked up Bob at a supermarket parking lot one exit north of Lakeville. We were all business—we planned on arriving in Somerville by six o'clock and having breakfast before Cleary's starting time an hour later. Otherwise, we'd bog down in the middle of Boston's rush hour, and there was no avoiding the city to get to Somerville. Leaving before sunrise made sense to us both. On the drive up, we laughed about the radio traffic reports that referred to rush "hour," which was really four hours, and "the expressway," where traffic came to a halt and inched forward in drabs and spurts.

I made sure I was on site when the materials were delivered, not only to check for accuracy, but because I loved the excitement of it all. When the truck dumped its load of sand and it sparkled in the early-morning sun, it looked like a mountain of gold to me, and now that I owned Argus, the gold was profit in my mind's eye. Fortunately, Cleary had taken on-site safety and security precautions, surrounding the entire area with chain link fencing and posting it with the name and number of the security company that guarded it nights and weekends. Bob warned me that the Davis Square area was a tough neighborhood and suggested I secure the cement mixer with a lock and chain each night. We also brought in tarps to cover the sand pile and other materials that were left on site.

Shortly after I arrived, a young laborer drove a truck up to the Cleary trailer and an older man climbed out. From his briefcase and stash of blueprints, I knew he must be Dan Tripp, the chief superintendent, so I introduced myself and immediately smelled the telltale reek of alcohol on his breath. I knew too well the look of an alcoholic: the bloodshot eyes, ruddy complexion, trembling hands, and familiar odor, and Dan scored 100 percent on all counts.

But Dan also scored high in job knowledge and expertise. By nine o'clock, I could see he was a master at running a professional operation from the bottom up. The work I was hired to do was clear enough, so after our brief conversation, I felt comfortable being on my own. Bob and I planned to spend the first week hauling concrete blocks into the basement area in preparation for Pete's arrival the following Monday. Given my first "real" job as head of Argus, I would act as owner, foreman, payroll clerk, bookkeeper, bricklayer, laborer, and gopher. I wanted control of everything, no surprises. And anything I expected my crew to do, I was willing to do myself. That's the kind of boss I wanted to be.

Lugging the blocks all week turned out to be great therapy for me and kept my anxiety level at an even keel. When Pete joined us, he and I partnered up on the block work, building the basement walls, while Bob acted as mason tender and laborer.

No matter how often I heard it, I always felt a rush of excitement when the cement mixer started up each morning. Its rumble was like the sound of a Ferris wheel when I was a kid and waiting my turn. The familiar sounds that followed—the "thump-thump" of block being stacked and cries of "mortar here!"—were like music to my ears. Once the linemen got working full speed, the sounds of the job blended together like a symphony. The repetition of brick, mortar, brick, mortar set the tempo, clicking away like a metronome, and the thumping of block and brick, block and brick sounded like a drumbeat. All the sounds made up the melody—the shouts of the men, the revving of the trucks, the creaking of the staging. Whenever I heard classical music overtures, I pictured a busy job site instead of an orchestra.

During the first two weeks I hit Dan with some questions, but he disappeared after nine each morning, leaving a foreman named Joseph in charge. Dan made no bones about it. He said he'd be on the site from seven to nine only, so that was the best time to catch him. After that, I could find him at the Oxford Club nearby. A laborer informed us that Dan spent his days in the bar nearest each and every job. Cleary was aware of their chief superintendent's habits, but retained him because of his seniority and superior skills. Dan always saw Cleary's projects to completion without incident, which was somewhat of a miracle since he was on the job site only two hours a day. He had lost his driver's license for good, so Cleary arranged for a worker to pick him up and drop him off.

I had met a lot of Dans over the years at the Belmont and in the union, and I got sick inside to see what alcoholism did to them and their families. Strangely, they maintained a normal life to some degree. From nine to three, Dan drank just enough so he could still answer questions and handle situations on the job. After that, all bets were off. But he arrived on time the next day and performed his duties. So sane and so crazy at the same time.

"That's terrible, drinking on the job like that," said Pete in all seriousness. "Hey, I like my whiskey, but you'll never catch me drinking before quitting time."

Bob and I exchanged wry glances, thinking of the many times we had seen Pete put down two or three beers, and sometimes a shot of whiskey or two, on lunch break. Was he kidding? Did he really think he didn't drink on the job? Or was it the alcohol speaking?

One day I had to hunt Dan down at the Oxford with a question only he could answer. When I left the bright sunshine and entered the smoky tavern, I could see nothing; I was lost in a vast smoky haze. I had recently become a nondrinker, as I wanted to be as sharp and professional as possible. Bars were not my hangouts anymore.

"Yeah, whadayawant?" asked a listless barmaid. I asked for Dan and she pointed toward the far end of the bar.

As I stumbled in his direction, I was overcome by a moment of truth. Ohmigod, that dead-eyed barmaid could be me, this dark, hellish bar could be my workplace, this dingy, dank place could be my life were it not for the fact that I'd walked away from it. Thank God, I had found a trade I loved. I didn't want to mess with that; I wanted to be the best I could be. I could have been this sour young woman and, in truth, I had come so very close.

I wanted to shake her and say—There's a world out there. Go for it! But you can't save other people. Hadn't I learned that by now?

Dan was stinking drunk but he took me on like a pro, even answering my questions with precision. He was a clear and concise drunk. I couldn't ask for more than that.

"Thanks, Dan," I said, heading out into the sunlight. Millions of people spend their days in dark taverns like this one, I thought, and I blew a kiss to the gods, grateful I was no longer one of them.

By our fourth week laying brick, Bob, Pete, and I were a team. Dan inspected our area every morning and gave it his stamp of approval. To my surprise, Chuck showed up on the job site that Friday with the union paperwork, and he took time to inspect our work as well. "Great job."

I felt honored he'd stopped by and given us high praise. That night I did the books, filling out the requisition form for Cleary so I could get reimbursed for my first month's expenses. I was no bookkeeper so I just used common sense. I listed everything I'd spent to date, including payroll, and made sure my backup receipts and time sheets matched the grand total. After three attempts, it came out right. This was my least favorite task, and I hoped to hire someone someday to take it away. Meanwhile, I gave the forms to Dan, and he casually said Cleary would send a check in four to six weeks.

Another two weeks and we finished the entire job. Both the block-work and the brick-work looked great, and Dan let Cleary know we excelled in all ways. Pete and Bob had given it their all and it showed. I was grateful beyond words for their help in getting me through my first official union contract as the owner of Argus Construction. When I totaled up the contract price minus the expenses, I realized I had made almost twelve thousand dollars in profit!

I submitted my final requisition forms in person at Cleary's New Bedford office and asked if the check from my first requisition was ready. It was and I scooped it up, eager to pay off the bank's twenty-nine thousand dollars and prove to my father I was a good investment. While there, I asked to speak to Paul Cleary to thank him for the opportunity he'd given me, but he ended up thanking me! And lo and behold, he offered Argus another job. I tried not to jump up and down like a kid as I listened to the details.

The next job would be more complicated and anxiety producing—this I could tell from a quick visit to the new site. GZA Drilling had hired Cleary to build a new business headquarters in Brockton. The company used super-large equipment, and a huge warehouse was included in the plans. I quickly estimated that I would need ten men. Ten men! What was I thinking? How could I be responsible for ten men? Not so long ago, I hadn't a clue about how to be responsible for myself.

Anyway, I took the plans home that night and called Paul the next morning. "I calculate a price of sixty-nine thousand dollars and a time frame of two months," I relayed with surprising confidence. He mailed me the contract and thus began another adventure.

Argus's job was to construct the entire building exterior in concrete block. I had enough cash left from Osco to pay the start-up costs for Brockton, and I opened charge accounts with my new Boston vendors.

Once again, I paraded in to see George Medeiros for advice on handling the unfamiliar aspects of the new job. George was at his best, offering bits of homespun wisdom.

"Listen, Lynn, don't ever let the size of a job scare you off. It's exactly like a side job, only there's more of everything. More materials, more men, more time, more paperwork. But when it's done, you get more money!

"You need to hire five men from the Brockton local, and I'm going to warn you about the laborers' business agent there. He's a guy named Lefty, and he's a son of a bitch. He's gonna try to give you the bottom of the barrel for workers, so stand up to him, give it right back."

Oh, Lefty, give me a break, I prayed.

Whiskey Pete and Bob Lynch gave the okay to work the GZA job, and I planned on working it myself, so I needed two more of my own crew to match the five I'd get from Brockton. I thought of Henry Atwood, the friendly man I'd met while working for MF, who took me under his wing on the Car Barn job. Henry and I did several side jobs together, and he was great at hopping from one task to another. I needed a jack-of-all-trades on this job, so I could concentrate on supervising and laying block myself. I called him at home that night and he jumped at the chance. He was between jobs and knew that a Cleary job was a good move.

Next I thought of Ted Murphy, the legend who could handle everybody else's botches on a job. If some of my guys were less than great, Ted would save the day. Also, if I couldn't lay brick as much as I planned to, Ted had the speed and skill to handle his load and mine, too. I was a little nervous about asking him, so Pete offered to do it. They saw a lot of each other on side jobs, and I thought Pete would get a yes.

But, no. Pete called the next day. "Ted's not interested. He said he'd never work for a woman."

I wasn't laughing. I was hurt, even though it was Ted's loss. Of course he'd never work for a woman! What was I thinking? I was thinking what a terrific opportunity for *him*. But now, I hoped he'd look at himself someday and see how foolish he really was. He lost himself a good job that day.

I figured it this way: If I provided regular work at good pay, union members would be happy to work for Argus. There was plenty of security in being a "company man," just as I had been with Anastasia Brothers. I had never forgotten Ted's statement that I was not tall enough, strong enough, or "man" enough to be a mason. By this time, I hoped he would have changed his mind, but underneath that hard-hat was a thick skull.

Time was running out. George Medeiros couldn't find anyone, and I didn't want to waste any more time on the phone, so I finally asked the Brockton local for six bricklayers instead of five. I still needed two laborers. I went to Lefty and prepared for the worst, but he was surprisingly decent.

"I'll send you two men next week. Nice meeting you, Mrs. Argus."

I giggled all the way home. As time went by, I got used to getting mail and messages for Lynn Argus. Another take on the name came from a bricklayer who hailed from Maine. "I thought you chose the name because 'I guess' is the standard reply to questions like 'Can you do this job for me?' " I often told the anecdote so the Argus name would stick like glue in people's ears.

Dan again acted as superintendent for Cleary in Brockton and ran a tight ship, then got tight himself at the nearest bar. By the end of the third week, all the kinks had been worked out, and I was pleased with the crew and their speed in laying block.

We finished the job three days ahead of schedule, and once again, Dan and Paul were pleased with Argus's performance. Cleary promised to call if more work came up. I asked Paul for a letter of recommendation I could use in pursuing other bid opportunities. He gave me a glowing review.

Tim and I went out to a real restaurant that night instead of the usual pizza parlor. And why not? After deducting expenses, I had earned a grand total of twenty-nine thousand dollars profit for my first two jobs with Cleary and I wanted to celebrate. If I kept that up, I could count on close to sixty thousand dollars profit for my first year. Tim hadn't been happy at his job for some time, but we'd agreed to wait and see how Argus went before he made any moves. Now he could give his two-week notice to Voke Tech and go to school.

The now-famous annual Fourth of July party drew the usual festive crowd, and we couldn't wait to tell them about our new paths. This year we served up shish kebab instead of hot dogs, and we added fresh-baked cheesecakes and a professional disc jockey. I also invited many co-workers and their families and Tim invited his friends from the gym-and-track club. Pam helped us get ready, but Jason was now a teenager and preferred to hang out with his friends. We missed the old mix and hoped this new group would work out.

And so they arrived—old hippies, marathon runners, tavern regulars, union brothers—you name it, we had it. Some were now married with children and others had moved away, returning only to visit. While Tim and I cleaned up the yard on Sunday night, we talked about the difference in our lives since we'd had our first party. Neither of us said it, but I knew we were both thinking of Sean, wishing he were still here with us, perhaps with a wife and children in tow. No matter how much time passed, we felt his absence, especially at times like this.

The next year flew by and just as I was consumed by Argus, Tim was consumed by school. Too much so, we both learned. When you've got your high beams fixed in one place, there's a blind spot somewhere else. We had some hard days coming up.

WHAT COMES AROUND...

Tim often talked about going to college and earning a degree in motor development, inspired by his sister Meg with her special needs. He needed something more fulfilling than custodial work at Voke. For the rest of that summer, Tim helped me with the multitude of tasks required to run Argus and in September, he started his freshman year at Bristol Community College in Fall River. His class schedule allowed him time to help me during the week, just enough to take the edge off.

I subscribed to the *New England Construction News*, a weekly publication that listed all the projects out to bid in the region. Vista Corporation had several listings for subcontractors in the Middleboro area, so I called and made arrangements to pick up plans and put in bids on three different jobs. Nine days after I mailed my quotes, I showed up at their public bid opening.

In order to meet federal and state regulations, most projects had to be publicly advertised, and sealed bids had to be opened at a scheduled time and place in front of a panel of officials and any contractors who wished to be there. This process was supposed to prevent favoritism and fraud, though these things were still prevalent. Much to my surprise, I was awarded all three jobs because I was the lowest qualified bidder. The profit margin I factored into my bids was fairly low compared to that of other companies, but I consciously bid low to get the work and establish myself in the industry.

The first Vista job was about the same scale as the last Cleary project, and I used the same Argus crew and added my old pal Jay Dias to the lineup. For the next two Vista jobs, I hired nine new men besides my existing crew. As I originally intended, I hired men from my union local, especially those who were good workers but didn't get regular shots at the best jobs. My friends from the early days with MF Construction, Phil and Carlos, joined up first. Next came Sam, Tony, Alex, Armand, and Francisco, all hard-working men grateful for steady work to get them through the year.

In order to make a good impression on the Vista jobs and continue building Argus's reputation, I needed to hire a few more topnotch masons and experienced foremen. Unfortunately, a great many men who qualified had strong personalities and big egos, which didn't threaten me personally but affected the atmosphere on a job. I didn't want the easy camaraderie already established at Argus to be compromised, but I also needed to move forward.

Brian Reed had been following my progress and said a quick yes to my offer of employment. Winter was approaching and work was getting scarce, so more and more masons were available. I always checked with George Medeiros before making an offer to anyone. If he didn't have any good opportunities lined up for the man I was pursuing, he gave me his blessing. George appreciated this courtesy and said I was one of the few business owners who operated that way.

When Brian was about to start the third Vista job, he quietly asked me if I would consider hiring his brother Frank, and I, gulp, fell silent at the memory. How could I hire someone who had disparaged and humiliated me when I was trying to make my way as an apprentice? On the other hand, how could I not? Wasn't this my chance to show character and an open heart? Hell, no, I wasn't a saint. But couldn't I take a chance?

And so it went, swinging this way and that. For sure, I was no longer the insecure apprentice who wilted under Frank's assaults, but inviting the enemy to be on my team was quite another thing.

Anyway, this is how I resolved it: I absolutely loved the idea of being Frank's boss. And as my mother always told me, "Keep your enemies close."

Brian explained that Frank had been a fun-loving guy at one time, but alcohol broke up his marriage. He stopped drinking cold turkey without attending AA or any other rehab program.

"He's what they call a dry drunk," said Brian, "as opposed to me, which I guess you could call a wet drunk."

I knew the term "dry drunk" referred to a person who didn't drink but still had unresolved anger, making him miserable to be around at times. Despite his attitude problem, Frank was an experienced foreman and a skilled mason, precisely what I wanted. I told Brian to go ahead, ask him. Ask him! I had made my decision.

As soon as I heard Frank's voice on the phone, I felt apprehensive, like I used to feel as a child when I heard Dad's voice or footsteps. I quickly reminded myself that the tables were turned and I was the one in the driver's seat. The conversation was awkward for both of us, so I was overfriendly, which made it worse. Frank nonchalantly agreed to work for me, but made it clear he expected to be made foreman if the opportunity arose. I thought about it briefly and said okay, so we agreed to join forces on the third Vista job.

The three projects went along as smooth as silk, except for the money—I had to literally chase down the owners for payment. More than once, I used the profits from the Cleary jobs to meet payroll, then waited for Vista so I could pay myself back. Brian, who had once ran his own business, told me I'd lucked out with Cleary because most companies he subbed for weren't good at making payments without some pestering. He gave me some tips on bill collecting, and I finally wrung out the last nickel and dime from Vista.

The small, modest memo pad in the top right-hand drawer of my desk began to take on great importance in my life. On the first page was my old goal: "In five years, I will have $100,000 profit in the bank." My signature and the date, May 26, 1982, followed. I had been faithfully repeating that goal every day and envisioning the goal as a reality.

The profit I made from each side job was listed on the next few pages. After that was an entry on the day I incorporated Argus Construction, August 9, 1983. Three pages later, I had listed profits from Osco, GZA, and Vista. It was now November 14, 1984, and when I deposited my final check from Vista, the total profit was $103,268. A ripple of joy ran through me as I realized I had not only achieved, but surpassed, my five-year goal in two and a half years.

Somewhere along the way, I had decided it wasn't a bad thing for women to make money. The thing about money, I was slowly learning, is not that you can buy stuff with it. Hell, I didn't have time to buy stuff and I didn't much care about buying stuff anyway. But money was giving me something I never had before—power, and power means options in your life.

I often thought about the women in my old South End neighborhood, how if they'd had a penny to their names, they wouldn't have had to stick it out with their drunken husbands. The men were the breadwinners and the women had no options. If women don't feel entitled to money, they should start practicing. I don't mind saying I was in awe of the fact that I was making money, saving money, and it was accumulating in an account. How about that? It was amazing. Hey, I was really doing it.

But there were costs too and, in the end, they had to be figured in.

That Saturday night, Tim, Pam, Donny, and I went out to celebrate my new-found wealth. Celebrating was something we hadn't done in a long time as I had little time for fun. "How do I look?" I asked Tim, feeling like a movie star in my sleek black dress and high heels, hair in a French twist, earrings dangling, sparkling.

"Like a million bucks."

We began, appropriately enough, with dinner at Dunfey's in Hyannis, where I'd received my apprentice contest award. Then we danced the night away to a live band playing all the latest disco hits. I went to bed that night blissfully happy—I had Tim, my work, and my little black notebook. And Freud wondered what a woman wants?

The next bid awarded to Argus was familiar territory—the old Sunset Hill project in Fall River that had gone bankrupt a few years before. I knew the site well and put in a detailed bid, mentioning in my cover letter that I'd worked on the site before. I had mixed feelings about going back there, remembering that musty basement with the motley demo crew. But the truth was, I was anxious about not having enough work. Now that I had a larger crew, I felt obligated to keep them working steadily, one of the overwhelming responsibilities of running Argus.

I also felt guilty about not spending enough time with my family and friends and especially missed my heart-to-heart talks with Pam. Now a Marion resident, Pam and I kept in touch, but her job as a crisis specialist for a Boston property management firm left her with a hectic schedule too, even turning her into a frequent flyer. How had we both gone from being hippies to successful businesswomen? Jason was in high school already, and he and Donny did some serious bonding while Pam was away on business trips. When we finally got together, we always ended up yakking about our careers and how tough it was to juggle work and a home life, too.

Meanwhile, as Jason reached college age, Pam was already dreading the empty nest; she would miss him terribly. And she felt him pulling away—she wanted to spend time with him, but he wanted to be with his friends. All very normal but painful, too.

Pam and I were like sisters, and Jason was like my own son. I admired the great job she did as a single mother of little means and how she had grown. We often went through the same trials and tribulations at the same time and knew each other's hearts.

One Sunday evening when we managed to get together for dinner, I was telling her how quickly Argus had taken off. She asked what I was doing in detail, and when I ran down the list—bidding, bricklaying, hiring, firing, supervising, bookkeeping, payroll, billing, errands, and business meetings—she said that from the sounds of it, the next thing on that list would probably be a heart attack. How eye-opening it is when someone else has to tell you what a load you're carrying! Clearly, I needed more staff support.

I called Clarence Whatmough, the most experienced superintendent I knew, and offered him a position with Argus. He had taught me a lot when I worked for him on the wastewater treatment plant project in Fall River. We agreed to meet and discuss it. Clarence was a real pro and I'd be lucky to get him.

"Perfect timing!" he said over lunch the next day. "How did you know? I've been with Westcott Company forever, it seems, and they're phasing out their masonry division, which I ran. I like what you have to say, but I'm getting close to retirement and want to scale down a bit. I'll talk to my wife and get back to you."

The next day he called back. "Okay, Lynn, I'll do it. I accept your offer." He also noted that Westcott had sent a lot of work out to bid. "Have you thrown your hat in the ring for the masonry subcontracts?"

No, I had not, so he mailed me some plans and I prepared bids for three of the jobs. I figured he'd put in a word for Argus and give us a good shot at it.

Well, as it turned out, more than a good shot. Argus got the call to do all three projects, all on Cape Cod: additions to the telephone company and town hall in Harwich and a new fire station in Yarmouth. All three jobs were in close proximity to each other, and my New Bedford local included the Cape, so I could use my own Argus crew and make up the other 50 percent through George Medeiros. A perfect situation! Clarence lived in Orleans, farther "down Cape," so he was happy to have a shorter commute than usual.

Once the word got out that Clarence was on board, I began getting calls from bricklayers asking if they could work for me. What a feeling! All three Westcott projects went off without a hitch, but how could they not? How can you top having Clarence, the former Westcott veteran masonry superintendent, acting as foreman for Argus? Clarence did much of the paperwork, too, a huge relief for me. The checks from Westcott arrived within two weeks of our submittals, the quickest turnaround time I had ever experienced.

Now that I was a bona fide business owner, I was shielded from the personal attacks I had endured as a worker, but my presence on job sites still caused a commotion. Hiring Clarence proved beneficial for Argus in more ways than one. General contractors were more comfortable dealing with a seasoned male masonry veteran than a twenty-seven-year-old female newcomer, and it put the Argus regulars and the union men at ease, too. Clarence could be trusted to run a job, so my workload became lighter.

On a Thursday night, after I deposited the last of the Westcott checks and paid the bills, I calculated my profit on all three Westcott jobs. When the adding machine spit out the final figure, I shouted, "Tim! Come here, quick!"

"What's the matter?" He hurried over to my desk and looked over my shoulder, as if expecting to see a big bug.

"Look at this!" I pointed to the adding machine tape, which read $150,000.

"What's that?"

"My total profit from the Westcott jobs!"

"Wow," said Tim, as astonished as I was.

"Tim...I think we're rich!"

"We're on our way, that's for sure."

Tim was excited. He was not against women making money, and he got a kick out of the whole thing, considering where we'd started. My making money was not a threat to his ego. It was *our* money.

By this time, we decided we needed a financial planner, since we didn't know anything about finances or investing. Until now, we had just left our money in the Argus account earning a standard rate of interest. We called our accountant, Dave LaPalme, and he referred us to an experienced investment specialist. During our first meeting with Steve White, we discovered that Tim had an aptitude for investing, an area I neither understood nor wanted to. Tim agreed to work with Steve in setting up an aggressive investment portfolio.

Tim was as quiet about pursuing his goals as I was loud about mine. He graduated with an associate's degree from Bristol Community College and began working toward his bachelor's degree at Bridgewater State College. Always active in sports, he continued to keep physically fit by working out at the gym, bicycling, and running road races. He kept a close watch on our new investment portfolio, and I felt confident that Argus profits would soon be earning profits of their own.

I had become a true believer in writing down and envisioning my goals since my success with goal number one. And now I was about to embark on goal number two, which also concerned money: "I will establish a $100,000 retirement account by December 1991." Not bad for a woman who hadn't hit thirty yet.

Jack Benevides had advised me to set up a pension plan, no matter how meager, as soon as possible. "Old age sneaks up on you," he often said, "so you'd best get ready for it now." Most of the older masons were big on pension planning. I was also aware of the serious injuries common to my trade and wanted to set a little nest egg aside, just in case.

I wrote down the goal in detail and put the paper in the top dresser drawer, just as I had done before. Next, I went about my little ritual, which may seem nutty but I found it incredibly affirming. I looked at myself in the mirror and repeated the goal out loud several times. Then I copied it onto my little memo pad, signed and dated it June 14, 1986, and put it in its place in the top right-hand drawer of my desk. Every day, I repeated my new goal to myself.

Clarence was a wise man and, as our work relationship thrived, I began to depend on him for his advice and consent. Above all, he felt Argus absolutely needed more office space and he was right—I had trouble finding space in our tiny home to lay out blueprints, and we were tired of moving piles of paperwork around to get to whatever was beneath them. Working from home made me feel like I never left the office, and now that Clarence worked at the house, our home had literally become the office. Tim was all for a move.

He located a nice little cottage for sale on Assawompset Pond, a reservoir within a few miles of our present house. We called the realtor and fell in love with the location. A good-sized lawn led up to a screened-in front porch at ground level. Outside the living room was a wraparound porch that met the water's edge and upstairs, a cozy bedroom overlooked the sparkling lake. A driveway ran alongside the cottage, which had been winterized the year before.

We decided to buy the cottage and use it as our main residence. Located off the beaten path, it was quaint and cozy, and the water view was calming, something I definitely needed at the end of a long day. Mugsy became a full-time water dog, spending hours walking to and fro in knee-deep water as he searched for minnows and other intriguing creatures around the pier. Every weekend, friends came over and we swam and had cookouts. The cottage was a perfect retreat, separating home from office.

Meanwhile, I struck up an instant friendship with a woman named Geraldine who lived next door and began spending time with her every evening, watching the sunset over the water.

"Life," she would say.

"Yeah, life," I'd agree, and we both knew what we meant after a hard day's work.

Geraldine was a quirky person, and she thought I was a flake, so we got along just fine. In her late thirties, she was divorced, with two grown daughters and grandchildren who lived in New Hampshire. She shared the cottage with her mother and brother. Her mother suffered from health and psychiatric problems, and her brother battled drug and alcohol problems. She was their principal caretaker, and her generous hands were full.

Geraldine was an interesting mix: smart and vivacious with an adventurous spirit but utterly lacking adventure in her life. She worked as a nurse in a local hospital, then did double duty at home. I was determined to bring some fun into her life and perhaps into my life, too. In the next months, we would attend a Madonna concert dressed in leather and lace, take a course in meditation, and go on a quest to find the best sushi bar in the Boston area.

Tim talked her into taking up body building to stay in shape, and she took to it like a fish to water, participating in local body building competitions. I stuck some pictures of female body builders from Tim's magazines on our refrigerator and glued photos of her face onto the bodies. We laughed ourselves silly.

One night on her porch, she looked at me and said, "I don't like myself much. I don't like my freckles. I don't like my stringy hair. And I'm sick of wearing these thick glasses. How am I ever going to get a boyfriend looking like this?"

I had no idea she wanted a boyfriend. "You know, Geraldine, there's lots of help out there today, beauty products and such. You need to make the most of what you've got, and you've got a lot." I was telling the truth; her intelligence alone should have attracted a good man. "Hey, I've got it. Let's do a makeover weekend and get beautiful."

We did exactly that. Took a weekend off and got facials, haircuts, and contact lenses for Geraldine.

"Ohmigod, I don't look half-bad," said Geraldine, staring in the mirror.

The thing was, she felt beautiful, and that made a huge difference. Then, sure enough, she met a friendly man in the health food store and accepted his offer to dinner. She hadn't been romantically involved since her divorce many years ago, so this was a really big deal. Pam and I took her shopping for a dress and makeup and got her all dolled up for her big night out.

When her date arrived, Pam, my sister Dawn, and I peeked out the window like worried parents and watched her go. An hour later, as we sat drinking tea and talking, we heard a car drive up. Good grief, it was Geraldine and her date!

We all ran to the door. "Wha...What happened?"

"Well, as we were driving to the restaurant, Ken told me he'd devoted the last ten years to searching for a 'Sasquatch-like' creature he believed lived in the woods of Bridgewater."

"What?" My mouth flew open.

"He showed me an article from a bounty hunter magazine with a picture of him dressed in a camouflage uniform and hat, and he was pointing to a large map marked with his 'sightings' of the giant creature."

"You're kidding," said Dawn, perplexed.

"The bottom line was, he was searching for a woman to help him in his quest and he wanted to know if I was the one. I politely said no and wished him well, then asked him to take me home because I had a headache. And I really did after that."

We roared so hard our stomachs hurt, and Geraldine joined in as we got sillier and sillier. The next day, I bought a copy of the *National Enquirer* with Bigfoot on the cover and a headline that screamed, "I was forced to have Bigfoot's Baby!!!" A young woman in a rocking chair held a strange-looking baby in a blanket next to an inset photo of Bigfoot himself. I glued a picture of Geraldine's head onto the woman's body, and she framed it and hung it on the living room wall. From then on, we concentrated more on friendship than romance. Pam, Dawn, and I, and our other friends, too, loved Geraldine and we spent many happy weekends hanging out together at the water's edge.

Our old Vaughn Street home now served as Argus's headquarters, and with the move came several benefits. We could write off a large percentage of the cost of maintaining the house as a business expense. The rooms could be divided into four offices, and the garage and yard were perfect for equipment storage. I decided to keep the storage space I rented in nearby Middleboro, since it looked as though Argus was on a growing spree.

A beautiful outdoor sign announced our new headquarters to visitors and passersby. Two beveled wooden posts painted a bright white supported a metal sign with a brick-red background and big black letters that spelled out *Argus Construction, Inc. Lynn Donohue, President.* I used a whole roll of film taking pictures of it for my portfolio.

Argus's next job was constructing the Edgartown Middle School on Martha's Vineyard, off the coast of Cape Cod. Rich Construction of Boston was the general contractor, and there was an extensive amount of brickwork to be done. The owner, Mr. Walter Rich, had been impressed with Argus's references from Cleary, Vista, and Westcott and wanted a firm that had experience on the Cape, where the native "Cape Codders" tended to be picky about hiring contractors who respected the tranquility of the natural surroundings.

Clarence knew the best Cape union men for the job and gave me his list of names. I looked at the list and froze. Ohmigod, Russell

Carleton was among them! My mind flashed back to that fateful day on the New Bedford bus terminal job when I'd almost quit masonry because Russell's verbal abuse was nearly destroying me. After Arnie convinced me to stay, I recalled walking by Russell and thinking—*Just you wait, you bastard, you'll be working for me someday.*

I shared my story with Clarence, who agreed Russell could be whiny and difficult, but he felt his skill level and good reputation as a Cape native outweighed the negative. Clarence also knew that Russell had been out of work for two months and would grab the opportunity.

"He'll behave himself, I'll see to it," he assured me.

It was another test of character for me. I had taken on Frank and it was working out well. He was doing his job and keeping his attitude to himself. But taking on Russell was a different story. He had treated me horribly and now I was considering hiring him, in which case I would treat him decently to boot. And why not? I was no longer his target. I had the power to be decent.

"Let's do it."

I arranged for the Argus crew to fly over to the island, and Clarence showed me how to calculate meal, hotel, and travel allowances. Most of the crew opted to stay on the island from Monday to Friday, then fly home for the weekend. The job, which required sixteen men, was expected to last for two months, so Clarence and I went over the figures twice to be sure we included enough money to cover the unusual extras like freight costs back and forth on the ferry. After all, the bricks needed to get there, too.

I chose to take the supply truck via the ferry to the island as needed, which gave me a perfect opportunity to talk with CEO Walter Rich. He was a wealthy man, smart and savvy, and I learned a lot about the ins and outs of owning a construction business. He was delighted with my inquisitiveness and full of tales about the lessons he'd learned on his journey to success.

One lesson stood out from the rest. He said I should always hand out paychecks myself—it made the employees feel important and appreciated when the company's owner hand-delivered their wages and also reminded them of who they were working for.

When the first week's paychecks were ready, I took the ferry over with the checks in hand.

Looking over the job site and seeing sixteen union men toiling away under the Argus Construction signage was a beautiful sight. My regular crew greeted me with enthusiasm, and I made sure to inspect and praise every man's work as I handed out the paychecks. I also wrote them thank-you cards to let them know how much their work was appreciated.

When I reached Russell, he looked flustered and his face turned beet red. He looked down and didn't say anything.

I thought of all the old stuff I'd rehearsed over and over in my head to inflict as much pain on Russell as he had on me, but now I had no stomach for it. It was all behind me now. I held out his paycheck, and, when he hesitantly reached to take it, I looked him in the eyes with a smile and said, "Nice to have you aboard."

He nodded and dropped his eyes again, and I quickly moved on to the next man.

Of all the lessons I have learned in life, the importance of forgiveness is the most powerful. I had seen firsthand how hatred and resentment could poison a life, and I was truly blessed to be able to let those bad feelings go. I had so much I wanted to accomplish and I didn't want anything to get in the way, especially myself.

I ran Argus differently from the companies I had worked for. Handing out the paychecks and praising each man for his work became enormously important to me, and it wasn't a power trip. It was about working people. How often are our construction workers praised? Almost never! Birthdays, marriages, new babies, I always made sure to send a gift and card. When a job ended, I took the crew out for lunch. I grilled them burgers at our Fourth of July party and handed out plump turkeys at Thanksgiving. At Christmas, I hosted a party and gave each man a generous bonus. I wasn't saying, *Look at me. Look how great I treat my workers.* I was saying, *Look at you. You guys are doing great. I can't tell you how much I appreciate your skill and hard work.*

In return, my crew became loyal and dedicated and there was more cooperation and less grumbling on the job than the norm. The men thanked me for the perks, and several wives said their husbands were very happy working for Argus.

It was not all a picnic, though. More than once, I got into difficult situations with some of the men, and they all involved the same issue.

They wanted their sons to follow in their footsteps and expected me to hire them. I did hire a few, against my better judgment. Trouble was, the young men, usually in their twenties, were more interested in partying than working and some had serious alcohol and drug problems.

"Try to talk to him," one of the fathers would say.

Talk I would, but I was in over my head. The sons listened politely but seldom changed their habits. I even took a few of them to AA and Narcotics Anonymous meetings in an attempt to "save" them. It was a complete failure. I sometimes had to fire them and retain their fathers, who then perceived me as "the bad guy" because I didn't do enough to help. I finally reached a point where enough was enough. This was a business, and I would have to keep my nose out of their personal problems and focus on work.

Another man I hired for the island job was Derek Ribeiro, the man who had been reamed out by Joyce for harassing me on the Westcott job in Fall River. How do you figure? The three guys who'd been nastiest to me ended up being in my employ. Was this karma at work? It almost seemed so, and the whole thing made me laugh. I took Derek on and we started fresh, or almost. I can't say I ever forgot how the three had treated me, but I could get past it.

Neither Russell nor Frank nor Derek ever apologized to me for their abominable behavior, but they eventually became my most devoted employees. By the end of the island job, Russell became so friendly and supportive, I received several telephone calls from Cape Codders who wanted to hire Argus based on his glowing endorsements. A great moment in my life. I forgave and everybody won.

FATE AND FAMILY

W hen the Fourth of July bash rolled around again, I located the guest list in a kitchen drawer, kept in a well-worn notebook. Names were added or crossed out as the years progressed and, as I looked over the list, this year seemed more poignant than most. The original guest list had grown shorter each year as many friends from the old days died as a result of car accidents, drug overdoses, and AIDS. A few were in jail. Others never escaped the downward spiral of alcohol and drugs and couldn't return to normalcy. They were living on the edge.

The remaining names fell into distinct categories—my work acquaintances or Tim's sports and college friends. As I went down the list, I could see how much Tim and I had grown apart and it made me achingly sad. Our family members and a few friends from our younger days were the only mutual connections we had left.

Had I been too busy to see what was happening? Was I so bogged down in work I couldn't see that Tim and I had less and less to say to each other? The thing is, I didn't really know when it started happening. Tim had always been supportive of me, but as he began to go to college and meet new people, he got more involved in his life and I in mine. Worse, I didn't know what to do to make things better. Underneath, we were both angry, the worst kind of anger, festering, the kind that spoke to unresolved problems from long ago. As children of alcoholics, we still carried that baggage. Unaddressed, it came back to haunt us.

Anyway, Tim was excited about his brother, John, coming to the party this year along with his Uncle Guy from New York. John had been on a path of self-destruction, going back to grammar school when he failed a grade while his twin sister was promoted. In high school he played basketball but couldn't compete with Tim. He began drinking, worked a while in factories, then entered a Job Corps masonry training program and became friends with a fellow taking the same course. There was only one apprentice slot open, and John was turned down by the union. By law, his friend Jerry, who was a minority, was accepted.

After that, John's drinking got out of control. He lived at home on and off with his mother and sister Meg and occasionally worked in the fish houses or drove cabs to earn money for alcohol and drugs. Handsome, with a great sense of humor, he always managed to find a girlfriend to take care of him for a while. When John wore out his welcome at most of the New Bedford bars, he moved to New York to live with his Uncle Guy.

Guy, a longtime alcoholic, was now sober, thanks to AA, and loved to tell stories about his "nine lives," having survived a sea-plane crash, a furnace explosion that damaged his hearing, and a shoot-out in a barroom brawl, where he was shot three times. He lived at the YMCA and worked part-time at Manhattan's famous Water Club.

After many failed attempts, he managed to convince John to sign himself into a detox center, where he stayed for six weeks. While there, John became involved with a nurse named Nina and when he was released, moved into her apartment . We thought that this was the beginning of John's new life.

When John and Nina arrived at our party, John's old friends were thrilled to see him.

"Hey, you look great, man," two friends said in chorus. "Nice to meet you, Nina. Hey, John's got himself a beautiful woman here."

Nina beamed, and she blended in like a member of the family. We sat up late into the night schmoozing about old times. Uncle Guy and Tim got caught up on each other's lives, and Geraldine endured more jokes about Sasquatch.

The party was one of our best, but Tim and I didn't sit around the next day and talk about everything as we used to. The silence was an awful strain and we both felt it. In each other's presence, we were suddenly lonely. As soon as the guests left, we fell into the gloom again and we didn't know how to make things right.

Months later, the phone rang at five-thirty in the morning. I jumped up, thinking it was a workday and I had overslept. But no, it was Sunday. Good grief, who could be calling at this hour? I heard Tim's mother crying on the other end of the line.

"John's dead. Ohmigod, John's dead. It was an overdose. I just got the call from a hospital in New York."

I gave the phone to Tim and we fell apart, re-experiencing the awful pain we'd gone through when Sean died. The days following were a nightmare. Tim's mother and father, long divorced, made the funeral arrangements together, and a lot of old hostilities came to the surface.

John and Tim had a long history. They were close friends who cared deeply about each other. John was two years older, the typical big brother, very protective of Tim when they were kids and proud of his athletic prowess and strength of character. No matter how John behaved or self-destructed, Tim admired his intelligence, worldliness, and Paul Newman-like charm and good looks. John was still Tim's mentor and best friend. His loss was immeasurable.

Tim and I grieved separately; we could not comfort each other. We were like lost souls living in the same house. Even in the face of this tragedy, we were individually desolate. We could not connect.

When the island job ended, Argus got so busy we had multiple jobs running at a time and hired on extra crew. Brian oversaw the weekend side jobs, which I never gave up. I even tried to work on them myself when possible. I didn't ever want to stop laying brick, and this was what side jobs were about.

Three big jobs were staring Argus in the face, and we had some serious juggling to do. Clarence became a full-time estimator in the Vaughn Street office. He no longer went out on job sites as superintendent or foreman, though he drove out to potential new sites to prepare bid proposals and make sure we were well-equipped. Nearing retirement age, he found his new responsibilities less physically demanding. Also, unlike me, he was very detail-oriented. My work style resembled a tornado that came and went. I got the big things done quickly but left a trail of unfinished details in my wake. Clarence cleaned up after me and tied up all the loose ends.

Frank and Brian became foremen. Brian oversaw a wastewater treatment plant project in Revere, while Frank supervised a job in Fairhaven, the conversion of an elementary school into senior housing. The job employed eight men for three months, and Argus realized a hefty profit. Frank received a good bonus for keeping expenses down. When Frank discovered I loved horses as much as he did, he invited me to ride with him a few times—he owned two horses. How funny that he had no respect for me as a bricklayer but admired me for my love of horses. Pam and I met him and his friends once at a country and western club and he went out of his way to impress us. We got hooked on country music for a while but didn't admit it to many of our friends.

As our friendship became less strained, Frank and I talked about the way he'd treated me as an apprentice, usually in a joking manner, but both of us knew it was deadly serious. Frank said he honestly felt apprentices needed to learn their trade the hard way, which told me he wasn't facing up to what had really happened.

As time went on, Frank and I developed a kind of love-hate relationship. I wanted my employees treated kindly with the utmost respect, and Frank believed in being a "ball buster" to get the job done. When he acted as foreman, he insisted on doing things his way, and I acquiesced. He always made money for Argus, so I put up with his mean attitude and tried to let it roll off me. Because the men knew I was a soft touch, they often came to me with complaints about Frank. I tried talking to him about toning it down a bit, but he refused. His philosophy was "life sucks and then you die."

Frank was a diabetic and a few months later he had several toes removed. Pam and I visited him in the hospital and brought him a tape recorder and a few Merle Haggard and George Jones cassettes. He was less guarded than usual after that but still kept his distance on the job.

Argus had accumulated so much equipment that I rented extra parking space across from the Vaughn Street office. I now owned six pickup trucks, two forklifts, a rack body dump truck, four mixers, and two air compressors. Business was booming and, even with Clarence manning the office, I couldn't keep up.

Payroll and bookkeeping had become especially complicated, and on certain jobs I had to submit "certified payroll" on a weekly basis. The design of the government forms was different from my own ledger payroll system, and I had to list each man separately by race, union local, rate of pay each hour of the day, and various other statistics. If Frank was on a Boston job on Monday morning, then checked on a New Bedford job in the afternoon, I had to pay him according to the region's union scale. If he acted as a bricklayer in Boston and a foreman in New Bedford, the rates of pay were different, too. Overtime calculations were a nightmare.

A second nightmarish form had to agree with the first one, which certified I was doing everything properly and required subtotals and grand totals of man-hours and locations in a different format. If the forms weren't correct, I didn't get reimbursed and I risked being audited. It was time to bring on a full-time accountant and payroll clerk.

My youngest brother, Mark, seemed like the perfect candidate and was looking for a job change. With a master's degree in accounting and obsessive about organization and accuracy, he agreed to set up shop in the Vaughn Street office the following week. I bought a computer, and in no time he designed an elaborate system on Lotus that would automatically calculate payroll by region, job position, and overtime hours. After the first month, Mark had completed his work way ahead of schedule, so I asked him to take on payable and receivable accounts as well.

Again, he worked the same miracles and I began to hear compliments about the professionalism and accuracy of my documents from government and union officials, vendors, and customers. Argus was succeeding not only in the field but also in its office system.

Because of our age difference and home situation, Mark and I hadn't spent much time together as children, so I hoped that working together would strengthen the bond between us. It didn't go that way at first because of my controlling nature and his desire to be left alone to do things his own way.

"You hired me to be the controller, so back off and let me control," he told me repeatedly. After a few months, I gave in and stopped looking over his shoulder. He continued to keep a good handle on things.

Although the business was doing well, I was plagued by a sense of impending doom. I worried obsessively about anything and everything to do with Argus. Even when I left my employees alone to do their jobs, I was still plagued with concern about every move they made. I leaped into new situations and then was overwhelmed with panic over what I had gotten myself into.

Even the weather was a constant source of anxiety. I stayed up late at night, bleary-eyed and overtired, waiting to see every change in the forecast, no matter how small. Tim threatened to cancel the cable service and remove the television from the house. But I knew it wouldn't help—I was worried not only about the current weather but also about the weather for the rest of the year, especially during the winter months.

"Geraldine," I said one evening when we were on the porch looking at the stars. "Why am I always so worried? I worry about the men, the weather, the payroll, even the national economy." And on I went till I nearly wore her out.

"Lynn," she sighed. "All the success in the world means nothing if you're too unhappy to appreciate it. What do you really have? It's a very hollow success. What's it all about, anyway? You're a victim of your own success and it shouldn't be that way. You need to rethink it—or get out."

At first I thought she was being a little harsh, but then I started listening. I wanted success, yes, but I had to rethink its form. I'd heard that meditation offered people a way to transform their thinking, but I'd never really tried it. Tim was interested too and discovered a meditation course being taught in Providence. Geraldine decided to join us.

We headed for Providence the next weekend. Geraldine dubbed our teachers "the ghosts" because of their ethereal demeanor. While we were supposed to be clearing our minds, all I could think of was work problems. In time, I learned to meditate, as did Tim and Geraldine. It turned out to be an immensely helpful tool, not only in my business life but in my personal life as well.

Meanwhile, my habitual high anxiety worsened things on several fronts, including my marriage. Tim and I had grown even further apart as we dealt separately with our grief over John. College life and his sports friends consumed Tim, and I was consumed by Argus. A few nights a week, Tim started going to a sports bar frequented by some of his friends. He began coming home later and later, and I wasn't home much except to sleep. The easygoing relationship we once enjoyed gradually deteriorated into arguments, complaints, and long silences.

Tim and I thought it best to separate for a while to assess our marriage. Tim stayed in the Vaughn Street house and I moved most of the office to the cottage. The split put Clarence and Mark in an awkward position and they tried their best to stay out of things. Further complicating matters, the country was in a recession and business suddenly dried up. I couldn't handle the pressure and responsibility of keeping my crew afloat without work, and I was overwhelmed with the chaos in my personal life. Argus began to flounder. I was so stressed, I lost a great deal of weight and people began commenting that I looked unhealthy.

Pam had problems too. Jason was attending college in Georgia and she missed him terribly. Donny's three young nieces moved in with them in Marion, which put a big strain on their marriage. Pam quit her job and signed on with another company that offered more money, but she was miserable with the workload. The stress affected her physically, and she underwent several surgeries for ulcerative colitis. Worried about her, I didn't want to burden her with my problems when she had so many of her own.

Thank God for Geraldine during this terribly difficult time. She came over to the cottage every day after work and we cooked dinner. She listened compassionately day after day, as I poured out my heart. Dear Geraldine was as comforting as a warm blanket.

"Lynn, if you don't mind, I'm going to sleep on your living room couch for a while 'cause I know you're afraid of staying in the house alone."

And for the next three weeks she did. She listened to my rantings long after she must have been sick to death of it all.

"Lynn," she told me one day, "I think it's time for you to begin meditating again."

She got me on a daily regimen of meditating each morning and made me eat fresh fruit and yogurt before I headed out each day.

Clarence had been through recessions before and assured me that things would get better, but I was guilt-stricken about not having any work for my crew. It was as if I were responsible for the U.S. economy! I was going to drive myself nuts if I didn't do something positive with my free time.

And then it came to me. I had always wanted to talk to the students in junior high school, especially the girls, about considering a career in the trades, but I had no time when Argus was busy. Now was the perfect time to approach the schools. I needed to stop staying home feeling sorry for myself. Could I do it?

"I am a bricklayer," I explained to several classes in the New Bedford school system. I told them about the Belmont, the newspaper article, the women-in-construction course, my first job, and on and on. At first, I felt nervous, but then it began to flow naturally. The girls, in particular, were all ears. Their minds opened, they asked questions, they loved the part about making money. I began to come alive again. Their positive response built up my self-confidence.

I began to calm down and begin a reassessment. It wasn't just my marriage that was suffering, my life was out of whack. How much time I had wasted worrying about things beyond my control! Things would be out of control anyway whether I worried or not.

I began attending AL-ANON meetings and worked on the Twelve Steps and the Serenity Prayer: *God, grant me the serenity to accept the things I cannot change, the courage to change the things I can, and the wisdom to know the difference.* I worked on letting go of the hurts from my father, my husband, and my co-workers that I had carried around for years.

Six months passed and the economy showed signs of improvement. After submitting bids unsuccessfully week after week, Argus was selected to construct an addition on an elementary school in Mattapoisett and I was able to call my crew back to work. Frank had returned to working for Empire and opted to stay with them for the time being, as did a few other Argus regulars. I marveled at my calmness in accepting the news and at the sensible way I made changes in the Argus roster.

Sadly, Tim's mother, Catherine, was diagnosed with cancer and had to spend several weeks in the hospital. Tim and I visited her daily and observed an unspoken truce that we wouldn't talk about our problems, just focus on his mother's needs. She passed away shortly after and we were grateful her suffering was over. We mourned her death.

Meg was devastated by the loss. Her mother had cared for Meg since birth, when she was diagnosed with cerebral palsy. Tim and his sisters coordinated a schedule so Meg would have round-the-clock care until other arrangements could be made. After she moved to an apartment in an assisted-living complex, with health-aide coverage, the house on Sycamore Street was sold.

Tim and I began to talk about the possibility of reconciling and agreed to try counseling. Separated, we missed each other terribly but we couldn't find a way to talk about our difficulties, nor did we have much insight into what was wrong. An experienced marriage therapist helped us discover what was really important to us and prioritize accordingly. Tim stopped drinking and we worked hard to make amends and rebuild our marriage. The most important decision we made was to start a family in the near future.

The Argus crew was glad to see us reunited and couldn't believe how calmly I handled things now. Business was booming again and Argus was back on track. We relocated the office back to Vaughn Street and hired an extra two dozen men to keep up with the workload. Three of our bids were accepted in the same week, and Clarence and I scrambled to coordinate the manpower and schedules. Two weeks later, we won a masonry subcontract from Turner Construction on a huge restoration project at the Charlestown Navy Yard. Clarence called Frank one more time, and when he heard about the Charlestown job, he agreed to come back and act as foreman.

An older woman at an AL-ANON meeting once said she was grateful for the bad times in her life because they were an integral part of the good ones that followed. I could see for myself how true it was. The period of separation between Tim and me had resulted in a stronger marriage bond, a clear plan for our future, and the beginning of a family. I had always loved him and felt lost and alone without him.

The hard times with Argus during the recession brought a healthy restructuring to the company and we were now making more profit in one month than we had in a full year. Having my entire life spin out of control for six months forced me to face the fact I couldn't control most events. It helped me to learn to "let go and let God."

Argus continued to make money week after week, thanks to the hard-working crew's diligence. Within three short months, the profits were phenomenal. After I made my weekly retirement account deposit on November 12, 1989, I asked for a receipt showing the account's grand total.

"Wahoo!" I shouted, which drew a few curious stares from people in the parking lot. The numbers said $100,152. This time, it had taken me only three years to meet my second five-year goal.

Frank was doing great as foreman on the Charlestown Navy Yard project, and everyone noticed his changed attitude. The chip on his shoulder was gone, and he was acting more like a team player. I'm not sure why it happened, but I was grateful for it. Meanwhile, other Argus bids had been accepted, and we were now working in five different locations.

When Argus first began, I made a point of being at the Vaughn Street office at 5:00 AM each day to meet the men as they arrived for work. As they loaded equipment onto the Argus trucks, they brought me up to date on how things were going on the jobs and in their home lives. Even though I owned Argus, I always felt guilty about not being out on the job sites all day, so spending this time with the men compensated for it and also let them know I cared about them. But why, I wondered, did I still feel guilty about everything? I was busting my butt trying to run the business. Did I feel guilty about not actually working on the wall? The only work I still needed to do was on myself.

The five jobs, as different as night and day, were scattered throughout the state. The Charlestown Navy Yard was still our biggest project and the only one in the Boston area. Another crew was building a new church in the West End of New Bedford. A third crew was building a new wing on the Bridgewater State Hospital.

Clarence had a small crew doing an emergency repointing job at a school library, and I was keeping an eye on a crew of ten who were working on a sewerage treatment plant in Falmouth. I had been feeling tired and queasy, probably from the stress of it all, but I hoped I wasn't coming down with something. I soon discovered that, in a way, I was.

I asked Brian Reed, acting foreman on the Falmouth job, if he could hand out the paychecks that day. "Yeah, sure. Is everything okay?" He knew I passed out the checks myself, heeding the advice Walter Rich had given long ago.

"Never been better—I just need to get home a little early today."

Tim usually arrived home from school by four-thirty and I wanted to be there. As soon as Tim put his books down on the kitchen counter, I called to him from the first-floor bedroom. "Tim, could you please give me a hand moving this bureau into the den?"

He looked puzzled. "Why? It's just fine where it is."

"Well, we're going to need that space for a bassinet."

Tim's jaw dropped as he began stuttering, "Wha…you mean… we're hav…you're preg…a baby?"

I was delighted at his surprised reaction and the next thing I knew, we were a tangle of arms and legs, hopping around the room, laughing and crying with joy.

"Lynn, you shouldn't be jumping around like this," Tim cautioned, and then in the next breath said, "Oh my God, I'm gonna be a dad!"

I told Tim about the three home pregnancy tests I'd taken, just to be sure, and about my visit to the doctor that morning. Everything was fine, the doctor assured me, and I was already nearing the end of my first trimester. We spent the next hour talking about our baby and getting used to our new roles as expectant parents.

Geraldine stopped by after work and was thrilled to hear the news. "Does this mean I can have all your size-six clothes?" she quipped. She stayed for dinner and later that evening we called family and friends. Pam rushed right over with her camera. After hearing all the details and crying lots of happy tears, she made me pose sideways, holding a sign that said "11 Weeks," as she snapped away.

"I'll take your picture every month so you'll have a photo album of your new expansion project."

Jason called from Georgia that night to congratulate us. He laughed when I told him it didn't seem so long ago that he'd been a baby. "That's just what my mom says all the time!"

"Congratulations, Boss," Clarence said the next day, "and don't worry about a thing—I'm a four-time grandpa, so you're in good hands." As the news spread throughout the Argus crew, everyone wished me well and told me to start taking it easy.

The Charlestown job was becoming more and more complicated. It was a "tight site"—difficult to get equipment and materials up onto the staging, and the new work area called for restoration work. Frank thrived on new construction projects but disliked repair and restoration, which was the work I liked best. Since all of our men were busy on other jobs, I decided to supervise the old-section work myself. Clarence and Frank protested, but knowing how stubborn I was, they soon gave up.

In the midst of all this, wanting a fresh start for our new family, Tim and I decided to buy a new home. Argus's profits continued to roll in and home mortgage interest rates were low, so we felt the timing was right. One of Tim's golf partners, a Lakeville man, had just put his home up for sale, a beautiful, expansive home he built himself. Shortly after, his wife filed for divorce and moved out. Bill was devastated, emotionally and financially.

We loved the house, located a half-mile up the road from our cottage, a two-story colonial with four bedrooms and several acres of wooded land. Bill was a carpenter by trade and every room in the house showcased his skill. One bath even had a built-in Jacuzzi, and the room above the garage would make a perfect home gym for Tim. We bought the house at a reduced price and Bill rented our cottage, a perfect deal for us both. We moved in just after I entered my sixth month of pregnancy and, for the first time, we hired movers. What a difference!

Our new neighbors across the street, the Garbitts, owned two horses with a stable and corral, and their teenage daughter Renee's bedroom was full of ribbons and trophies. Fulfilling a long-lost dream, I purchased a beautiful Morgan horse, Susie, and she boarded with our neighbors. I rode her every day along a wooded path that ran through the woods behind our house. This gentle horse seemed to know about the baby-to-be, taking extra care to give me a smooth ride.

Frank was handling things well on the Charlestown project and the profits kept rolling in. I continued to work as I always had, but drew looks from some men on the job site that reminded me of my early days as an apprentice. There I was, almost six months pregnant and climbing up on staging, looking like I had a hard-hat under my waistband as well as on my head. I felt great and had the doctor's okay to continue working, but Burt, Turner Construction's chief superintendent, was worried. As I climbed down from the staging one morning, he called me over to his trailer.

"Have a seat, Lynn. You want some water or something?"

"No thanks, I'm fine. What's up?"

He hemmed and hawed for a minute and then said, "Lynn, you know I think the world of you, but it's risky, you working here when you're…you know…" His voice trailed off.

He seemed embarrassed to talk about my pregnancy. It was funny but the same men who boldly talked about and ridiculed every part of the female anatomy amongst themselves were humbled by my growing midsection.

"What I mean is," Burt continued, clearly flustered, "there ought to be rules about this sort of thing…you know…your, um…but there aren't any rules, I checked with the union. So just be careful, would you please, Lynn? I'd never forgive myself if you took a tumble off the staging or slipped on the ice."

In truth, I was more concerned with Burt's blood pressure than I was with my own health, so I assured him I was following doctor's orders and would certainly be very careful.

During my final trimester, I tired easily. I gave up climbing the staging but continued to visit the Charlestown job four days a week, and, as my energy diminished, I turned over certain administrative duties to Pam. She worked with Mark on certified payroll and accounts payable. Since my due date was getting closer, Clarence and I decided to have some fresh seafood on Friday at Dewey's Restaurant, up the street from Argus, and plan a strategy for my one-week maternity leave.

The weathermen, who predicted a major snowstorm later in the day, were off by a few hours. At noon, the snow began coming down thick and heavy, so Clarence picked me up in his Explorer with its four-wheel drive, I watched him wolf down his baked scallops, but after a few bites of broiled scrod, I felt queasy. Oh, shoot, I thought, ignore it, ignore it and get with the program. But sometimes you can't will yourself back to normal, and this was one of those times. Things got worse.

"Clarence, I gotta go," I whimpered in a pathetic voice.

"Are you okay, Lynn? Should I call somebody?"

"Uh, no. We'll have to do our talk on Monday." He drove me home and I slowly made it upstairs to bed. A half-hour later my water broke. Tim and Pam had "baby beepers" and I paged them both. My "labor day" had clearly arrived two weeks earlier than expected. Tim came barging in and called the midwife with details. "Go to the hospital now!" she ordered. It was near Boston, an hour's drive in good weather.

When Pam arrived moments later, we sped off in Tim's Jeep, jittery about traffic and plodding our way through the storm. Tim drove like a trooper, and we arrived at the hospital with time to spare.

Labor seemed endless, but with Tim and Pam as my coaches and a great midwife who had welcomed many babies into the world, Kelsey Lynn Donohue was finally born. We laughed and cried with joy as she let out her first lusty howl.

"She's beautiful."

"Gorgeous," said Tim.

"An angel," said Pam, as we looked lovingly on this piece of work. The midwife praised me for only yelling at my helpers once, and not until the very end. As the snow continued to fall, the world outside our window looked like a fairyland, and we settled in for the night. We were truly in our own little world, thinking about this miracle, the arrival of this beautiful new baby. Kelsey's bassinet was next to my bed, and Tim and Pam slept on roll-away beds nearby.

A week later, I went back to work part-time, and so did baby Kelsey, who occupied a nursery at the Argus office. I wanted to work, yes, but I wanted her to be with me too, so why not? I did both. Several men from Argus sent flowers and baby gifts, and I laughed when Clarence presented Kelsey with a tiny yellow hard-hat. Though I was sleep-deprived, I felt wonderful, way up there, in awe, touched by the gods and moved beyond words by this new life. Tim felt this way too, as if something incredible had happened and our lives would never be the same again. Surprisingly, I was more determined than ever to make my business succeed so our new little daughter would have every opportunity in life.

Clarence and Mark proved to be a great team, taking the reins of Argus and moving ahead while the crew labored mightily to finish all five projects in record time. Rare it was to have so many bricklayers employed in a New England winter, and word was spreading about Argus's professionalism and swiftness at completing work. The days of begging were over. Masons and laborers were calling us to come on board. We had to feel optimistic when we were already receiving calls for spring and summer work from general contractors.

Meanwhile, my third five-year goal was crying to be written. I could hear the refrain buzzing in my ear—*Do it now, not later, NOW.*

That's the way goals are. You reach a goal, you pat yourself on the back, you take a rest. But new goals are always waiting to be born.

I took out my trusty little memo pad and wrote: "January 29, 1993—In five years, I will pay off the mortgages on all three of my properties." As in the past, I began repeating my goal aloud every morning and periodically throughout the day. I also began a journal about Kelsey, recording the little details of her daily life. Busy as I was, I always wrote at least a few words every night so I would remember her precious infancy forever.

NEVER CAN SAY GOODBYE

The Argus team kept things running smoothly for the next two months while I worked on an as-needed basis, spending as much time with Kelsey and Tim as possible. Geraldine stopped by often, doting on Kelsey like a proud aunt and filling us with anecdotes about her own two girls when they were small. She also cooked dinner, did housework, and helped us adjust to being new parents. She was our fairy godmother.

Me, I lived a double life, shifting roles from Argus president to new mother many times daily and often combining the two. "If Gilly could only see you now," said Clarence warmly as he watched me balance the phone on my shoulder, tenderly cradling Kelsey in my arms, and talking to Gilly, a general contractor, about a cement delivery.

Argus didn't need any headaches now, but a bad job arrived in the guise of a good one, and we took it on. Argus won the bid by Johnson Construction to do masonry work on a new BJ's Wholesale Club in Framingham, a sprawling suburban city between Worcester and Boston. On the way home from Boston, where I'd driven Geraldine to have the numbness in her right arm checked out, I stopped at the BJ's site to introduce myself and sign the contracts.

The superintendent, Douglas Smart, looked at me with a seemingly permanent scowl etched on his face. "Who's your foreman? I'll be dealin' with him from here on in. I got enough problems on this job already and I don't like dealin' with skirts."

My eyes were blazing, but I tried to keep control. "I'll be overseeing the job," I politely told him, "and you'll be dealing with me, like it or not." As I exited the door of the trailer, he delivered one more punch, but feebly.

"I've had it with this lowest bidder bullshit."

I turned back to look at him. "Excuse me?" I said sweetly, but he turned away.

"Oh, Geraldine," I groaned when I got in the car and told her about the incident. "Are we ever going to get out of the Stone Age?"

"Why didn't you call me in? I could have threatened to sic Bigfoot on him."

At that moment, Kelsey smiled in her sleep and we laughed at her perfect timing. Had I been by myself, I might have brooded all the way home. Friends are so therapeutic. We unburden our hearts—they listen and put things in perspective. Sometimes they only have to be there, their loving presence is enough. Without our friends, we would all be lost. Geraldine and Kelsey gave this otherwise depressing moment a certain lightness of being and I began laughing too.

My first encounter at BJ's only presaged worse to come—it was all downhill from there. Frank acted as foreman and was in constant conflict with Douglas Smart, who couldn't get along with anyone. The two almost came to blows one day when Douglas informed Frank that the Argus crew had put up an entire wall with the wrong materials.

"Look, it's right there in the plans," Frank shouted, laying out the blueprints.

"I informed you that the plans had been changed," Douglas retorted.

I believed Frank. He was a pro and didn't make mistakes about these things. I tried to recoup the cost of labor and materials from Johnson Corporation, but was told I should have double-checked with them before my crew began. The general contractor had the final say, so Argus took the loss. Worse was yet to come.

In early April, with Kelsey in tow, I took Geraldine to Boston to a follow-up doctor's appointment. The numbness in her arm had continued, and we knew only that it wasn't carpal tunnel syndrome. Meanwhile, her doctor had ordered an MRI and CAT scan and we'd hear the results today. Kelsey entertained us on the drive with her wide wonder at the world and utter delight in her own being, cooing and ahhing and ooohing, then dissolving into laughter. Her antics diverted us from our central mission. It's never fun to go to the doctor, but it's even harder when you're getting test results or dealing with a mystery illness. When Geraldine went in the office, Kelsey and I settled down in the waiting room, and I looked for something to keep her entertained. Minutes later, a nurse summoned me in.

As soon as I walked in and saw Geraldine's grim face, her shocked expression, I could tell the news was awful.

The doctor was kind, and I couldn't imagine it was easy for him to deliver bad news to anyone, but he looked in my eyes and was calm and straightforward. "Geraldine's numbness is caused by three malignant tumors rapidly growing in the left side of her brain. I recommend immediate surgery, but there's a good chance the tumors will return."

I sat in stunned silence as Kelsey began to wail. I just wanted to get out of there. Out!

Dear God, it can't be. Geraldine and I were in shock as we exited the office. On the way home, I babbled on about thinking positively and getting a second opinion, but I didn't even half-believe myself. Always the clown, Geraldine made a few wry comments, then sat quietly looking out the window at the April sky. The promise of spring and new beginnings was everywhere, the trees budding alongside the highway, grass poking its way through dead ground, and here and there wildflowers showing their colors. Oh, spring, you are such a mockery! I dropped Geraldine at her house and told her we would beat this thing. She smiled and said thanks.

When I got home, I cried and poured my heart out to Tim. He immediately went to the phone and called his sister Maureen, a nurse, to get a referral for "the best brain surgeon in Boston." Three days later, Geraldine entered Brigham and Women's Hospital and had surgery performed by the doctor who had operated on Ringo Starr's daughter a week earlier. Following surgery, the doctor gave us a brief, somber report.

He looked weary, his white hair tousled, his face lined and serious. "Well, we removed the majority of the growths, but I was unable to reach one tumor that had grown into an inoperable area. I expect it will enlarge before too long." I stood there in silence and didn't ask any questions. I knew what he was saying anyway.

After two weeks of recuperation, Geraldine was back at the gym, walking the treadmill and going up and down on the Stairmaster. She was determined to maintain the life she had, in moderation. For us, life went on—it always goes on. There's no stopping it. Kelsey was christened on Sunday, with beaming godparents looking on—my friend Pam and Tim's friend Jack. At the reception, Geraldine danced away with her new boyfriend, John, as if all were well. She hadn't had a date, a romance, a boyfriend, in years, and John had just walked into her life a few months before and swept her away. And he didn't flee after her diagnosis, he was hanging in there for the duration. A spirited, good-humored guy, he adored Geraldine and was helping her live life to the fullest.

"Thank God for John," I said to Tim. "Sometimes I think he came straight from heaven," and I squeezed Tim's hand because, after all, we were alive. He and I and Kelsey and Geraldine and Pam and all these people I loved were alive, we were here, celebrating this grand event. And I knew I would hold on to this moment forever.

The BJ's nightmare continued. The first two months were filled with miscommunications and general noncooperation between Johnson and the subcontractors. At times, Frank was so miserable I feared he would quit, so I surprised him with the gift of a week's stay at a dude ranch in Texas. Joey Burba, an experienced brick steward, filled in at the site, and when Frank returned he was tanned and smiling. I knew I had done right and he would stay the course.

"If Douglas gives me any crap, I'll hog-tie him," Frank joked, describing the roping skills he'd perfected at the ranch.

But the mishaps continued. Witless Douglas allowed the plumbing subcontractor to dig a deep ditch around the perimeter of the building foundation. The "big dig" occurred the very day before we were due to erect staging in the same area, and Douglas knew it, or he should have. In construction every minute counts, and when you make a plan, your men and materials must be ready. Argus took a loss on several truckloads of cement and a week's payroll for twenty men who had to wait around until the plumber finished his work and filled in the ditches. At the end of four months, hallelujah, the job was over. The men knew it had been difficult, but they didn't know Argus had lost fifteen thousand dollars on the deal. Clarence gently pointed out that I'd learned two important lessons: never bid a job too "tight" and always check on the reputation of the general contractor before you put in a bid.

The wonder of Kelsey helped me get through these difficult months. At six months, she had begun imitating my facial expressions, from my no-nonsense scowl to my gushy smiles directed only at her. Geraldine was a frequent visitor, and I tried to act normal in the face of her worsening symptoms. The tumors were growing again, and her doctor suggested a round of radiation and chemotherapy as a last-ditch effort. I searched for books on alternative treatments, even ordering shark cartilage from Nebraska that I'd heard about on an infomercial.

The responsibility of trying to keep the Argus crew employed through hard cold winters, when jobs were in short supply, was overwhelming. I never saw my men as separate entities but as people with families to support. Work meant their families would have a good winter too. So I was ecstatic when Norcross Corporation hired us to do the interior brickwork in both a new shopping mall in Plymouth and a bank branch in Seekonk. It was enough to keep everyone working through the winter.

Two days before Thanksgiving, with Kelsey in a backpack, I handed out turkeys and bonus checks to the crew, thanking each man for his service and wishing him a happy holiday. What a thrill it was to see them laughing and being buddy-buddy with each other, genuinely happy to be working for the woman who supposedly would bring nothing but grief to the brotherhood.

Geraldine's boyfriend, John, took her to chemotherapy and radiation treatments, but the tumors continued to grow and do their damage. Her coordination and speech rapidly deteriorated. When she wasn't hospitalized, or too tired to move from the couch, she exhibited remarkable powers of the human spirit. Tuesdays were reserved for Geraldine. Every Tuesday afternoon we went adventuring, usually to Boston to eat sushi at Copley Place or to a matinee in the theater district. What a break—these adventures were as much for me as for her. I was blessed to be able to help in this small way during this long winter.

While she was undergoing an especially grueling week-long session of chemo in December, Pam and I visited her in the hospital and found her lying on the bed in T-shirt and running shorts with jogging shoes on her feet, looking ready to do a marathon. "Going somewhere?" we asked.

She told us as best she could that when the I.V. was removed once a day, she walked up and down the stairwells for exercise. We shared her hospital dinner, read aloud from a *National Enquirer* we bought as a gag, and took turns trying on her new wig, crafting outrageous styles and giggling like schoolgirls. As Pam and I were leaving, the nurses at the desk told us we were good medicine for our friend. We talked and cried on the drive home, deeply moved by Geraldine's courage.

Tim and I planned to host Christmas dinner for our families, celebrating our first Christmas with Kelsey in our new home. On Christmas Eve, our closest friends arrived for a buffet lunch—Pam, Donny, Jason and his fiance, Geraldine and John—and we opened gifts. Geraldine's determination to be there amazed us, though her speech was unintelligible and she had lost mobility on her right side. She never complained about the unfairness of it all, but privately Pam and I complained plenty to each other.

After everyone left, I began cleaning the house and preparing for the next day's festivities. The phone rang over the noise of the vacuum and I ran to pick it up. It was my sister, Dawn, sounding very upset.

"Dad's had a terrible accident and they're airlifting him to Boston. Can you come?" I passed the phone to Tim so he could get directions to the hospital while I ran around in search of my purse. Tim stayed home with Kelsey and I jumped in the car, trying to stay calm enough to get to the hospital in one piece.

The news could not have been worse. Dad, now sixty-nine, had gone up a ladder onto the roof at the Belmont to clear some vines that were blocking a gutter, causing water to run into the parking lot. He was concerned about someone slipping on the ice. When he tried to descend the sixteen-foot ladder, it slipped out from under him and he plunged through the open cellar bulkhead below, landing face first on the cement steps leading to the basement. He tumbled the rest of the way down the stairs and was knocked unconscious. When he came to, he was covered in blood and couldn't move. Slipping in and out of consciousness for twenty minutes, he called intermittently for help and was finally heard by a woman walking her dog.

Four specialists at New England Medical Center evaluated his condition and gave us the news: his nose was broken, his teeth were pushed through his gums, and he had deep lacerations over his face and head. Then came the really bad stuff: his spinal cord was severed, he was paralyzed from the neck down and may have broken his neck.

His heart was enlarged and if he survived the night, he might need open-heart surgery in the morning to prevent a heart attack before they could deal with the paralysis.

Dawn and I sank into our chairs and wept. Irene, Dad's girlfriend, stood grim and silent. My dad, the workaholic, always on the go, paralyzed? That is, if he made it through the night.

"Is he conscious? Can I see him?" The doctor hesitated and said yes, but only for a moment.

That's not my dad, I thought as I looked at the man on the bed, but he opened his light blue eyes and tried to focus them on me. I choked back my tears. His eyes were locked onto mine, searching, and I knew I had to be strong.

"What's wrong? Did I break something?" he whispered in garbled speech, wincing in pain.

I opened my mouth, but no sound came out.

His eyes pleaded as he fought with all his strength to whisper a few words, "Lynn—I can't move—tell them I'm not a wheelchair case!" My grief doubled at his words, and I slowly said, "Dad, that's up to God now, not the doctors."

He closed his eyes and I left the room. Dawn and Irene planned to stay the night, but I had to get out of there before I suffocated. I said a hasty goodbye and walked rapidly toward the exit. My hands, my cheeks, my jaw tingled, and my thoughts were incoherent as I pushed the door open and stood outside, gasping for air. A nurse came over and said, "Take a deep breath, miss, you're hyperventilating." She stood with me for a few minutes until I was breathing normally. I thanked her and went to my car.

I know Dad had caused a lot of grief in our family and inflicted pain that would never go away. He had been a cruel father in many ways, but in the last few years he had tried to make up for it. He gave me a job when I needed one, and he showed tremendous faith when he backed my business loans with his signature, an act that could have bankrupted him if things had gone wrong. He had tried to show love as best he could, in his own way. I believe he had been so hurt in his own early childhood, he did not know how to feel or express love. The responsibility of fathering a young family overwhelmed him and put him over the edge. He lashed out at his wife and children.

I'm not making excuses for him, at least I hope I'm not. But as his daughter, I still loved him in spite of everything. I could afford to be generous of heart. I had won the battle over all the bad stuff in my life and was fulfilling my dreams. What Tim and I learned from our troubled childhoods was knowledge of how *not* to be. We loved Kelsey beyond words, paid attention to her, and provided a loving home. She was immersed, surrounded by love. I know things don't always work this way—the sins of the father are visited on the sons and all that. But this I know: Tim and I had triumphed over the circumstances of our early lives, and we took a certain wisdom with us into our adult lives. So, at the hospital, I felt nothing but grief for my father, who lay in that bed paralyzed.

I have no recollection of the drive to or from the hospital. As I told Tim the story, I became increasingly upset, and he urged me to get some rest. Before I lay down, I had the strangest thought—Call Whiskey Pete, call Whiskey Pete, call…The refrain kept going through my head. Pete was "born again" and had become a new man, sober for almost a year and a deacon at his Pentecostal church. Between sobs, I told him what happened and asked him to pray for Dad. He promised he would.

After I fell asleep, Pete's wife called and told Tim they had put the call out on their church's prayer line and over fifty people were praying for a miracle. Tim stayed up for a while, tending to Kelsey and preparing an overnight bag for me to take to the hospital the next day.

At six-thirty on Christmas morning, the ring of the phone awakened me from a deep sleep and the memory of my father's accident rushed over me. I put my hand on the phone and hesitated, thinking, he's dead—the injuries were too much for him to survive. When I heard Dawn's voice, I prepared myself for the worst.

"Lynn, the diagnosis has changed," said Dawn, sounding exhausted but hopeful. "Dad's heart is okay—he's always had an abnormally large aorta, apparently. They did another MRI and his spinal cord no longer looks severed, only pinched, so the paralysis may not be permanent."

"It's a miracle," I said through tears.

Pete was happy but not surprised at the more optimistic picture. "I've heard many testimonies like yours, and I can tell you God is faithful and He does answer prayers."

"Thanks, Pete, and thank everyone at church for me too."

On Sunday, I went with Pam to her church to thank those who also prayed for my dad. The doctor had no medical explanation for the drastic turn of events, but acknowledged he had seen the power of faith many times before. My faith was strengthened and I began reading books on spirituality.

After three weeks in the hospital, where he endured numerous surgeries to repair his face and body, Dad was transferred to the Braintree Rehabilitation Hospital for three months of intensive physical therapy. I visited him every morning, bringing him samplings of his favorite foods and pictures of the family. He still could not move his body, so I fed him as I read him the daily newspaper. Then I'd massage his hands, arms, feet, and legs with Bag Balm, a cure-all for dry, chapped skin and bedsores.

Knowing he'd been spared a lifetime of paralysis, I began to look at his condition with a small ray of hope. Concerned about his facial appearance, he nevertheless looked better every day and had even begun to look like his old self a bit. I had faith he'd get back his mobility and good looks soon. Family and friends visited him throughout those difficult months. I brought Geraldine to visit, and it was heartbreaking to see her condition worsen as my dad's improved.

Somehow I managed to keep things running smoothly at Argus, and the mall and bank projects were fairly routine, a perfect follow-up to the BJ's nightmare. I kept up with my normal duties, working late into the night at times to stay on top of it. Energy I had, and it didn't abandon me now. Energy kept me going.

Meanwhile, a big change was taking place at the union. Over the years, many of the small local chapters had merged with the larger Boston local so they could pool their resources, funds, and staffs. Though the locals no longer kept a functioning office, they kept their autonomy. New Bedford had recently merged with Local 3 in Boston, which now encompassed the eastern half of Massachusetts.

Seeing the local office shut down, the scene of so many of my losses and triumphs, brought a lump to my throat and, saddest of all, was Addie's retirement. Though we never discussed women in masonry, I knew she was my cheerleader. Her face turned on like a light bulb whenever I had business at the office with George. "How's my girl today?" she'd say, the way a mother would, and I'd reply, "You mean, before George or after George?" and she'd laugh.

George Medeiros held a big retirement party for her and nearly everyone in the local turned out to wish her well. She took me aside. "Lynn, I hope you know how proud I am of all your accomplishments. Do you realize, to this day, you are still the first and only woman bricklayer in Local 39? It's been twenty years since you first walked into my office, can you believe it? I'm going to miss you very much." We hugged and got all choked up and promised to keep in touch.

If it's possible for a party to be fun and melancholy at the same time, this was it, the end of an era. Most of the bricklayers sat and talked about old times, and several men told me they were impressed when I won the apprentice contest and cheered again at my courage after my fall on the Com Electric job. Could it be? The thing I had longed for in my heart for twenty years—to be recognized as a member of the brotherhood simply because I was a good mason—was actually happening on the day the office closed and the union merged. The guys accepted me. If my heart was soaring, it was because I had done so much more than earn my stripes in the brotherhood. I had educated myself in the field of construction and moved on.

Kelsey, already a year old, was thriving, and no matter what happened at work her existence made the world right for me. Tim and I delighted in watching her grow. Her lively, vital being, her overwhelming presence, her first steps, first words, smiles filled our lives and put everything in perspective. I still saw Geraldine every Tuesday, but our adventures were over. She was no longer able to go out. She could not walk or talk, though she understood everything we said to her.

A blustery-cold March arrived and with it came one of the biggest jobs I had ever bid on. The town of Barnstable on Cape Cod hired Callahan Brothers as general contractor for a new high school, and the project's size offered a potentially huge profit margin. I was eager to put in a competitive price. Clarence, Mark, Frank, and I brainstormed for two weeks and finally had a proposal we were comfortable with. We each found it helpful to have input from the group so we wouldn't miss any important details. Once the bid was accepted, we'd be locked into the price, and an omission on a job of that magnitude could prove very costly.

I invited my mother to the bid opening, and we had lunch at a little restaurant in Barnstable Village before the action. While Mom and I talked, Kelsey sat in her highchair eating carrot strips and wiggling her nose like a bunny. Just looking at her brought me instant happiness. Then, while Mom and Kelsey walked in the park, I strode over to Barnstable town hall and made my way to the meeting room upstairs. Three men sat at a table in front of the room: the town clerk, the president of Callahan Brothers, and the town manager. In front of them were several piles of bid packages from subcontractors. The town clerk read through the required legal notices, and the process began. Plumbing work came first. As the town purchasing agent opened the bids, he read the name of the company, checked the paperwork for accuracy, and announced the bid price. The town clerk wrote the information down and, after the last bid was opened, announced the lowest bidder.

The process was repeated for carpentry, electrical, excavating, and landscaping. Finally, the masonry bids were opened. I fidgeted in my seat, my nerves jumping. If Argus won, it would be a significant feather in my cap and I would then have the experience and credentials to enter a much more lucrative playing field of profitable jobs. Clarence, Mark, and I had sweat over the bid for days and had come up with a final price of $2,000,000.

As things progressed, I jotted down the bid amounts and the names of the companies, which is standard practice so you can become familiar with your competition and their bid ranges. After a while, it was easy to predict who would be highest bidder, who would bid ridiculously low and be disqualified, and who would stay in the running. Although I saw a lot of men I knew, there were at least six masonry subs I was not familiar with.

The highest bid was $3,800,000, but most of the others were more in line with mine. I was distracted when my beeper went off and I missed two of the bid prices. Not wanting to interrupt anyone, I put down two question marks and went on from there. Finally, the last bid was opened. There were fifteen bids, the clerk reported, and the low bidder was Argus Construction. I had to restrain myself from cheering. Some of the other contractors congratulated me on my way out, and I ran to the park to tell Mom and Kelsey.

"Good news," I announced later at a hastily called meeting of the whole Argus crew. "We've been awarded the high school subcontract!" I couldn't wait to get the words out—what could be better than delivering good news to a hard-working crew? Everyone was overjoyed, knowing they had steady work for a year at good pay. I ordered pizza, and we laughed and talked, grateful for our good fortune.

On the home front, Dad was doing remarkably well. His long stint at Braintree Rehab was over and he was home. Dad had never allowed anybody to help him with anything, but he was in a new world now and totally dependent. Fortunately, he shared his house with Irene and she became his principal caretaker. A special wheelchair van took him to physical therapy sessions three times a week at a Fall River hospital, and homemakers and health aides arrived at the house daily. Dad was determined to walk again.

"I can see that strong will runs in the family," said the doctors and health-care workers who saw Dad and me together, practicing leg bends and stretches. His speech was back to normal now that his facial operations were over and he was getting used to his new false teeth. I visited every few days, and he always said the same thing. "I'll be out of this wheelchair soon."

On Tuesday, I called John to tell him what time I'd be there to see Geraldine. "She's not up to it today, Lynn," he told me. "Things are not good—she's taken a turn for the worse. I fear she is nearing the end." I promised to call the next day but it never happened. At three in the morning, John called with the news that Geraldine had passed away. I drove to their home in Weymouth and found Geraldine's two grown daughters sitting at the table lost in grief. John gave me a hug and said, "She's at peace now," and he led me into their room and left me alone to say goodbye.

Geraldine was lying peacefully in bed, a colorful silk scarf wrapped around her bald head, and in her hands, her favorite flower—a red rose. She was forty-three, so young, and her life spirit now stilled. I touched her hand and, my tears made puddles down my face and onto the quilt.

"Oh, Geraldine," I cried softly, "you were so brave. I don't know how you got through this without giving up. I'll miss you so very much. I'll never forget our long talks and all the funny stuff we did—the makeovers, the sushi trips to Boston, and, ohmigod, those wicked aerobics classes where they called you the bionic grandma. I'll always remember your goodness and the wonderful things you did for me. Goodbye, dear friend."

I kissed her gently on the forehead and asked God to take her safely to a new life.

The world seemed bleak and empty as I drove home. At the lake where Geraldine and I had shared so many good times, I pulled off the road. The sun was beginning to rise and the morning mist floated off the water as two swans swam gracefully by. Suddenly, I felt a rush of energy pass through me, and Geraldine was everywhere. She was in the early morning light, in the rising mist, in the dance of the swans, but most of all, she was inside me. My whole being was filled with her presence, her voice, like a soft whisper, saying, "Write it down...don't let it go unsaid." Her spirit slowly receded, and I felt an overwhelming peace and a new determination to live life to the fullest. Life was, after all, such a gift. Geraldine knew that, she taught me that.

At a church ceremony, we celebrated her life and the inspiring way she had lived, then gathered at John's sister's house to share stories about her more irreverent side, her fiery spirit, and her hilarity. How she had touched all our lives! A week later, I discovered I was pregnant again, and I believe it was no coincidence. "This baby will have your spirit, Geraldine." I looked up at the sky, feeling the soft wind on my face. It was a sacred moment, for I knew her spirit was in me and would flower again in my child.

CLEAR HORIZON

After months of dealing with Dad's accident and saying a long goodbye to Geraldine, it felt good to immerse myself in Argus again. Argus was tough, hard, inanimate, and didn't make me cry, at least not at the moment. Tim and I were excited about the new baby, and I needed to stay healthy and get through the sad times without crumbling. Work is very therapeutic in that way. I missed Geraldine terribly and talked to her often. I talked with Dad a lot too. He was now walking with a cane, enjoying the balmy July weather and planning his return to a fuller life.

The Barnstable job was going smoothly. Callahan Brothers was a large, experienced firm that operated by the book, which made our job easier. On two occasions, the company's president drew me aside and praised our work, and the Argus crew beamed when I passed on the compliment. Requisitions were paid promptly, and I paid a lower cost for materials because we purchased in great quantity. Every month I deposited the balance from each reimbursement check, after expenses, to fund the coming month's material costs and payroll. With fifty men on the job, I expected a few mishaps, but so far, so good. We just kept working, and before long the Barnstable job was done. I thought of it as an early Christmas present, a job well done. Argus had completed the work two months ahead of schedule, much to Callahan's delight.

We received letters of praise from both the architect and Callahan Brothers stating that it was the quickest and most professional masonry job they had ever seen. The Barnstable town officials were happy also and invited me to lay the last brick myself at a special ceremony, unaware that I was more than eight months pregnant and could not climb the staging. I made a speech at the ceremony instead.

I knew the money was looking good but, yikes, I didn't know how good. When I calculated the earnings and expenses from the Barnstable job, I ran the numbers through three times to be certain I hadn't made a mistake, then I just sat back and stared—$385,000 profit. Could it be? Indeed it was, and I did a little victory dance around the room as I realized my third five-year goal had been surpassed in three short years. The next day, I paid off the mortgages on all three properties—the Argus office, the waterfront cottage, and the Staple Shores Road house.

Clarence made copies of the architect's and general contractor's letters and passed them out to each man, along with a letter of thanks from me.

"I feel like I just won the Super Bowl," Russell said. "Thanks for everything, boss."

Was this Russell speaking? The following week, I hosted a retirement party for Bob Lynch and invited the whole Barnstable crew and their families. I felt so indebted to him for becoming my first employee and wanted to do a bigtime party as a fitting tribute. We hired a comedian for entertainment, and about a hundred people turned out to pay their respects.

Daniel Cullen Donohue was born on New Year's Eve, and from his first feisty cry I felt Geraldine's high spirits alive and well in him. Once again, Tim and Pam coached me through labor and delivery and kept me distracted with a comic debate about whether the baby would be a last-minute tax deduction or the first New Year's baby. Tim had gone with the tax deduction and won.

Pam went home to stay with Kelsey, and Tim remained at the hospital with me for the next two days. We thought Kelsey might be jealous of the new baby, but when we brought him home, she looked at her tiny brother and said, "He's so cute!" then kissed him on the cheek. At her second birthday party two weeks later, she proudly showed Daniel off to her guests. She had settled easily into her role as big sister and especially liked to "read" to him. Her favorite book was *The Three Little Pigs* and she'd point to the pictures and tell him the story. When she got to one particular page, she'd say, "And this little pig made his house with lots of bricks, just like Mommy," which made me feel as tall as the Empire State Building.

Callahan Brothers informed me they wanted Argus to sub on three more projects in the coming six months and I said yes, yes and yes. Clarence and I managed to get all three jobs up and running while I kept Daniel close by in the Argus nursery and Tim looked after Kelsey at home. I was able to place all fifty Argus men on the three Callahan jobs and no one had to be laid off. Argus had the key to the city in Callahan's eyes, and the jobs went off without a hitch.

Tim and I had been looking into a private school for our children when they reached kindergarten age, and the one we liked was located in Pocasset, a thirty-minute drive from Lakeville. The cost would be high and the commute difficult.

Pam understood our desire for good schooling, but she thought we were nuts. "You're going to spend a fortune, and your kids won't even know anyone in their own neighborhood—they'll be commuting an hour each day to another town. Why not move to a town that already has a great public school system, like Marion?"

Marion? We had lived in Lakeville for twenty years and had some good friends here, but we were less than thrilled with the public school system. We decided to explore Pam's idea. After all, that's where she and Donny lived and they loved it.

A short time later, the town of Lakeville made a serious blunder and we felt more urgency to move. This rural farming town was run by "good-old-boys" who were sometimes shortsighted. This year the town was over budget and the selectmen decided that nothing much happened at night so they would close the police station on weeknights and contract with the Middleboro police for emergency calls. An article on the "new hours" even showed up in the *Boston Globe!*

"Why not just send the thieves an engraved invitation?" Tim joked.

They didn't have to. Three nights later, the Argus office was broken into. The front door was battered and a stereo and television were taken. Luckily, the computer and safe were secured with a deadbolt in another room. The insurance company paid for the loss, but we were disenchanted that the culprits were never found. A week later, the selectmen voted to bring back the police, after being deluged by complaints from townsfolk who had been robbed in the interim.

Marion, an old-money town with a fine harbor, was also the site of a famed prep school, Tabor Academy, that welcomed students from all over the world. The Marion public schools and many of their teachers had won numerous awards for excellence, and the college entry rate for high-school graduates was something to brag about.

This we wanted for our children! Besides, Pam had launched a tireless campaign to convince us to move there, sending us copies of the *Annual Report*, newspapers, and magazine articles that extolled the town's virtues.

Tim and I hooked up with a Marion real estate agent and looked at five homes in different parts of town, falling in love with one in particular. The house exuded charm, on a winding country road and an acre of land. When I saw that the finished basement had a built-in office, that was it. The neighborhood was alive with young couples and children, play groups, and get-togethers.

Best of all, Pam and Donny lived just a hop through the woods. Though Pam and I had been best friends for over twenty-five years, we always had to commute to see each other. After I showed her the house, the first thing we did was to time ourselves as we walked through the woods to her house. "Only seven minutes!" we exclaimed excitedly.

"Oh no, we're really in for trouble now," joked Donny.

"Yeah, double trouble," Tim chimed in.

"Well, just think of all the money we'll save in long distance calls and gas."

We listed our Staple Shores Road home with a Lakeville realtor and laughed our heads off when Russell came over and buried a plastic statue of St. Joseph upside-down in our front yard.

"Go ahead, laugh all you want—it works, I tell ya." He wiped dirt from his palms. Two days later, the second person who looked at the house bought it. "I told ya, that upside-down St. Joseph thing works every time," Russell responded when he heard the good news.

On the day of the closing on the Marion house, I walked up the steps of the Plymouth County Courthouse with excitement and awe. "I never thought I'd be walking into a courtroom under these conditions," I said reflectively to Tim.

"What do you mean?"

"I mean, not charged with anything!" and we laughed heartily.

"You've come a long way," Tim said with a smile, and we exchanged a quick hug before heading in.

We were early, so we sat on a carved oak bench in the spacious lobby and I thought about my long journey. I thought about the red-brick walls at the Belmont Club I'd stared at day after day, never dreaming that bricks like those would one day lead me down the road to financial freedom. I thought about my pal, the buffalo head, stuck on the wall of the Belmont forever. I thought about all the buildings I helped to create and about the memories I had every time I drove past them—the crisp mornings when I jointed off and the mortar was thumbprint hard, the pride I took in my workmanship, the camaraderie with my co-workers, the famous and infamous stories from each job.

A secretary read our names and interrupted my reverie. The lawyers were a bit taken aback when I told them I intended to pay off the mortgage and closing costs in cash. My first real job had been at the Belmont earning meager pay and bar tips in small bills and loose change, and it was important to me to incorporate that humble beginning into this important event.

We moved into our beautiful new home in June, just in time to enjoy Marion in summer. Pam and I wore a path through the woods going back and forth between each other's houses. The neighbors welcomed us, inviting us over to get acquainted and trading off play times for the children. Within a few weeks, we felt like longtime Marionites.

The alarm clock rang at four-thirty on Saturday morning, and for a moment I was that young woman from years ago, about to embark on her first day as an apprentice bricklayer. The gentle tug on my arm brought me back to the present as Kelsey whispered, "Come on, Mom, it's almost time!" She was already dressed and I groggily pulled on sweat pants and a long-sleeve shirt.

"Come on, Daniel, it's time to go!" Kelsey whispered gently, but his eyelids were still heavy with sleep. I scooped him up, blankets and all, and carried him out to our Suburban van. Kelsey trailed behind me, dragging her sleeping bag.

I carefully settled them into the back of the Suburban atop blankets and sleeping bags and slowly drove the short distance to Silvershell Beach. Dan was awake now and said, "Good morning, Kelsey," and "Good morning, Mommy," in his cute little singsong voice.

The beach was deserted, and I backed the van up to the edge of the sand. Hopping out, I opened both rear doors and climbed in between my two beautiful children, rearranging the blankets as we nestled against each other and looked out over the peaceful ocean. As we sat there in quiet anticipation, I thought about how my struggles had all been worth it and how, against all odds, I had realized my dreams.

"Here it comes!" Kelsey suddenly cried out, pointing toward the Bird Island lighthouse at the rising sun. "Look at the pretty colors—I see purple and blue."

Daniel sat up and craned his neck to see the glorious sunrise. "I see yellow and orange!" he crowed.

"What do you see, Mommy?" Kelsey asked.

"I see a big, beautiful sky that goes on forever."

Every so often, you're entitled.

Brick by Brick,
A Community Organization

I am fortunate that I have been able to change my direction and build a successful life for myself, thanks to the many people who helped me along the way. Now, I would like to do something for others caught in a similar struggle.

Brick by Brick, A Community Organization has been established to help sponsor education and apprenticeships for people in southeastern Massachusetts struggling to build a career. Someday, they will have their own success stories to pass on.

For information on the Brick by Brick Foundation and how you can help, contact:

brickbybrick@neaccess.net • tel. 508-990-9090

ABOUT THE AUTHOR

Brick by Brick is Lynn Donohue's first pub-
lished work. A native of New Bedford,
Massachusetts, Lynn became the first female
member of the International Union of Bricklayers and Allied Craftworkers Local 39,
working on construction projects from Cape
Cod to Boston.

Photograph by Gretje Ferguson

After a decade as a bricklayer, Lynn
founded Argus Construction Corp., a firm
which began with two employees and a pickup
truck and grew into a multi-million-dollar business with more than
50 full-time employees.

Ever mindful of her roots, Lynn established the Brick by Brick
Foundation in Greater New Bedford to help high school dropouts and
others struggling in their careers. Today, Lynn teaches workshops and
speaks on entrepreneurship and personal success. She lives in Marion,
Massachusetts with her two children.